Spanish Swans

Pablo Gómez

Iponymous Edition
First UK edition published in 2015
By iponymous publishing Limited
Swansea United Kingdom SA6 6BP

Los Cisnes
Issued under license from Libros del K.O.

A CIP record for this book

Is available from the British Library

Cover photograph © Swansea City FC

(EBook) ISBN 978-1-908773-92-0
(Physical Book) ISBN 978-1-908773-93-7

www.iponymous.com

Swansea University
Prifysgol Abertawe

Translated from the Spanish by Laurie Munslow, Lisa Matthews, Andrew Patton and John Ablett with very special thanks to Dr L.H. Davies and all the staff and students at MA Translation with Language Technology at Swansea University without whose help this book would not have been possible.

CONTENTS

PROLOGUE BY ROBERTO MARTÍNEZ

The city of Swansea and the country of Wales have been an important part of both my personal and professional life. Since my arrival in Wigan, when I was just twenty two years old, I have become steadily more and more hooked on British football. It is a very honest sport which is alive with a great deal of passion, as the Spanish players featured in this book have been able to experience first-hand.

Now, when I see how Swansea City play, I feel a great sense of pride and satisfaction. Without wanting to detract from the importance of the work of Paulo Sousa, Brendan Rogers, Michael Laudrup and Garry Monk, I think that Swansea's current state of success is the result of many years of hard work and the maintenance of the ideas that have been sown into the club's philosophy since 2007.

The central idea of this philosophy consisted of finding a formula by which the team could compete alongside other clubs without having to spend the same amount of money as they did. In order to achieve this, a change to the old philosophy was needed, focussing on a possession style of play in order to create a formula which would allow us to grow, year after year.

Today this is a style which is recognised for the success it has brought both Barcelona and the Spanish national team, but back in 2007, to many people it came as something of a shock. There was a great contrast between Welsh football and the leagues beneath the Premier, where it was always a widely-held belief that playing good football alone was not enough for a team to ascend higher in the leagues. Although football may be a results-driven industry, I don't believe that a team's playing style is something irrelevant or that one should focus only on the scoreboard.

In order to pin down the necessary technical and tactical aspects which this new philosophy required, we sought the inspiration which Spanish and, to a certain degree, Dutch football could offer us. These were two footballing cultures which could contribute what was needed to our philosophy in order to overcome the prevailing concepts within the British game.

Since this time, the team has achieved results, winning a League Cup and spending three sensational seasons in the Premiership. Now I see people such as Àngel Rangel or Ashley Williams play and I remember the excitement and passion with which they sealed their contracts, in the same way in which we all began our pursuit of the Great Dream. Something similar happens to me when I see Leon Britton play, someone who changed his style of play for the good of the team, going from an extremely offensive to a highly controlled player within this possession style of football (he was also my roommate during my time as a footballer at Swansea).

Life's coincidences are truly remarkable. I always dreamed of bearing witness to the beginning of Premier League matches at the Liberty Stadium and as fate would have it the first game Swansea would play at home after their rise to the Premiership was to be against Wigan. I was proud to be sat on the bench at the Liberty that day. Swansea played in the exact same way as we had in the past and so even though I obviously wanted my team to win, it was a very emotional match.

In all honesty, I must confess that I have not maintained a direct line of contact with anyone at the club since I left in 2009. Things were complicated. I didn't want to interfere; the group needed to be focussed and to maintain the same level of commitment. It was, however, such an intense relationship that I still hold a lot of affection for them. I have had some very special times, both in my role as player and in my role as coach. That last-minute salvation of 2003, becoming captain of the team so shortly after arriving at the club, playing at the new stadium wearing the captain's armband... I will never forget these, as well as many other, special moments.

In addition to this, of course, there are the people. In South Wales the people are very open, highly patriotic... they make you feel very good. I immediately connected with the fans, who live football and rugby with a great passion, as a way of fighting against the almighty English. They have made me feel as one of their own. Within the club as well there are many people that deserve recognition, although their work might not be visible to the outside world – Susanne Eames, Huw Lake, Alan Curtis... this book also aims to do justice to these people.

Huw Jenkins, the team's chairman, deserves all the credit for his defence of the team's philosophy, both in sporting and economic terms. On the one hand, the choice of coaches has allowed the cultivation of the possessive game and this has been faithful to the idea which was forged in 2007. On the other hand, however, in terms beyond that of results, the austerity imposed on a financial level has been another great success of the club.

I will be forever grateful to Huw for giving me the opportunity to be coach, especially given the circumstances in which this took place, when few would have given the chance to someone with no experience on the bench, someone who was still a football player and someone who did so at an inferior level. With him we created something truly special and I know that we could work together again at any time.

I thank Pablo Gómez for his effort and enthusiasm in compiling our history in this book and I would like to sign-off by sending a big hug to the whole family of Swansea City, especially to the Spanish Swans that star in the pages that follow.

Roberto Martínez

CHAPTER 1

SWANSEA, THE RAINY CITY

They would arrive at Bristol airport most of the time and London the rest, almost always by night (due to the flight timetables), usually from Barcelona, in economy class with EasyJet or Ryanair, going unnoticed, just like any other normal passenger. Hearing the sound of windscreen-wipers is a virtual guarantee on the journey by road to South Wales, as you drive the 86 miles from Bristol (down small sections of the A38, the M5 and the M49, before travelling a good portion of the M4) which is more than double the distance from the English capital (and almost the full length of the M4 itself).

This journey marks the beginning of the adventure for the first Spanish Swans who followed in the footsteps of their forerunner, Roberto Martínez, who just four years previously, in 2003, had established the vital connection between Swansea and the country more commonly known to the wider world by its simplified image of bullfighting and Flamenco. The ignorance and confusion over Spain as a country was so much so that in their first photograph with the Welsh club Guillermo Bauzá, Àngel Rangel and Andrea Orlandi all appeared wearing Mexican sombreros, repeating the mistake of the infamous "The Three

Amigos" picture , taken with Roberto Martínez, Isidro Díaz and Jesús Seba when they signed for Wigan in 1995.

Lakie

Each new Spanish signing for Swansea begins their journey by settling themselves into a white, eight-seater van which awaits them at the airport in either Bristol or London. The van is driven by an endearing man, known to those within the club as Lakie, who has driven an incalculable amount of miles taking players to and from their destinations. Throughout the years that Huw Lake has worked at Swansea City there have been more than fifty different signings for the club. He began taking on this role as driver back when Kenny Jacket was manager and he has continued doing so throughout the reins of Bob Martínez, Paulo Sousa, Brendan Rodgers, Michael Laudrup, and Garry Monk. His role is one of liaison officer – which is to say, he is the man whose job it is to help the players with all of their off-field needs, from helping them to find a place to live to giving them advice by phone should they be caught breaking the speed-limit by police. Who better to solve any unforeseen problems than an ex-player himself, having shared many years on the field with Colin Pascoe, Alan Curtis and John Benjamin Toshack (the latter he defines as "a quality midfielder – slow in his legs but fast in his head"). Lakie can attest to a handicap common to all of the Spaniards he's picked up over the years on their first journey with him: an extremely sparse knowledge of English. Even though Lakie himself is a friendly and extroverted sort, the language barrier which existed within the vehicle was nothing short of impenetrable. "Rangel sat in the back, he spoke zero English. Neither Orlandi nor Pintado spoke a single word on the entire journey. I taught Bergara a few words, but I also advised him under no conditions to say these words to a referee lest he be sent off", he recalls, smiling, surrounded by training bibs, cones and balls in the humble little equipment shed on the training ground. Iñaki Bergara arrived in London with an English phrasebook pinned under his arm, such was his fear of the language, and as soon as he offered his first, tentative 'hello', the brief response of his chauffeur, a brief 'hi', already left him feeling highly confused. Many Spanish players confess that it went completely unnoticed when the road signs began to appear in two separate languages: "Welcome to Wales" at the top, and "Croeso i Gymru" underneath, as reads the first welcome signs into the country of Wales.

In the darkness of night it is also difficult to appreciate, especially through the rain, the industrialised nature of nearby Port Talbot, birthplace of Anthony Hopkins. "It's darker than the actor himself!" exclaimed Xavi Cruz, brother-in-law and right-hand man to Rangel, as he exchanged jokes with Lakie, who was sat in the front of the white van on one of his many journeys to the city which has changed the lives of so many Spanish players. Fourteen miles after leaving behind the chimneys which were once one of the largest steel industries in Europe, weary with the tiredness of the two journeys – by plane and by road – the new Spanish signings of Swansea City FC set foot in their new home.

The Stadium and Marina – First Stops

The Liberty Stadium is open twenty-four hours-a-day virtually every day of the year, always available so that any player can show off their moves and meet the people, but also so that they can use the ice baths if, for example, they have pulled a muscle and need to get fit for match day. It's a real community resource beloved by the Swansea public. All you need, even if it is the day before a big match, is the 'ok' of Susanne Eames, Swansea City's Football Utilities Co-ordinator, who makes sure that all materials are ready on stand-by in the locker rooms and also is endowed with the power to grant clearance with security for anyone to enter the hallowed grounds of the Liberty. This is one of the great benefits of being a club with a limited number of employees, it's almost like a family, with no rigid protocol procedures or any intermediaries.

In the era of Roberto Martínez, these circumstances meant that even at one or two o'clock in the morning Lakie's van would make its first stop at the hallowed grounds every time it entered the city with new reinforcements. To catch a first sight of the Liberty Stadium at such an hour makes an impression. Some Spanish Swans are pleasantly surprised by the modern exterior façade of the stadium, others by its perfect turf or its cosy stands, and others still by the walls of the tunnel which connects the locker rooms with the pitch which are covered with portraits of coaches and players, among them hangs the portrait of Rangel. Roberto Martínez had everything very well prepared. Presenting each new recruit with a stadium which surpassed the expectations one would presuppose of a League One team was quite a coup de theatre. But there was more to come. Huw Lake had been given instructions that the new recruits would spend their first day in the Bay Area, the coach from Balaguer wanted to impress on them the gorgeous location and give them a taste of their new residence.

Guillermo Bauzá and Àngel Rangel, the first Spaniards to join Roberto Martínez's project, were near-inseparable during their initial period in Swansea. In the first few weeks they went together everywhere, in car or by foot. They ate at the same places. They went from first of all sharing the same hotel, then to sharing the same flat and finally the same room at the team training camp. Not even for Angel's first interviews did they leave each other's side, since Guillermo was there, serving as his interpreter. His high level of English was also vital for Rangel, so that he could open a bank account and so that he could buy his first British mobile phone – a Samsung on contract with the operator O2. At the beginning, Orlandi opted for a very simple Motorola with a prepaid card which cost him less than ten pounds. From the outset, Rangel decided to take his Mercedes ML with him to Swansea. Bauzá, meanwhile, shared an old, grey Ford Puma with Dutchman, Ferrie Bodde – which Roberto Martínez had loaned them so that they could practice their driving. Later, Orlandi would also make good use of the same car: "Bussy had it as his 'racing car', a test car. I learned to drive with him. And if we gave it a little bump, we wouldn't say anything to Roberto and it would be fine". It stayed that way until the day that Bussy broke down in the middle of the motorway as he was on his way to pick up his partner, Angie. The car had struck many a curb in its lifetime, and had many a tough time on many a roundabout. In these first months the Spanish players had to overcome the challenges posed by driving on the left-hand side of the road. Later, they had got so used to driving in Britain that they faced the same challenge when they returned to visit Spain!

Bauzá and Rangel lived for one week in the Marriott, a luxurious hotel situated by the side of the docks, around three miles from the Liberty Stadium. The other new players spent their first nights in Swansea, if not in the same hotel, in others such as the Village or the Dragon. In the latter, equally as luxurious as the Marriott, situated more to the north of the bay, the second Spaniard to be incorporated into the team, Orlandi, stayed for just four days until he decided to move into the first place that Lakie showed him. Coincidentally or not, it was next door to the new residence which his two compatriots had decided to share in the Marina.

"The Marina is a very nice place; it's in the city centre and it's not far from the training grounds and the stadium", points out Huw Lake. This privileged area, also close to the beach and the yachting harbour, is mainly comprised of recently-built developments of flats and houses in which all the Spaniards were setting up home. In this way they were forming a sort of neighbourhood community which could have been aptly named 'Los Cisnes' (Spanish for 'The Swans').

Albert Serrán, who arrived in mid-2008, remembers fondly that through one of his windows he could see Bauzá's balcony, through another he could see Orlandi and Fede Bessone and Jordi Gómez's residence was also very nearby. The relationship between all of them was growing ever more and more special. During the first few months they spent a great deal of time in each other's company, more so even than they had done in Barcelona, where several of them had been teammates, but in Spain they all had their own circle of friends and family, in Swansea they were all thrown closer together.

One snowy day Bessone, Jordi, Serrán, and their respective girlfriends met up with each other. They made a snowman and they threw some snowballs against Andrea Orlandi's window, who then peeked outside and returned back inside without saying a word. "Sometimes he gets in a bad mood and you don't know how he's going to react", says his good friend Serrán. Orlandi himself explains that they had played this joke on him just as he had managed to finally get some rest after two sleepless nights. They were living in each other's pockets: they had lunch and dinner together they helped one another with day-to-day problems and difficulties, they shared rooms in the training camps and they went on group excursions in order to get to know the surrounding areas of Swansea.

Wales' Second City

Although it is the second largest city in Wales, surpassed in population only by Cardiff, the country's capital, the feeling one has when one knows Swansea is of having arrived in a small town, the locals call it a "village". This feeling goes against the grain when you note the giant screen in Castle Square or the nearby, modern shops and Zara store – features typical, these days, of a considerably larger city.

One of the first Spanish players to arrive in Swansea, Andrea Orlandi, noticed this difference the most at the beginning, having arrived from such a large city as Barcelona. The way in which houses extend back across the hills around Swansea gave him a false impression – "Although the city has more than two hundred thousand inhabitants, there is no large urban core – instead everything is very focused within the bay".

For Jordi López, who joined in the summer of 2009, the place was just too small – he had come to play from London's Queen Park Rangers – while for Óscar Brau, a native of a town much smaller than Swansea, the size issue was no inconvenience at all thanks to the friendliness of the people and he felt himself very much at home since his arrival in mid-2008.

Bauzá, who is an optimist and quite pragmatic to boot, cites many different offerings which the area provides and for him they are more than enough to live well and be happy – "It has a coastline; it has a university; it has a small centre and quite a lot of activity. It's another thing if you're seeking grand sights. or grand cities, such as London, Madrid or Barcelona". The Spaniard tried to adapt fully to the local culture. He bought guidebooks and travelled a lot in the surrounding area, which helped him to get to know the society's background, its history and its people, more – "The people's character has a lot to do with their history. A knowledge of this history allows you to see the differences between the Welsh and the English – you get to understand the rivalry".

Speaking of guidebooks, the Lonely Planet guidebook caused much controversy in Wales by referring to Swansea in the English version of its book as "an ashtray of a place". In its 2004 edition it was forced to modify this content. In its new version it states that the Welsh city combines the charm of tradition with sophistication.

Gorka Pintado notes a significant difference in the character of the Welsh outside and inside of the stadium: "in contrast to the vibrant atmosphere that they create on the stands of the Liberty Stadium, in their daily lives they are people with a culture that is very different to the Spanish – somewhat colder and a little boring. Their mentality leads them to do little outside of their homes and virtually all businesses close after five o'clock in the evening. It's baffling!"

Swansea is known to some as the birthplace of the actress Catherine Zeta-Jones, who owns an expensive mansion close to Mumbles Cricket Club, and the late Dylan Thomas, of whom it is said that Bob Dylan borrowed his stage name. Or perhaps football fans would better be able to place Swansea on a map thanks to Italian striker Giorgio Chinaglia, who was raised in Wales and began his career with a brief stint in Swansea before moving on to make a name for himself with Lazio of Rome and then, much later, to the New York Cosmos. However, surely nothing has made the name Abertawe – the city's name in Welsh – more universally known than having a football team in the English Premier League. The name Abertawe means 'the mouth of the Tawe', which is the river which crosses the city from south to north and also borders the Liberty Stadium.

Swansea's strategic location on the coastline of South Wales, to the west of England, made the city an industrial centre and significant port during the last two centuries. Its importance made it a target for aerial bombardment during the Second World War and its most important buildings were destroyed in the year 1941. The remains of the castle, located in the centre of the modern town, gives an understanding of the level of damage caused at this time. Although many locals say that the Luftwaffe haven't caused half as much damage as the local planners at the City Council.

Its large role in the copper industry led to the city being dubbed with the nickname of 'Copperopolis', but Swansea was also a major trader in terms of wine, wool, fabric, animal skin and coal. There was a system of canals and trains to carry the coal from the mountains in the centre of Wales to the coast. The port of Swansea was one which was rather famous. Its splendour, however, suffered after the Industrial Revolution, after which the use of coal fell into decline.

Bauzá is the player who is best known as an intellectual among his fellow players, always with his nose in a book when his fellow players were killing time with card games at training camps. His opinion of Wales helped educate his fellow Spanish players – "It has its natural, green side, with its cliffs and coastlines, which now they are trying to promote, and also it has this other side of society consisting of small towns which were purely mining towns and which have been in decline for around fifty years or more."

Roberto Martínez states that Swansea maintains the essence of being a typical British city, especially in terms of housing. However, due to the fact that it is a coastal area and because of the undulating green countryside and predominantly grey climate, it is difficult not to feel oneself transported to any corner of northern Spain – or even, he adds, the coasts of Italy or Croatia, so long as the weather is sunny, which, however, is an unusual circumstance.

Jordi López lays testament to the sad fact that the terrible local climate forces one to contemplate Swansea's beautiful beaches from the inside of a car or to roam them forever accompanied by a raincoat. Who can fail to be reminded of the video for 'Yellow', the first hit song for the band Coldplay? It's true that it was shot in Studland Bay, 160 miles away, but the same effect could have been achieved, for example, in Rhossili Bay, one of the best beaches Bergara has ever known – "There are also beautiful, surfer-type places, such as Caswell. I spent two very nice years in Wales following a difficult situation in terms of football. A door closed and a window opened up for me, in this case, a window with a sea-view".

Swansea is surrounded by water in almost three quarters of the region. This is ideal for Bauzá, a surfing fanatic – a sport which is as difficult to reconcile with football as it is useful for shaking off the pressures of everyday life. And for the Majorcan Serrán, it's only thanks to the use of a wetsuit and a kayak that he has gained the bragging rights for having, one time at least, bathed in the icy Welsh sea.

The Omnipresent Rain

Travel agencies would rub their hands together with glee at the prospect of the marvellous Gower Peninsula were it not for the meteorological conditions which thwart the plans of tourists seeking to enjoy its majestic landscapes with good weather. Orlandi's personal experience in this regard, the Spaniard who has worn the Jacks' shirt the second highest number of times, is very telling. He wasn't able to enjoy a straight week with a temperature of more than twenty degrees until September of 2011 – "It would be twenty four degrees and we would be 'roasting'. I have had horrific summers". He handles this absence of heat in summer even worse than the low temperatures throughout the rest of the year. "What hit me the most when I lived in Vitoria, is that it truly is cold", says Bergara, in order to put the harshness of the Welsh winter into perspective.

The almost daily need of an umbrella gives testament to a news article from 2004 which asserted that Swansea is officially the wettest British city, at a cost of around £550 million to its inhabitants each year. The cancellation of events, wear and tear on clothes, replacement washing machines and heating bills are the main reasons for these costs.

The copious amount of rainfall was not an obstacle for the more pragmatic and optimistic of the group. When it came to the bad weather (and other inconveniences) Óscar Brau put on a brave face – "I knew I was going there to work and so I didn't let the climate, the customs nor the different meal times make me think about returning to Spain".

Rangel acknowledges that being a father makes it easier to spend so many hours at home, while Bussy took the opportunity to fill his life with intellectual pleasures and studying. Perhaps the Spaniard got his theory on the excessive rain in Swansea from one such reading session – "On the west coast of the United Kingdom all the areas of low pressure release rainfall as soon as they make landfall". While almost any human being could despair at these conditions, Bauzá considered them a blessing for his profession – "You arrive at the grounds and the terrain is in perfect condition: green, wet grass which allows for the practice of a super-fast style of football. This is not possible without rain everyday".

CHAPTER 2

SWANSEA CITY, A CENTENARY CLUB

The club was founded under the name Swansea Town AFC in 1912, and only adopted its current name of Swansea City Association Football Club when the town was granted city status in 1971. In that year its population surpassed two hundred and fifty thousand inhabitants, whilst in the decade of the club's founding the figure was around one hundred and eighty thousand.

The club's first professional encounter was against the best possible opponents – Cardiff City. A one-all draw sparked a fierce rivalry that day, the 7th September, 1912, at the Vetch Field – a ground named after the plant, which is similar to cabbage, which once grew there. The fans held a lot of affection for this old ground, in spite of the toilets which were so bad that they became known as the absolute worst in the Football League, so bad that they might well have been the inspiration for the filthy toilet shown in the infamous scene of the film Trainspotting. The famous hamburgers of the Vetch Field were also of some notoriety, but in this case for the right reasons. The stadium hosted matches until May 11th, 2005, the date it said its final goodbye with a 2-1 victory over Wrexham in the final of the FAW Premier Cup. As captain, Roberto Martínez lifted the cup on that historic day. The club's next encounter, a Swansea-Fulham friendly, was played at the Liberty Stadium on June 23rd, 2005.

Throughout its construction it was called White Rock Stadium; later they asked both the public and the media to call it New Stadium Swansea in order to make it more likely to attract a sponsor. Upon completion they sold the naming rights of the stadium to the company Liberty Properties. It was a practice that was beginning to establish itself as a new means of funding throughout British football – a few months before, it was announced that Emirates Airlines would be the sponsor of the new Arsenal Stadium in London.

The Legendary Swans

Standing outside the Liberty Stadium, which is shared with the Ospreys rugby team, stands a bronze statue which was donated by fans in order to pay tribute to the Golden Boy of Welsh Football – Ivor Allchurch. Born in 1929 in Swansea, Allchurch wore the club's shirt throughout two stages of his career (1947-'58 and 1965-'68) and his sporting exploits led to him being honoured as a Member of the Order of the British Empire (MBE). The legendary Bobby Moore said in his day that Allchurch, who died in 1997, was one of the best attacking midfielders he ever faced on the pitch. The ability to play ambidextrously, lightning speed, a powerful strike or an elegant movement were some of the hallmarks of his game. Veteran fans still speak of his final season during which he scored twenty-one goals at thirty eight years of age and of the encounter with Arsenal in the FA cup, in which his presence was almost as big an attraction as the opposing team itself.

The successor to the Golden Boy of Welsh Football in fans' memories is Alan Curtis, who is currently a member of Garry Monk's coaching staff and also served both Brendan Rogers and Michael Laudrup in the Premier League. Throughout the seventies and eighties, Curtis played for the Swans, Leeds United, Cardiff City, Southampton and Stoke City – in total, five hundred and seventy games and one hundred and sixteen goals. He was a member of the Swansea team when it managed to rise to Division One (the highest division at the time) with his friend John Toshack at the helm, a season (1981-82) in which the three points for a win system was implemented for the very first time.

The team began its adventure in the Top Flight with two consecutive wins and by October 22nd, 1981, the club reached first position for the first time in its history. They rose twenty points in the league after beating Stoke City away, a team which was already known, even back then, for its physical prowess, as Curtis himself recalls ruefully. The Jacks remained in the top six of the league for the entire season, finishing in exactly that position and finishing higher in the table than the likes of such clubs as Leeds United, Aston Villa and Southampton. To date, this has been Swansea's best performance. It was short-lived, and the following year they fell back to Division Two, and a further division drop in 1984 marked Toshack's final farewell. As well as Allchurch and Curtis, the club celebrates such players as Wilf Milne, Reg Weston, Robbie James, Roy Paul, Mel Charles, Wyndham Evans, Herbie Williams, Harry Griffiths, Billy Lucas, John King, Joe Sykes, Geoff Thomas, Mel Nurse, Cyril Beech, Trevor Ford, Frank Burns and Bob Latchford – all of whom were instrumental in the clubs history and footballers of great importance in their time, although in some cases this can be attributed more to sentimental factors, as few of these players were ever actually capped for their country.

All of these players are represented on the Robbie James Wall of Fame, which was opened on the 12th September, 2012, on the front wall of the Liberty Stadium. The idea for the wall arose at a 2011 Season Awards dinner, in which it was agreed that for each year over the next decade places would be added for ten new players. The requirement for inclusion on the wall, regardless of the number of appearances or goals scored, is that any new honouree has contributed to the current culture and individual identity of the club. During the centenary season (2012-13) members of the Swans Trust formed their 'ideal eleven' from players drawn from the entire club's history. In this ideal team, Roger Freestone is the goalkeeper; Angel Rangel, Mel Nurse, Ante Rajković and Mel Charles form the defensive line; Ivor Allchurch, Robbie James, Cliff Jones and Leon Britton are in the midfield; Bob Latchford and Alan Curtis appear as forwards. Alan Curtis agrees with many of the names selected by the Trust but does not include himself in his ideal Swans eleven. Curtis finds room for Wyndham Evans, Ashley Williams, Dzemal 'Jimmy' Hadziabdic and Leighton James.

Eirian

Eirian Wyn, club employee and Swans aficionado, adds a more recent name to the list of his personal favourites – "If I had to choose my three favourite players they would be Robbie James, Mel Nurse and Lee Trundle". This Baptist minister, in addition to coordinating the events held with the club mascot (Cyril the Swan) for match days, played a key role as host for the first Spanish players who arrived under the persuasion of Roberto Martínez. With some he has forged a special relationship, and it is no coincidence that in Amposta (Tarragona, Spain) there lives a small boy named Eirian, which in Welsh means 'brightness'. That little boy is the nephew of Rangel, whose sister became pregnant on one of her many visits to Swansea. Xavi Cruz, Rangel's brother-in-law and right-hand man, took delight in giving his son a different-sounding name. Moreover, in choosing this name the Rangel family paid a small tribute to Wales and to Eirian Wyn himself, who has always played a supporting role for Àngel and who had himself gently suggested his own name for the baby.

The two Eirians got to meet each other in person in January 2012 at Swansea's training grounds. It was as though they had already met, many times before. Neither the language nor the age difference presented a barrier between them. The adult of the two adored the experience and the child, who was then just two and half years old, was amazed by the magic tricks his namesake performed for him. How could this Welsh minister have ever imagined this scene, when years previously, as a young man, he travelled much of Spain by motorcycle (the same bike with which he would arrive at parties at the Vetch Field in the seventies). It was thanks to this adventure that today he speaks something of the language and this allowed him to communicate with the first Spanish Swans and to forge a lifelong friendship with their families.

The Swans, the Jacks

The team mascot is, rather obviously, a swan. It couldn't be any other way. It must be mentioned that the name Swans is used in reference to the club as well as the fans, but also the name Jacks, or Swansea Jacks, is used. One is made well aware of this latter name when the stands of the Liberty Stadium audibly rumble with the trademark chant of the fans "Who are we? Jack Army". The Welsh are known for their famously big and splendid voices. Even John Steinbeck, Nobel Prize winning author, mentions this fact in some of his work. The intensity of their singing grows exponentially to the rhythm of patriotic pride when they sing their favourite verses: "And we were singing hymns and arias, "Land of my Fathers", "Ar Hyd y Nos". The Welsh comedian and singer Max Boyce wrote this song and it has been a famous anthem since the seventies, livening up many a Welsh rugby match. In more recent years it has also gained prominence among Swansea fans, so much so that Max Boyce himself sang the song live from the pitch of the Liberty Stadium in 2011, on the eve of the first Premiership game played in Wales.

While it is true that the Jacks had competed in the highest league of English football before, with John Toshack as the figurehead of that first major milestone, this was achieved at the beginning of the Eighties, before the highest league became known as the Premier League – a move which was made with the objective of generating higher revenues for its clubs, which became independent of the English Federation and the Football League.

There are three possible origins of the term 'Jack' as a name for the inhabitants of the city of Swansea, as well as for the fans of its football team. According to the first version, the name was used in honour of local sailors, referred to as 'Jack Tars', who gained a good reputation in the 19th Century and were named due to the tar which was used to protect them from the harsh elements out at sea. A second possibility is that the name was borrowed from a certain black dog, a retriever, who saved around twenty people from drowning in Swansea docks in the early nineteen thirties; at the time the dog became a hero whose exploits were splashed all over the press and even today there stands a monument in his honour in the city. The third and final option, which seems the least likely, is that the name originates from the name of the lunchboxes of miners from the surrounding areas, which were made of tin.

A Modest Club

A quick glance at a list of the club's wins show us Swansea's place in history and its remarkable recent upward trajectory. It's quite a showcase with three championship victories in the current League One or Third Division (1924-25, 1948-49 and 2007-08), one in the current League Two or Fourth Division (1999-2000), two Football League Trophies (1994 and 2006), ten Welsh Cups (1913, 1932, 1950, 1961, 1966, 1981, 1982, 1983, 1989, 1991), two FAW Premier Cups (2005 and 2006) and one League Cup (2013).

Swansea's recent trajectory is all the more remarkable when the limited financial constraints of its creation are taken into account. It's impossible not to be surprised the first time one arrives at the training facilities of what is a first-class club only to be presented with the sight of the whole squad and coaching staff at breakfast or lunch in the cafeteria of a private sports and fitness centre, rubbing shoulders with members of the public and fans who pay a monthly membership fee to use the facilities. Swansea FC were considered just another patron of the facilities and were possibly the only Premiership club, or European Division 1 club, which didn't have their own locker rooms or facilities at their training ground – something which didn't happen until February 2013, well into their second season in the Premiership.

The training centre's parking lot and a small local road on which fans would often stop their cars to watch the training sessions were the only things which separated the training field where the team exercised from the outside world. It was in this way that, for a long time, the club prepared for encounters against multimillionaire opponents such as Manchester United, Manchester City, Chelsea and Arsenal. The team was provided with a private room for physio treatment, but the sauna, swimming pool, showers and changing rooms were all shared with other members of the gym.

Guillermo Bauzá once said that although the other members were respectful, the players didn't feel free to talk amongst themselves in the changing rooms. Albert Serrán remembers once encountering a stereotypical hooligan with a large Chelsea tattoo in the showers – for a team in the Premiership, this is something which he felt must have seemed very odd to his teammates as it did him at the time.

It was due to instances such as this that, as Serrán remembers, at the beginning the players didn't shower at the gym – "You would leave your house having already changed, enter the training grounds, and, because you didn't really want to go to the changing rooms with the fans there, you would go home to shower and you would wash your kit yourself". For the first few years things stayed this way, until Brendan Rogers decided that the players shouldn't have to be washing their own kits in this way, and so as a result they finally began changing in the gym before and after each training session.

Another drawback was that of having one solitary training camp in an area with such bad weather conditions, which made it necessary at times for the team to train on artificial grass, something which Bessone lamented – "When you've had injuries and you've been training on that artificial surface for three weeks, it's difficult. But I don't complain because I prefer that to training on a dirt field".

The First Welsh Club in the Premiership

Some Welsh clubs compete in the different categories of English football, something which, for various reasons, the two most powerful Scottish clubs – Rangers and Celtic – have never achieved, preferring to stick within the Scottish divisions. In the 2010-11season, Swansea City managed to rise to the Premier League, while Cardiff managed to do the same in 2012-13. The 2013-14 campaign was a historic one because for the first time in history there was a Welsh derby played in the Premiership. Newport County also managed a promotion in the 2012-13 season, but in their case to League Two. Within the four professional categories of English Football three other Welsh clubs can be found: Wrexham, Colwyn Bay (both in the

Football Conference) and Merthyr Town (Division One South & West of the Southern Football League).

Two decades previously both Swansea and Cardiff passed on a move to the Welsh League, the other clubs did decide on a move home and the Welsh Premier League was founded in 1992. Apart from financial motives, Roberto Martínez alludes to other competitive reasons, "The Welsh League exists and is improving, but it is still not professional. Some clubs are, but the majority are not. For this reason, the best Welsh clubs are competing in the various English Leagues. Football in Wales is alive with passion and intensity; it's a way of fighting against England".

There are also reverse cases, such as The New Saints FC, who will compete in the Champions League 2013-14 having been proclaimed champions of the Welsh Premier League in March of 2013. The club's full name is The New Saints of Oswestry Town & Llansantffraid Football Club. Oswestry is the English town where the team play its matches, and Llansantffraid-ym-Mechain is the Welsh town, situated around thirteen kilometres away, whose union was forged with the former in 2003.

The island of Great Britain is home to Wales, England and Scotland. The three countries, along with Northern Ireland and other smaller island territories, constitute the United Kingdom. Ireland, which shares its island territory with its northern neighbour, is independent of this state, the full name of which is the United Kingdom of Great Britain and Northern Ireland. It is governed by a parliamentary system with its headquarters based in London and three decentralised national assemblies based in the other respective capital cities (Edinburgh, Cardiff and Belfast). But even once one has understood all this, one realises that England, Scotland, Wales and Northern Ireland compete separately in the World and European cups, as their respective football associations predate that of FIFA. Contrarily, in the Olympic Games all of these nations compete together under the name of Great Britain and Northern Ireland.

Bauzá notes the Welsh desire to be recognised by the International Olympic Committee and illustrates this point with an example – "I remember that there were doubts and criticisms towards Welsh players such as Bellamy or Bale when they began to talk about their possible inclusion in the British team at the London Olympic Games". In the end Gareth Bale didn't attend, citing a back injury, and during the tournament there was some controversy among the English fans at the refusal of the Welsh players (the captain – Ryan Giggs, Craig Bellamy and the Swansea players Neil Taylor and Joe Allen) to sing the British National Anthem, 'God Save the Queen'. It must be added that among the various football fans of the British Isles that it was not only the Welsh that harboured negative feelings towards the British team selection, with some protests taking place prior to the 2012 Olympics.

Rivalry

In this same context, however, the Welsh are not critical of the fact that some of their footballing representatives compete within the English structure; in fact, they feel a sense of pride at having a team in the Premiership, while at the same time recognising the rivalry which exists with the English clubs.

Some of these English fans can be heard to sing "England, England" when the Swansea players emerge onto the field. When this happens, the Jacks respond from their seats with chants of "England's full of shit!", according to journalist Tim Lewis, who has been covering the current state of Welsh football for many years. However, Lewis notes that "because they are a new team in the top category, they are generally treated very well in other stadiums". For example, Liverpool fans applauded the Swansea team in their encounter at Anfield in the 2011-12 Premiership.

This being said, some followers of Welsh football do complain that playing in an English footballing structure means that sometimes a Welsh club will encounter prejudice or discrimination, especially in a fight for promotion against powerful English clubs. Lewis has no doubt in placing the rivalry between Swansea and Cardiff higher up the scale than these other rivalries with English clubs. On the 23rd September 2008 the first derby in nine years took place between the two teams in a clash in the League Cup. The tension which had been building up for so much time was reflected in the excessive euphoria that erupted among the Jack supporters, as well as the energetic celebration of the local players after their winning goal.

That Tuesday night called for a lot of overtime for dozens of police officers dressed in yellow reflective vests, some on horseback or with dogs. The television programme 'Cops with Cameras' captured races, provocations, shouting, arrests and numerous other incidents on the streets of Swansea after the game. These types of circumstances, as Roberto Martínez has explained, are the main reason why derbies tend to be held at midday, according to police guidelines, in an attempt to minimise alcohol consumption and thereby prevent these types of incidents.

The sense of pride it evokes in the inhabitants of Swansea at being in the Premiership is multiplied several times over at having achieved this before Cardiff. The capital is probably a superior city not only in terms of size – its club has always been superior in terms of its budget, its training facilities and in any other aspect you'd care to mention. Cardiff was the number one candidate for promotion in the 2011-12 season of the Championship, which is why Swansea's historic promotion hurt so badly for Cardiff fans, who had to wait two more years for their time to come.

In short, Swansea's story can be seen as being profoundly linked by three different factors: its rivalry with Cardiff; its position as a Welsh club competing within an English footballing structure and its humble circumstances and status.

CHAPTER 3

2002-2006: ROBERTO MARTÍNEZ, THE PIONEER

Swansea suffered a crushing defeat against Cardiff in the final of the FAW Premier Cup in the 2001-02 season. It was almost the lesser of two evils for the Swans at the time. In the early years of the century the situation in which Swansea found themselves was disastrous, not only on account of their £1.4 million debt, but also due to the mass departure of players and the numerous managerial changes all incurred in a very short space of time. In 2001, the business Ninth Floor sold the club to the managing director of Swansea City, Mike Lewis, the only person to make a firm offer. Mike Lewis recalls that he had no interest in keeping his stake of the business, which he acquired for one pound, the same price for which, that October, he would in turn transfer The Swans to an Australian group fronted by Tony Petty.

Roberto Martínez remembers all too well these events; "Petty wanted to use Swansea as a source of business income but he decided not to put any money into the club. The Fans, realising what was happening, united together and paid for a number of things to keep everything going".

The Swans Trust

There is a famous story that tells of how two cartographers arrived in a Welsh village to measure the summit of a mountain that was the pride of the local people. However, these retired military officers determined that it was some metres short of being a mountain, that it was no more than a hill. Faced with humiliation, the villagers joined forces and carried buckets of earth to the summit, increasing the height, and gained official recognition that their mountain was indeed a mountain and not a hill. This story, which was brought to the screen in 1995 as 'The Englishman Who Went Up a Hill But Came Down a Mountain' and starred Hugh Grant, shows us a little of the determination of the Welsh. Swansea's supporters had to demonstrate similar obstinacy to ensure that their side were kept afloat.

In 2001, protest marches of up to two thousand people lined the streets, from Castle Square to the Vetch Field, with the aim of ousting Petty, who was notorious for nefarious business practices and financial misconduct. The protests continued in the stands.

Much of the support was garnered from the Swansea City Supporters Trust. The group's origin dates back to May of that year with the first meeting held in Port Talbot, and arranged via the internet. There was one clear objective: to save the club financially and ensure that it remain in the hands of the local community. After further meetings, the Swans Trust was officially inaugurated in front of six hundred supporters at the Patti Pavilion on the 27th of October 2001.

The Trust, proudly displays on its website, the letter of support received from John Toshack, considered an icon of the most glorious period in the club's history by most fans. In a fax from Spain with a Real Sociedad letterhead, the team he was coaching at the time, and signed in his own handwriting, Toshack wished them luck and success in their efforts to save the club. Up to a thousand people attended some of the meetings, as well as television crews and journalists. Months of fierce struggle ensued, but the Trust never lost faith, not even when the initiative led by former player Mel Nurse failed in its attempt to take Petty to court. Petty was later responsible for the debt collectors who turned up at the Vetch Field to seize goods, for unpaid tax bills and for failing to pay the players' wages at Christmas. Furthermore, during his first week in charge, he attempted to sack seven players from the team and reduce the salary of another eight.

External pressure and debts forced Petty to cash in and try and sell the club, otherwise he was faced with the prospect of being left with nothing. In a moment of impulse Petty picked up the telephone and asked David Morgan, one of Swansea City's current associate directors, if he wanted to buy a football club. Without hesitating, Morgan, Steve Penny's lawyer, Tom Jones and the aforementioned Mel Nurse attended a hotel in Cardiff, where they handed over £25,001. The symbolic pound represented the pound that Petty had paid to take the reins of The Swans. The meeting, which continued for four torturous hours, reached its climax when the four negotiators scraped together loose change from their pockets to make up the agreed amount and handed it to the club's now former owner, whose parting shot was to toss the coins on the floor.

So, at the beginning of 2002, the fans could celebrate the departure of Tony Petty with the same energy with which they had shouted and brandished placards with messages like "Petty Out" (which can still to be found on the internet, with a black background and the slogan "TWAT").

Little more than a decade later, the club was valued at a little more than £60 million, and the Swans Trust keeps its fighting spirit intact for the good of the club. In 2012, The Trust was instrumental in leading a campaign across local media and social networking sites to prevent a famous fast-food company from opening an establishment on land adjacent to the stadium, land which had been set aside and which was intended to be used for the future expansion of the Liberty.

According to Alan Lewis, one of its members, all of their actions respond to three fundamental objectives: maintaining a professional football team in Swansea, democratically electing an executive director who represents the fans vision and sits on the Swans board of Directors, and bringing the club closer to the local community.

With a view to fulfilling this final objective, the Trust organizes two or three meetings a year – some of which are attended by the chairman and the manager – so that the supporters may ask whatever questions they wish. In addition, so that the fans can get to know the players, they promote events like the annual bowling game (Ten Pin Bowling Night), in which twenty six teams, comprising of six fans per team, each contributing £10 per fan, participate in a bowling tournament with a Swans player joining each team.

The weighting of this association, where each of the approximate 15,500 members pay an annual quota of €12, is shown in the ownership distribution of Swansea City, which can be found on the official webpage (only those who own ten percent or more are shown):

Mr & Mrs Martin Morgan - 22.5%
Brian Katzen - 20%
Swansea City Supporters Society Ltd. - 20%
Huw Jenkins - 12.5%
Robert Davies - 10%

The high percentage belonging to the Trust is because its contribution has reached £30,000 over the years, after having initially contributed to the survival of the club with a payment of almost £50,000. Huw Cooze, a graphic designer born in Swansea and who helped the team right up until the end of the 1970s, is the Supporters Director on the Swansea City board.

Huw Jenkins, the fourth on the list above, was chairman from 2002 and continues to be; "At the time the only objective was to save Swansea City and improve the financial situation."

Support for the club, back then, was at an all-time low around the City. Since taking up the reigns, the growth has been progressive in every aspect – on a sporting, economic and social level. Jenkins concedes that one of the key factors for the rapid growth is as a result of keeping the same people involved who were in charge of the club almost a decade previously. The first local committee that started to manage the club in February 2002 was formed by Martin Burgess, Leigh Dineen (current vice-president), Huw Jenkins (current chairman), Brian Katzen (current executive and second highest shareholder), and the aforementioned David Morgan (current associate director) and

Mel Nurse. Four of the six continue to this day to be involved in leading the club.

One of their first actions was to return the money to the group of supporters who had contributed funds through shares. No information regarding the remaining fifteen percent shareholding features on the official Swansea City website, this was shared between Leigh Dineen's businesses and John Van Zweden's companies.

Changes

Despite all the changes in management and governance the situation was far from secure. In fact, the following 2002-03 season, was far from easy on the pitch, although the end of the season was probably a turning point. Nick Cusack, who had arrived the previous football year, was dismissed on the 19th September without having managed many games at the old Vetch Field. When Brian Flynn replaced him, Swansea ranked bottom of the Football League for the first time in the clubs history. Swansea sat in ninety-second place, bottom of the four leagues: above them were twenty Premiership clubs, twenty-four in the Championship, twenty-four in League One and twenty-three in League Two.

As well as the arrival of Flynn, the ninth manager in seven years, other people were also instrumental to Swansea's survival. Two of them, Leon Britton and Alan Tate, would go on to play for Swansea in all four of the professional leagues over the ensuing decade. Whilst the Spanish Swan, Roberto Martínez, was made captain just a few weeks after his arrival. Roberto, many years later, would become manager and implement the foundations of the definitive plan, the attractive football that has become the clubs identity and philosophy.

Roberto joined Swansea at the beginning of 2003 from Walsall, convinced by a conversation he had with Flynn. What can one say to convince a player to join a side languishing at the bottom of the lowest league? Well, there were two strong arguments which tilted the balance: Swansea City's history and, above all, the aspiration to avoid relegation whilst playing good attractive football. The Spaniard's eyes lit up when he heard mention of this latter point: for a technical midfielder, the proposal offered an oasis in British football, which back in those days was considered a wasteland of possession football, everything was about the long ball game.

The Catalonian footballer travelled down to Swansea one Thursday night in January, but the following day he had to return to Walsall, where he remained, waiting expectantly for negotiations to conclude. The following Tuesday he was able to make the return journey to Wales where he was contracted to remain until June of that year. The Spaniard had nineteen games in which to help his new team. The Swans were six points clear of safety and the odds from the betting community were stacked heavily against them, pointing to clear relegation. The media and the fans feared the worse and wondered which team would be relegated along with Swansea.

Alan Tate and Leon Britton who had joined a few weeks before Roberto, from Manchester United and West Ham respectively, must have asked themselves quite what they had got themselves involved in. Little Britton, a nickname he acquired as a result of his short stature (1.65 metres) and very similar sounding to the well-known comedy show Little Britain, played a key role within Swansea from the outset. "When I joined, we were the lowest in the table," Britton recalls. "After teammates like Tate and Roberto were signed, we played very well the final months and stood a chance in that final game."

The midfielder, who during his first months in Swansea played mainly on the right side, began his career with Arsenal until West Ham paid £400,000 to sign him as a young player, the highest transfer fee paid for a sixteen-year-old at that time. Another promising youth in English football, Michael Carrick, was Leon's roommate at the Hammers school back in those early days.

The lack of opportunities in the first team at the London club meant he was released to Swansea City, with whom almost a decade later he would make history, by debuting in the world famous Premier League, with the highest percentage rate of successful passes recorded throughout the major European leagues, even outperforming the international Spaniard from Barcelona, Xavi Hernández. Despite the different roles they played for their clubs, Welsh fans would compare them to each other and, some pundits in the local media nicknamed the

English player 'Xavi from the Valleys'. During the 2011-12 season, a photomontage in the FourFourTwo football magazine contained an illustration of both Xavi and Britton with the following caption: "One of the two is the best passer in Europe. The other plays for Barça".

The endearing Lakie (Huw Lake, the club's liaison officer) proudly commends Britton's performance against Bolton in October 2011 - where he completed one hundred percent of his passes, something which no midfielder or attacker had achieved in the Premier League for six years - and inspired the creation of shirts with 'Leon 100%' emblazoned across the front. Thomas Butler, his teammate between 2006 and 2012, would go even further with an illuminating comment on Twitter; "Britts hasn't lost a ball since he was five years old, and that was because he had a cold that day." The footballer himself plays down his own achievements and acknowledges that he doesn't risk too much through his combinations and his aim is to always take an opportunity to pass to a teammate and create space.

These attributes are highly valued by Premier League managers and in a study carried out in March 2012 they voted Leon Britton the third best midfielder of the competition, after David Silva and Yaya Touré.

Both on and off the pitch, Britton instantly hit it off with the first Spanish player to ever play for Swansea and they became lifelong friends. He remembers Roberto, who was his roommate, as a typical Spanish footballer on account of his skilful technique and as a midfielder who enabled the team to play differently in League Two where tackles and long passes were common.

Likewise, Britton emphasises that he was a fantastic captain, with personality on the playing field and ample experience, adding that he was always cracking jokes to create an upbeat atmosphere in the changing rooms. He is ever mindful that Bob only ever did two things in the lodgings: watch a lot of football and sleep at least eight hours every night.

The Final Relegation Battle

With the economic situation a constant source of worry, during Roberto Martínez's first few months, tension reached an all-time high. Roberto explains the drama caused by fear of relegation; "Relegation in League Two is the most difficult, because you lose professional status; employment by the club would be tough and full-time employees would become hourly workers. We were risking the club's very future."

With two encounters left to play at the end of that 2002-03 season, four clubs were in danger of occupying the two relegation spots: Carlisle United, Exeter City, Shrewsbury Town and Swansea. The Welsh side won 1-2 in the penultimate match against Rochdale, rescuing the whole season. That match was the culmination of 3690 minutes of league football played that season. This was a miracle for a club who were written off only four months previously. Those decisive ninety minutes that brought the season to a close were played on the 3rd of May 2003 in front of 9583 spectators at the Vetch Field.

With a typically British 4-4-2 formation, the eleven first team players to face Hull City and who bore the responsibility of maintaining professional status as well as the club's survival, were as follows: Neil Cutler, Lee Jenkins, Kristian O'Leary, Alan Tate, Michael Howard, Jonathon Coates, Leon Britton, Roberto Martínez, Lenny Johnrose, Kevin Nugent and James Thomas.

Hearts were racing until the final whistle. It was a game of high quality and a penalty taken in the eighth minute by Britton resulted in a bicycle kick by the wearer of the number 35 shirt, which set up the opening goal for Thomas. Amid the local euphoria, Roberto Martínez made a gesture asking for calm when he embraced the goal scorer, showing, even then, that he possessed the qualities of a manager.

With no time to savour the goal, the Vetch Field was left flabbergasted when Hull drew level only sixty seconds later. Then further tragedy befell the old playing field in the twenty-fifth minute, when the visiting team shot ahead with another goal. Both goals were the result of defensive failures, possibly due to nerves and pressure over what was at stake. Tensions were eased thanks to another vital penalty in the last moments of the first half, which meant that half time was somewhat less traumatic for the Jacks.

Early in the second half, Johnrose secured the hosts' lead (3-2) by firing home a loose ball into the goal after a majestically taken free kick by Roberto, who was wearing the number 27 shirt and captain's armband.

The defining moment of the encounter, however, was yet to take place. A loss of possession in the centre circle by Hull, and some skilful play by Thomas controlling the ball allowed him to pass the line of defence with a short sprint. Time stood still in the fifty-seventh minute, with the ball rolling in ideal circumstances for the forward, with only the rival goalkeeper waiting ahead. In that moment, all the agony over the possible loss of professional status vanished in a split second with one subtle piece of play. The Swans' dreams were realised as the ball was chipped over the goalkeeper's head into the corner of the goalmouth in a move that would have done justice to a Premiership star, the final 4-2 win was secure.

Thomas was lauded as the hero of the evening as the Swans were rescued thanks to his hat-trick. Thomas, who is retired from football due to injury and now works for the Welsh Ambulance Service, recalls how he couldn't sleep for two nights before the decisive final match; "As a local boy, I knew how important it was for the people of Swansea." The forward scored six goals in the last six games of that season playing as a centre forward, this was after a dry period of twenty two games, which he blames on Flynn's decision of forcing him to play on the left wing.

Immediately after the match, a mass of supporters flooded onto the field and helped ease all the tension that had been accumulating those previous months. The Stadium resounded with a joy and jubilance which would not be felt again until, almost a decade later, fate would once again smile on the Swans in the month of May with a 4-2 result and a hat-trick and entry to the top flight. But that Hull match continues to be one of the most important and emotional matches in the clubs history ensuring its very survival.

This objective (or some might say miracle) was reached thanks to the improved performances on the playing field, but also due to the many bonding experiences engineered between the players through their numerous meals together at Paco's, a Spanish restaurant, in central Swansea, which became their second changing room and home away from home. The owner of this establishment - located on The Kingsway (and previously situated on St. Helen's Road) - couldn't have begun to imagine the significance of the letter he sent to Roberto Martínez as soon as he knew the player was in Swansea, inviting him to eat at his restaurant.

Roberto, Captain

Roberto Martínez is the brother Jordi Cruyff never had. That is what the former Manchester United footballer says about the godfather of his children, just before adding that Roberto going to Swansea, a club so far from salvation, scared him a little; "We had a chat during which we agreed it was better to play for a small club than to sit out matches at a bigger club. Going to Swansea changed his life. He was soon made captain. He was fresh blood and he sent out optimistic messages in the changing room. Furthermore, he was really responsible for helping his teammates improve."

Roberto himself recalls how Brian Flynn made him captain some games after his debut, and how significant it was in British football. "It is rare if you have spent so little time playing for a team, and even more so if you are foreign. It's unusual, but it was a very unusual season". In fact, the initial objective was promotion. But this plan soon started to go sideways, which brought about many changes. The manager replaced many players, the captain was injured and the role of the defensive midfielder from Balaguer, on and off the pitch, had a significant impact on the final outcome.

Barely two days after the decisive encounter against Hull, and despite the fact that his transfer deal with the Welsh club had ended, Martínez publicly supported Flynn's continuation as manager, whom he assured, the fans, was the ideal person to manage the pressure and guide the players in the right direction. His continuing involvement with the team didn't even require a contractual agreement which was noticed both in the changing room and in the stands. The Spaniard was always greatly loved by the Jack fans, and he always identified strongly with Wales, whose sentiments and grievances were comparable to his native Catalonia.

The Battle for Britton

The weeks that followed the end of the season were going to be decisive. Much of the team were there on loan, and their continuation was complicated. The preservation of their professional status would mean nothing if the players didn't remain in the team. In this vein, the Swansea City Supporters Trust and their blessed tenacity would again play a vital role.

To help pay Leon Britton's wage, members of the association would walk around the stands, during match days, with buckets asking for donations. This fan led movement was named "The Battle for Britton", and resulted in a new two-year contract for the player. West Ham, surprisingly, didn't ask for any sum of money for his transfer, though they did include a clause securing a percentage share from a prospective sale. Supporters had voted the diminutive midfielder the best player of the season for his twenty six games played in those decisive final months. The efforts made by the Swans Trust to keep the player in the team are a reflection of just how much loved he was by the Jack Army.

In June 2003, Britton confessed that he thought the match against Hull City had been his last as a Swansea player, but he was delighted to stay connected with the Welsh club. He felt indebted to Brian Flynn for having had the opportunity to play in a premier professional team and get a run of games under his belt.

The manager publicly returned the compliment and felt relieved that one of the side's saviours had remained at the club: "Leon played an important role in the club's continued survival and, in the future, he will contribute to our success. To be able to sign him is an incentive for everyone. If we could also sign Roberto that would be the icing on the cake."

According to a pamphlet published by the Swans Trust, at that time, financial assistance from the organization would enable the signing of Brad Maylett, Andy Robinson and Lee Trundle as well as keeping Britton and Martínez at Swansea.

Phil Sumbler, current president of the Trust, would years later claim that, although Tony Petty wasn't the best thing that happened to the club, quite the reverse, with time it would become apparent that his era galvanized the club, bringing together an impassioned group of people who were aware that the club's existence was in danger and were willing to fight to ensure survival. Likewise he believes that those dark days enforced financial prudence which would become one of Swansea's hallmarks.

The Following Seasons

The beginning of the 2003-04 season went well. Swansea reached the fifth round of the FA Cup for the first time in twenty four year. With things going well on the field it made it difficult to predict that a change of management was imminent. It took place in March. Swansea's position in the middle of the table did not please the managerial body, which had also started to grow tired of rumours circulating about the players. Author Geraint H. Jenkins explains how some of the staff's unbridled social life negatively affected team performance on the playing field.

The departure of Brian Flynn, declared a hero after the game against Hull City some months previously, was brought about by some lacklustre performances in the following matches. The team had to forget about making the promotional playoff positions after losing six games on the bounce. Kenny Jacket was brought in and guided the team to tenth position in the league.

The addition of the former Welsh international footballer to the club brought about a change in philosophy, the aim was to introduce more direct football, with more experienced and physically stronger players brought into the side. This style was very different to the one known as the 'Swansea Way'. Although there are those who believe that this expression which refers to the Welsh side's thrilling passing game was coined only recently, some place its origin back to the sixties or seventies, and some attribute it to the Toshack era in the early eighties. Journalist Tim Lewis is not sure of the exact origin, but confirms that a tradition of identifying Swansea City with good play has existed for some considerable time, although he doesn't forget that the team went through some darker periods, especially in the nineties.

The following summer, various defenders arrived to support that new style espoused by Jackett, which was made perfectly apparent in the 2004-05 season and reflected in the results: a clean sheet of seven consecutive home games.

This stylistic turning point undermined Roberto Martínez's position at the club and was contrary to his characteristics. Roberto found himself progressively demoted, since the coach was an advocate of a box-to-box midfielder. With regards to the collective performance on the field, what happened was the flip side of the previous year. A fairly poor start provoked a lot of criticism of the manager, although rapid further progression finally clinched that much-yearned-for and celebrated promotion. Two one-goal margins of defeat in the final two games secured the triumphant promotion, the two goals were the work of Adrian Forbes. Among his eleven goals as a Swan, the winger will always remember both the last league goal in the history of the old stadium (1-0 against Shrewsbury on 30th April in front of eleven thousand five hundred spectators) and the goal that would secure their promotion to League One. The visiting fans barely had to wait thirty seconds to celebrate the cross-shot fired by Forbes which secured a 0-1 win against Bury on the 10th May. On that historic day, Roberto Matínez played ninety minutes. Kenny Jackett remembers that promotion as one of the best moments of his career, a fantastic achievement for him and his players, but also for all the members of the club who had stuck by it through the dark times. The players' celebration at Gigg Lane field was ecstatic. Willy Guéret, still in his goalkeeping outfit, was arrested and taken by four officers to the police station for climbing onto an area which posed some safety risks. His teammates did not want to return to Wales without him, therefore they went looking for him after attending to the media, and he was later released thanks to the intervention of Jackett. Guéret had to pay an £80 fine for a public order offence. On the journey home, each member of the team sang a song on the bus. When the goalkeeper took the microphone, his choice was "Please Release Me" by Engelbert Humperdinck.

It was a fine finale to the last season at the old Vetch Field, which closed its doors in style, with a victory of 2-1 for Swansea in the FAW Premier Cup final against Wrexham. The opposing goal was scored by the Spanish player Juan Ugarte. After scoring sixteen goals that season, the former striker from Real Sociedad was wanted by Swansea and thanks to mediation by Toshack he was very close to signing, but finally he declined the offer after realising that he didn't know his future coach too well or what manner of football he wanted the team to play.

Ugarte would have been the second Spanish player in Swansea's history, after Roberto, who had recently been delighted to raise the Welsh Cup as captain for the first time and subsequently re-sign with the Swans as a first team player. Jackett had advised him to go to another team for the 2005-06 season. The footballer from Balaguer did not heed Jackett's advice, preferring to stay at the Swans in order to have the opportunity to compete in the new league. Furthermore, he hoped that the dimensions of the new stadium (The Liberty), which was considerably wider than the Vetch, would favour his style of play. His qualities were demonstrated with the goal he scored against Nottingham Forest at the Liberty on the 24th of September 2005: Roberto chested down a loose ball in the penalty area, controlled it and skilfully chipped it into the opponent's net. Martínez had a generally good season playing for the team.

Despite being recently promoted, they failed to capitalise on their good run of form. The Welsh side won against Brentford in the semi-finals of the playoff, but on Saturday 27th May, they lost in the final against Barnsley in the cruellest of ways: 4-3 in penalties, after a 2-2 draw within the regulation time. Swansea had notched the first goal with a great bicycle kick and then a long shot facilitated by a mistake from the goalkeeper, but a free-kick saw the game go to unpredictable penalties. The Spanish midfielder had to watch the game from the Millennium Stadium stands in Cardiff, along with 34,000 Swansea supporters.

He would however play in that very stadium in front of almost 30,000 fans for the last seven minutes in the 2-1 victory against Carlisle United, then leaders of League Two, in the Football League Trophy which took place on Sunday 2nd April.

Another trophy showcased that season was the FAW Premier Cup, won in March against Wrexham again and with the same results as the previous year (2-1). Roberto took to the playing field after eighty-two minutes. Those were his last great moments as a Swan. The club decided not to renew his contract at the end of that season.

Roberto, to Chester

He was not short of offers, both from League One and League Two. Finally, he decided to move to lower league Chester as an act of allegiance to the Welsh club with whom he had experienced so much: he did not want to play against a side for which he had been captain. Since his debut on the 1st February 2003 at the Rushden & Diamonds playing field, Roberto represented the Jacks in one hundred and twelve league games, with a further ten as substitute and another seventeen appearances in Cup matches, scoring a total of six goals.

The Catalonian footballer values his three and a half seasons playing for the Welsh club. Historic redemption in his first half-season, a stable preservation of league status in his first complete season, a promotion to League One the next season, and, in the last season a penalty defeat in the final playoff of Championship promotion: "We won the Football League Trophy too, so my time at Swansea was very good. Furthermore, we moved to the new stadium and I was captain in the first match played there, as well as the last match at the Vetch Field, something that always carries important emotional connotations," adds Roberto to summarise his playing days at Swansea City.

A twenty-two year old Roberto had originally embarked on his great British adventure at Wigan. Isido Díaz and Jess Seba accompanied him, the first Spaniards after Nayim who tried their luck with football in the UK, all taking advantage of the Bosman Rule. Roberto was the first Spanish player to notch a goal in the emblematic FA Cup, and he'll always remember how he was voted best footballer in Wigan's history by the fans.

"We had a distinctive style to what is typically seen in these islands, and people remember us fondly." This recognition was shared by journalist Andrew Kirby, who compared seeing

Martínez play - the signing of whom would see better times at Wigan – to the sun shining after years of grey skies.

From Wigan, Roberto moved to Motherwell in Scotland, then Walsall and finally Swansea City. Also, in 1999 he started to collaborate with a television station as a commentator for Spanish football. With that track-record behind him, thirty-three year-old Bob Martínez started the 2006-07 season playing for Chester. Not even he could imagine that a few months later, in February, Swansea would welcome him back.

CHAPTER 4

2006-07: FROM PLAYER TO MANAGER

Roberto Martínez decided it was time to seek out some new challenges, fifty miles north of Swansea. Although his dreams as a player lasted little more than half a year in the service of Chester City gracing the playing fields of League Two. The club's history itself was to be almost as short thereafter. Just three years after the Spanish midfielder left, drowning in debt and roaming through the wilderness of non-professional football, Chester City disappeared on the 10th March, 2010, after one hundred and twenty-five years as a club. In just two weeks, supporters of the club created Chester FC, a new entity which today retains the blue and white colours of the original club and who were the celebrated champions of the Conference North in 2012-13. Meanwhile, in Swansea, expectations were high after having been so close to the Championship the previous year. The physicality and directness of the 4-4-2 game that characterised Kenny Jackett's style was losing favour in the press and among the fans, who never understood why he discarded beloved players such as Roberto. The fans admired Roberto, not just for his playing skills, but for the pride with which he wore the captain's armband. Even though the team was nearing the play-offs and had achieved a great victory against Premiership team, Sheffield United, in the third round of the FA Cup, the growing level of criticism became unbearable for the manager. This is how he put it to the club on Wednesday the 14th February in a phone call which left Huw Jenkins very upset. The Swansea Chairman went public with his surprise, admitting that only two days prior to the announcement, of Jackett's departure, he had had a meeting with Jackett in which not only had he not raised any doubts over his position as manager, but both had approached the possibility of strengthening the backroom staff. The decision to end the manager's contract was taken by mutual agreement.

The doubts of one of the fifty candidates

The Gaffer, as Martínez is known, was surprised to receive a call from Huw Jenkins, and even more surprised about the content of that call, so surprised in fact that he can't precisely remember the exact date, but thinks it was in late January and before his name had appeared in the press linking him with the vacant position. In English football it is standard practice to send a CV and apply for the position of manager at a club, something which Roberto did not do before having to confront the most difficult decision of his sporting career. Although he was available as a player, Martínez wasn't able to sign for any team apart from Chester during that month of February because the winter transfer market had already closed. If he was to become Swansea coach, he would be obliged to be only that and therefore hang up his boots. Roberto went through a period of self-doubt, he loved playing football, and was not sure whether he wanted to sacrifice the chance of ever playing again. He would also lose the bet he had made with his father that he would surpass his professional longevity on the field. Roberto believed that he could still perform on the pitch at a high level for two or three more years, Jordi Cruyff encouraged him to accept the proposal – "He wanted to go to Swansea, but the decision to quit playing can't be made in a matter of two hours. The majority of people in his circumstances would have continued playing, because he was a star at Chester, and considering the good condition he kept himself in he could have continued playing for some years," explained Jordi, who after his illustrious career as a player gained a lot of experience as Director of Football with AEK Larnaca in Cyprus and as head coach of MAccabi Tel Aviv. In those days, Roberto and Jordi spent a lot of time debating what it would mean to be in charge of both friends and teammates. Roberto saw only advantages: he personally knew ninety per cent of the workforce first-hand; he knew the strong and weak points of every person and he believed he knew how to motivate each person in order to get the best performance from everyone. Jordi Cruyff, Johan's son, was very sceptical about Roberto's reasoning, but changed his mind after his experiences in Cyprus – "In my job I had a good relationship with the players because they knew that I had been one of them and so they would always fight harder for me than they would have for another". Rumours soon spread among the fans that Roberto could be making an appearance on the bench at the Liberty Stadium. Although he had been idolised as a player by the fans, there was some disagreement about the prospect of him becoming coach. Some doubted him for his lack of experience and didn't believe he would be able to establish authority over his former teammates. Those Jacks that were waiting for him with open arms, however, praised him for the footballing brain that characterised him as a player, as well as his general knowledge of the game, the club and the city. Those close to Roberto, for their part, harboured no doubts. They had believed for some time that with his charisma, his knowledge and his footballing mentality there was an excellent coach inside the man from Balaguer. His former coach at Walsall, used to have him nearby in the dugout, when he wasn't on the field of play, so that the Spaniard could share with him the observations he made. Roberto used to studiously make notes, in a notebook he always carried with him, of all the training sessions and matches, as Jordi Cruyff describes – "He's always wanted to study the methods of and to learn from his coaches. He has documented every training session from his last years as a player: different series of exercises, sprint exercises, endurance, possessive plays, even the field measurements of various pitches… he dedicated time each and every day to detailing every pertinent fact about football and what achieved the best results." This desire and predisposition to absorb and accumulate knowledge extended beyond the pitch. For example, Roberto and Jordi both undertook a postgraduate degree in marketing at the ages of twenty five and twenty six, whilst playing for Wigan and Manchester United respectively. There was support, for Roberto, in the Swansea locker room, some players were keen, ahead of a definitive decision being made, that he got the appointment. The defender, Alan Tate, didn't give much importance to Bob's lack of experience as a coach and believed that his passion for football made him the right man for the job. On the 21st February, 2007, Chester hosted a League Two game against their opponents, Bury. Nobody could have guessed that Roberto, voted the man of the match for that fixture, had a meeting arranged the very next day with the Swansea chairman in a nearby hotel. A day after the meeting, on Friday the 23rd, Roberto received a message asking him to join Swansea City as soon as possible. It was noon and Chester's team bus was preparing to leave for that day's fixture, and so there were some minutes of confusion… would Bob, the team's captain, travel to play another game in League Two or would he stay behind to become the new manager of the Swans? In the end, Chester's president accepted his departure and the team left without the Spaniard, whose presence was sorely missed as that Saturday they lost 1 – 0 to Swindon. "I accepted because I knew the club and ninety per cent of its staff, I had a good relationship with the fans and I knew that possession football and my ideas could fit with the philosophy of the club. It was the right decision," Martínez later said. In retrospect, he thinks that Swansea was probably the only club that he would have agreed to manage at that stage of his career. That Friday as he drove the three and a half hour journey that he had made, in reverse, eight months previously, the Spaniard's mind was filled with ideas: style of play, the evolution of the system, player profiles for the future, his relationship with former teammates and many other things.

Jenkins' Chosen One

Out of the fifty aspiring candidates for the position, Roberto Martínez was the one chosen. The statement announcing his hiring made it clear that after having interviewed several different candidates, the decision had been unanimous – "We were sure that Roberto was the right man for the job. Many people in the world of football had recommended him to us, including John Toshack, who offered him any help or advice he might need." Toshack and Martínez had come to know one another in their work as commentators for Spanish League games on Sky television. On occasions they travelled together from Wales to London, exchanging their opinions and ideas on football. Roberto had impressed John, especially when he spoke about Real Madrid's style of play back during his first period with the team in the Spanish capital. The Welshman remembers clearly the words he used to advise Swansea's chairman, Huw Jenkins – "I told him that I already knew Roberto, that he had been at the club as a player and was a consummate professional who was very studious in his approach, and I also reminded him that I too had become a manager without any coaching experience behind me." Those in charge at Swansea secretly hoped for just this outcome, that the Spaniard would become a new Toshack, and emulate the success the club had enjoyed three decades previously. Roberto's name was in the mix from the beginning, but he was quite surprised that Huw Jenkins would select him for the job. The Spaniard, at thirty three years old, was returning just eight months after the club had decided not to renew his contract as a player, and replace the coach who was instrumental in showing him the door. Roberto is only too aware of the rumours, circulating at that time, that as a player for Swansea he built a good rapport with Huw Jenkins and they shared many a footballing conversation. According to the rumours this supposed trust and close friendship had sparked a negative reaction from Kenny Jackett. As a result of this, so it has been said, he didn't look favourably upon his midfielder, apparently he also took exception to the level of influence Roberto had in the locker room. Martínez himself explains that during his time as a player he didn't have a relationship with the chairman, with whom he says he only had one chat towards the end of his final season as a player, however he does admit to having a very harmonious relationship with Jenkins since his return to Swansea as manager. On top of this, he insists that his relationship with Jackett throughout this period was a good one, despite the contrast between their styles. Years later, destiny would intervene and the paths of Kenny Jackett and Roberto Martínez would cross once again. It was a duel from the benches in the semi-final of the FA Cup in the 2012-13 season, a clash which was fought at Wembley Stadium. Jackett led Milwall, a Championship side, while Martínez was in charge of Wigan, a Premiership team. The student surpassed the master on two fronts: he coached a team from a superior category and Wigan won the match 0-2, reaching the first cup final in the team's history. The press recounted the shared history of the two from their days at Swansea and in a press conference prior to the semi-final Jackett was effusive in his praise of Roberto - "He was a magnificent captain and the best professional I have ever seen." He also confessed that he had always thought that Roberto had the potential to become a high-level manager and made a justification, almost seven years after the fact, for not renewing the midfielder's contract with the Swans – "You make different decisions, such as trying to bring in younger players. It was a situation in which we were looking for progress." The newspapers reminded him of past events with such headlines as "Kenny Jackett head-to-head with Roberto Martínez, the captain he sold."

As soon as Swansea's proposal was accepted in 2007, Roberto defended himself against the criticisms of his lack of experience, assuring everyone that he would compensate for the deficit in experience with enthusiasm and hard work. The Welsh press focussed on him being a great communicator both on and off the field. It has been noted that this ability might have been crucial to his success when interviewed for the position by Huw Jenkins, who was impressed when Roberto produced an entire dossier he had compiled in which he analysed the strengths and weaknesses of every member of staff. During the decisive interview, he also won him over with his ideas of the game and his aspiration to imitate the youth policy of some Spanish clubs. An early inkling of his ideas about the game could be understood by observing Roberto as a player: he always played in front of the defence, it was the way he could go after the ball the most in a 4-4-2 and after the defensive midfielder in a 4-4-3. "He didn't like to go for goal with big strikes, he wanted to try to approach the goal with touches and combination passes. He had a good inside strike, with a good turn, and he didn't score many goals but the ones he did were good, those which appear on television," explains Jordi Cruyff. "He also deserves a lot of credit for adapting so well to the complicated 'box to box' football, which demands that you constantly run many kilometres from area to area, especially in the lower leagues of English football." This adaptation of the English style was a good thing and helped Roberto to become highly professional – Roberto admits it forced him to watch his diet and always sleep the necessary amount of hours. The primary objective of the club was to firmly establish the new philosophy of play ahead of the next season without risking the fight to make the play-offs in the months that remained of the current campaign. The Board was convinced that Martínez was the man who could get the team to play what today has become commonly known as the 'Swansea style'. Together with the chairman, he put together a short, medium and long term plan. He had it all in his head and now was an opportunity to put it all into practice.

A New Era

A few hours after Roberto Martínez signed his contract as manager, Swansea played away to Yeovil. Kevin Nugent, assistant to Kenny Jackett, led the team provisionally for the second time that Saturday 14th February, with Roberto taking notes from the stands on the 1-0 defeat which left the team ninth in the table, five points away from a play-off position. In his notebook, he wrote that one of his primary tasks was to reignite his former teammate's joy of playing. His first contact with his new charges was a few hours before that game, something which did not sit well with some players who stated that it wasn't the ideal time as it affected their concentration for that important league fixture. But, aside from this, what feelings were there in the Swansea locker room at the beginning of this new era? Leon Britton, Roberto's good friend and former roommate, remembers the oddness of the situation – "The first time we spoke with him as manager was a strange sensation for us all." From this point onward, the relationship changed dramatically between Roberto and all of the players, and for good reason. Roberto firmly believes that a manager cannot have a close friendship with any of his players. The Gaffer had twelve matches ahead in which to guide the team towards the play-offs and promotion. Swansea had won only one of the previous nine encounters, but in the twelve that followed the Jacks would significantly improve upon this record. Although he had little time with which to make his mark on the team – the next encounter was to be held almost immediately, the following Tuesday – Swansea beat Rotherham 1-2 at home. In the starting eleven, there were only two new faces compared with the previous match. For his debut as manager at the Liberty, the fans received him with a standing ovation, which turned into frustration with the game and the score (a goalless draw against Leyton Orient). Still, Roberto remembers the excitement of that day, especially his entrance onto the pitch from the locker room tunnels. After this, he concentrated on the game and envied his players, to the point where he imagined himself kicking each ball from his position in the technical area of the stands. Then came three consecutive wins for Swansea (2-0 against Tranmere, 2-0 against Chesterfield and 2-1 against Northampton), a loss (2-0 at Millwall) and a tie which felt like a victory of sorts as Swansea emerged the stronger after not yielding to Bristol City, who were second in the table and playing at home. A decisive final encounter arrived after having scored a further ten points in the four previous fixtures (victory by 3-0 against Port Vale, a 2-2 tie away at Bournemouth and two further victories by 2-1: Brighton at the Liberty Stadium and away against Carlisle). In the final match of the season Swansea were hosting Blackpool, a keen rival who had already secured a place in the playoffs, but could earn automatic promotion if they won and so had everything to play for at the Liberty Stadium. The Swans kept one eye on Oldham, who were looking to seal a playoff position, they had seventy-two points and were sixth in the league. Swansea were on the same points but were seventh in the league. Roberto, who without Tate and Painter due to injury, selected the following starting eleven: Guéret, Amankwah, Austin, Lawrence, Iriekpen, Britton, O'Leary, Craney, Robinson, Trundle and Duffy. Although all started well, with Iriekpen's 1-0 opener at fourteen minutes in, Morrel in the twenty-fifth and Parker in the thirty-second made it 1-2 by half time. Trundle, the local hero, made it 2-2 in the forty-seventh minute, but then missed a penalty shortly after.

The miss didn't affect his teammates too much, as Iriekpen put the team ahead in the fifty-fifth minute. The joy was short-lived, however, because one hundred and twenty seconds later Morrell found the equalizer and in the sixty-first minute the very same player made it 3-4. In just six minutes, Blackpool had turned the score around. At this stage of the match, Bob Martínez called upon a young seventeen year-old who had yet to make his debut in a league competition. A couple of minutes after this substitution, Morrell scored a fourth goal in the seventy-eighth minute, raising the visitors' advantage even further, Parker then sealed it, to the groans of the Swansea faithful, with his second goal. The Jacks finished seventh, with seventy-two points, three below Oldham, who had only been able to snatch away the vital final playoff position winning by a goal difference of four. However, since the arrival of the new manager Swansea's league points told their own story and hinted at good times ahead: since the end of February, the team had accrued twenty-four points out of a possible tally of thirty-six (seven victories, three ties and two defeats).

The Debut of the Young, Clean-booted Welshman

That young man of seventeen years of age who made his debut in League One wearing a Swansea City shirt that 5th May 2007, would come to be, five years later, an important part of one of the biggest clubs in the Premiership. The man in question is Joe Allen, who had already played a few minutes under Kenny Jackett some months previously in the FA Cup and the FAW Premier Cup, when he was still only sixteen years old. "Joe had been part of Swansea since he was nine years old, and with the way he handled himself he always reminded me of Guardiola and players of that style," remembers Roberto Martínez. On 14th August 2007, Walsall players laughed at Allen's lightweight physique when he emerged from the locker room tunnels onto the pitch at the Liberty Stadium for a League Cup match. By the end of the encounter, with Swansea winning 2-0, the young midfielder was named man of the match and his opponents realised that this was a man albeit with the body of a child. Not content with having given him his debut in the Football League in May, in August Roberto gave the then Wales under-21 international the opportunity to sign his first professional contract. Allen made statements to the press saying he was living the dream, but he also showed his maturity by adding that he had much hard work ahead of him. The Spanish manager stated how much he valued having such an important local talent in the team and that he saw a bright future ahead for the only member of Swansea's locker room that spoke Welsh. For home games, the young players made coffee for the technical team and prepared the boots of those in the first team. Martínez always considered this youth squad member to be special and soon recognised that he had star quality, and he made sure to treat him gently when he made his debut – "That day, Allen turned up as just another member of the youth squad. I didn't want to say anything to him beforehand so that he wouldn't be nervous, so he would sleep well the night before, and so I didn't tell him that he was up until he'd finished completing those tasks." For his part, Allen remembers receiving the news after he had trained with those who weren't to be called upon on the morning of the match. The midfielder thinks that he played quite well against Blackpool, despite entering the pitch in the final twenty minutes with the score against them.

The Conceptual Phase

At the end of the 2006-07 season, the prelude to the beginning of 'Spanish Swansea,' the team still held with the 4-4-2 formation so characteristic of British football. Although Roberto had been introducing many ball exercises into the training sessions, his game plan was still in its conceptual phase. Something he did establish from the start was certain new routines for the players off the pitch, such as sharing two meals a day together in the club's facilities. He also resurrected a tradition of which he, together with Kenny Jackett, had been the architect on one of the club's journeys to Lincoln. Each member of the team had to stand on a table to sing with a spoon, or a similar object, that served as a microphone. As a player Roberto sang 'Beauty and the Beast' and upon his return as manager he opted for 'It's a Heartache', by the Welsh singer Bonnie Tyler. From this point onwards, each new addition to the team knew what was expected of them on their first outing with the club when some of their new teammates would begin thumping their glasses on the table towards the end of each meal. Swansea maintain this tradition to this very day and Bob took it with him to Wigan, his next destination as manager, because he considers it a good exercise for the group dynamic: the new recruits can integrate with the rest and the team becomes more unified. In his initial assessment before that summer, Roberto opted for a push on the playoff places – the short term objective, though not obligatory, was decided in the plan he developed together with Huw Jenkins. At the same time he was slowly sowing the seeds of change in the style that he wanted to be the team's own – the medium term, priority objective. Bob was convinced that this was the path the club needed to take in order to grow. He only needed more time, to plan a complete season from start to finish and players that met the right profile to fit in with the philosophy of play that he had in mind. Roberto wanted to build a firm foundation that would help the team to achieve the dream of reaching the Premiership within four years – the long term objective. Something which he definitely noted during that final quarter of the 2006-07 season were the differences between the life of a player and that of a manager – "A footballer trains for two hours a day, and that changes a lot when you become manager because you have to dedicate yourself twenty four hours a day so that twenty four players can enjoy football." A manager's tasks in Britain are significantly different to those of a manager in the rest of European football. Roberto had to spend his time taking care of all the club's outings, making arrangements with travel companies, the structure of the youth team, managing budgets, the signing and selling of players… all on top of preparing and delivering daily training sessions, or deciding upon team selection, line-ups and approaches. He fully expected the summer, and pre-season, as exciting as it would be, to be chock full of hard work.

CHAPTER 5

2007- 2008: SPANISH SWANSEA AND PROMOTION

"If we had had twenty British players
It probably would not have worked"
(Leon Britton)

Planning and Objectives

Swansea's managerial staff began to scout in many different leagues (Scotland, France, Germany ...), but they were already certain of what they wanted to accomplish. They endeavoured to keep the framework of Welsh and English players who wanted to make technical and tactical improvements, alongside Dutch and Spanish players. Half of the new players came from both those countries: arriving from Spain were Guillermo Bauzá (free), Àngel Rangel (€15,000) and Andrea Orlandi (free), while Dorus de Vries (free) and Ferrie Bodde (€60,000) were Dutch.

Roberto Martínez recognizes that forming that team was by no means an easy task, since Swansea was the seventh poorest club in League One; "I had to be very financially creative." The departure of Lee Trundle, the most distinguished player between 2003 and 2007, played an important role in the economic balance of that summers transfer market.

Trundle, who scored around twenty goals a season, had revealed he wanted to leave to have the opportunity to play in the Championship, and he did so when an offer of £1 million came from Bristol City. This was a record sum for Swansea City, and facilitated the arrival of up to ten key players who would implement the change in playing style.

Roberto, who had played alongside Trundle in the past, was aware of his reputation: "He was a superb forward. At that moment, the transfer to Bristol, seemed to be the end of the world for the Swans, but it turned into something truly positive. It was a radical change in the history of Swansea City."

In contrast, Andrea Orlandi wasn't aware of Lee Trundle's prominence. When he was signed by the Welsh club, the number 10 shirt and anything after 35 were the only ones available. As Martínez had always liked and encouraged him as a player, he chose the number 10 shirt under the recommendation of the managerial staff. At his first match, he noticed a certain tension in the changing rooms when his teammates saw him brandishing the shirt. They might have been surprised by his audacity, but the newcomer was oblivious to the fact that number 10 had previously belonged to the side's star player. Later, when Danny Graham was signed by Swansea and requested this shirt, the club would ask Orlandi to renounce it.

Roberto Martínez wanted the pre-season objective, apart from team training, to be the consolidation of the new group of players. This is how it worked firstly in Swansea and subsequently in training courses carried out in Sweden- where there were three daily sessions per week – and also later in Holland. The more limited the resources, the more time that was needed for planning. For this reason, as well as managing the team in those twelve final matches of the 2006-2007 season, Roberto also had to prepare for the future. Ferrie Bodde attended the last fixture against Blackpool, and was invited to get to know the club, the facilities and the atmosphere of the Liberty. Other players, such as Orlandi, also accepted the offer to visit the city and get to know both the training grounds and the stadium. They were sufficiently enticing to convince those who were unsure about making the move to Swansea.

A few signed immediately, other discussions were not concluded so quickly and the signing of some players left a lot to be desired. For example, Swansea had to sweat for over a month to solve the problems concerning Jason Scotland's work permit - a player whom Roberto Martínez said had a magic touch, entertained the public and could conjure up a shot from nothing. This was a pretty apt description of the forward from Trinidad and Tobago who came to Swansea from the Scottish League and enthralled fans with his mercurial talents.

The newcomers were convinced and fully bought into the club's vision. The plan was to reach the Premiership in four years, words that Roberto had repeated time and time again in every interview. The coach reveals why he set that progressive timeframe of objectives: "The biggest leap is from the Championship to the Premiership. It is not enough to pay any price and then sign a totally new team to survive in the best league in the world."

The Spanish landing

The first new Spanish player was Guillermo Bauzá (Bussy). His recruitment was set out months before, when he was playing for the subsidiary side, Espanyol. He had six months left to finish his contract and he thought it would be impossible to find a place in the first team due to the overbooking of forwards. It was even very difficult to be considered for the line-up in the Copa del Rey or the Copa Catalunya. Ahead of him were Tamudo, Pandiani, Ewerthon, Corominas, Jonathan Soriano and even De la Peña.

Bussy, only too aware of the situation, made his point very clearly to his manager at the end of 2006: "I told him in December that I was interested in playing abroad for professional and personal reasons." Also, he had fond memories of Britain, where in 2001 he was proclaimed European champion with the Spanish national under-16 team, alongside Fernando Torres as a forward.

Roberto Martínez kept in touch with Espanyol's manager, Paco Herrera, who he had known at Liverpool. In addition,

Bauzá formed part of the list of players that Bob and his staff had observed whilst scouting in Spain. Roberto himself quickly realized that Bussy would make a difference in League One on account of his tactical knowledge. This sparked the significant interest and initial talks began: "I spoke to my agent, I spoke to Roberto and I didn't hesitate, even though I didn't know where I was going. I took a whirlwind tour with my manager to get to know the city, the stadium and the coach. They decided to make me the offer and I decided to accept it."

It was a straightforward process: the player wanted to go abroad whilst the Spanish transfer market offered Swansea good options at inexpensive prices. The talks with his new coach already made Guillermo well aware that the British League One could not be compared to the Segunda División B, the equivalent category in Spain. Bauzá recalls how Roberto was friendly and personable at the dinner they had with the team's head of scouting and the striker's representative in La Parilla, a modern restaurant located in the marina. There, they spoke about football, and the manager told them his plans and his personal history. He also told them that a sufficiently large new stadium had just been completed and that there were a group of investors in which he had a lot of confidence.

Bussy fondly remembers the tough beginnings: "Each experience was interesting: requesting a mobile phone card, looking for a flat, finding an internet provider ... In a different country, all of these details help you play better if you obtain them easily." In that sense, the first Spaniards worked together to overcome all of these small issues and formed a very strong bond.

Friends of Bauzá say that he takes everything, including football, in his stride. He has matters on and off the playing field very much in order, and even enrolled in medical genetics at Swansea University. It was a decision that came as a surprise to those at the club, but for him it came naturally. Aware of the ephemeral nature of any sports career, he wanted to invest his spare time in the future, and believed that the university also benefited from his reputation as a player. "Academic study and physical exertion are connected and are mutually beneficial, because the more you use intelligence in football, the better. Both football players and doctors have to make quick and accurate decisions at certain times. And both professions are very high-pressure," he once told the Diario de Mallorca newspaper.

His teammates describe him as peculiar, independent, intelligent, studious, outgoing, friendly and a bit absent-minded. The first words uttered by Britton about him were "long-haired and a happy person," in fact, 'Peludo' is one of his nicknames which is Spanish for 'Shaggy'. "If you know him, you like him, if not, it is pretty difficult to understand him," explains Orlandi. Fede Bessone considers him his best friend for giving him support whenever he needed it, such as when he lent him money until he received his first British payslip.

Ángel Rangel, Roberto Martínez's second Spanish signing, also began his footballing journey in Wales on the first day of that pre-season and came as a result of a scouting trip to Catalonian soil, although he was very much on the rebound at that time. Around March, Roberto attended a Terrassa-Benidorm match (a Spanish Segunda División B game) to observe visiting forward Jorge Molina, currently playing for Betis, though he ended up focusing most of his attention on the local right winger. A glance into the future of a player destined to become one of the greatest of defenders: "One must always give one hundred percent," says Rangel and many Swan's fans will give testament to that fact.

When he first met him in person, Àngel was surprised at the age of his new manager. His telephone voice had mistakenly led him to imagine him as larger and wearing glasses. Martínez acknowledges how impressed he was with Rangel's football skills the first time he saw him in action. He thought he was an excellent player that had somehow fallen off the radar of the large Spanish teams: "He had great physical capacity and knew how to deal with one-on-one encounters. He was also fast, and his ability to pass the ball first time was truly amazing."

Rangel also believes that the fact he was a less expensive player - specifically some €15,000, a large part of which he admits to having paid from his own pocket - played to his favour. Xavi Cruz, his brother-in-law and confidante, explains that the money was being debited from his weekly wage. Roberto states that he was one of the best buys of his career, and Iñaki Bergara confesses that he is one of the footballers who surprised him the most.

Rangel, who everyone now views more as a Welshman than a Spaniard, has a temperament and competitive nature that means he can sometimes be a bad loser. Gorka Pintado, one of his teammates, claims that you very quickly realise when he is annoyed. But, above all, his colleagues stress that he's a very good person and is reliable on the pitch, "When you don't know who to pass to you give it to him," says Albert Serrán.

The Spaniards received a lot of help and attention from Roberto Martínez, who paid Rangel a nice gesture at the very beginning of the preseason: "July 7th was my sister Pepi's wedding and she was devastated because I couldn't attend. I asked Roberto about it and he didn't have a problem." He was at the family home at two o'clock in the morning the day before the wedding, he woke her up and gave her a big surprise: "I attended the wedding and was back in Swansea in time to travel to Sweden."

Bad start to the season

The 2007/08 season kicked off on August 11th and Swansea started with a 2-1 defeat at Oldham, against the very team from whom they had snatched the sixth and final playoff position just three months before. More than one thousand five hundred Welsh fans travelled three hundred and twenty-five kilometres for four and a half hours to the town next to Manchester to accompany the team. Rangel is all too aware that the incidents that took place during this match tarnished, not only the result, but his debut in British football. He recalls that they warmed up without any problems and that Swansea were defending the goal next to where their supporters were seated when, at the start of the game, everything unravelled: "Suddenly there was an avalanche of policemen. The referee stopped the match and about seventy people from both teams came to blows; they had jumped over the barrier that separated the home and away supporters. The police, some on horseback, brought the situation quickly under control, in two or three minutes."

The eleven first-team players were the same which, a week earlier, had defeated the Spanish First Division side Levante 2-0 in a preseason friendly played at the Liberty Stadium. De Vries, the Dutch goalkeeper, was in goal; Rangel, Lawrence, Tate and Painter formed the defence. Pratley and Bodde were the two sweepers, with Britton on the right and Robinson on the left. Further up the field, Darryl Duffy accompanied Jason Scotland.

The 4-4-2 formation was still being used, De Vries, Rangel, Bodde and Scotland played their first game, whilst possession was unfavourable for the Swans on that first day (forty-nine percent). Oldham went ahead in the third minute, thanks to a penalty, and during added time in the second half made the final score 2-1, cancelling out Scotland's goal which he scored in the fifty-fifth minute subsequent to a move by Rangel.

Just three days after the start of the season, Swansea defeated Walsall 2-0 in the first round of the League Cup. That encounter, during which many changes were made to the line-up, featured Bauzá's debut as a first-team player and was also the first complete match for the young Joe Allen, who assisted in the first goal and was Man of the Match.

On August 18th more than seventeen thousand spectators - almost three times as much as the match against Walsall, attended the first league match of the season at the Liberty. Their performance against old rivals Nottingham Forest fell considerably short with the Welsh team hammering two balls into the goalposts, resulting in 0-0. The game's final minutes were dominated by the Spanish players, with a tackle by Bussy and a good performance from Rangel. Although six near-misses was not the start they had hoped for, Britton said the match had been very well played. He added that the only thing lacking was a goal and it was difficult when the rivals visiting Swansea came with the sole intention of achieving a draw.

Bergara and the goalkeepers

The Jacks and Walsall crossed paths soon after with a second encounter and second victory for the Swans in eleven days, this time in their stadium with a 1-3 win. Walsall's initial goal was trumped by Robinson's two goals and another by Scotland, who scored his third goal in four games. Roberto Martínez drew attention to the achievements the new Swans strategy was having on the field of play. They had decided not to include a replacement goalkeeper. This allowed him the flexibility to use other players on the pitch. He considered this to be low-risk given the few times his goalkeeper was sent off or injured.

Iñaki Bergara debuted as goalkeeping coach which coincided with that first league victory. He did so with an anecdote that reflects British respect for the pitch and rules. When he and the players went to warm up, a man told him something in English that eluded his understanding, and he had to consult with the Gaffer. He spoke of some rules according to which the players had only fifteen minutes to tread the little area in the box or else the club received a warning and Bergara a personal fine. "I learned later on that there was a prize for the best groundsman, hence the need to preserve the small area. Gardeners pay great attention to those kind of details." He is still advised from time to time that he cannot warm up with three goalkeepers at once. Iñaki likes to bring another player along to the games in case of any setbacks, as well as providing good future experience for new players to familiarise themselves with the professional environment.

Iñaki Bergara joined on August 22nd, when Swansea had already played three official matches. He had spent the previous year playing for Athletic Bilbao, where a day prior to the start of the season the club fired Javier Clemente as a result of differences between him and the club president. After the change in the first team's backroom staff, Bergara was offered the opportunity to stay and carry out other duties, as his contract did not end for another year. However, he opted to take the time out of football, partly because the previous year had been such a difficult one.

It wasn't until the following summer that he received a call from his friends and representatives Vicente Biurrun and Iñaki Ibáñez. They both informed him that a Spanish manager at Swansea City was scouting for a goalkeeping coach. Although his mother was ill, Bergara took the leap and ventured on a journey into the unknown without having even the slightest knowledge of the English language: "I was not proficient in the language nor did I know what I would find there. I had a couple of telephone conversations with Roberto of whom I had known only through hearing stories about The Three Amigos. I had a good feeling, I spoke to my wife and children and thought - I'm going, I'll see and if I don't adapt then I can always come back."

Roberto Martínez stresses that Iñaki has a unique working methodology quite different to what is followed in British football. The arrival of someone with his characteristics was decisive in shaping the role that the goalkeeper was going to acquire in Swansea's new style of play. The first Spaniards highlight the vision that the Dutch goalkeeper Dorus de Vries brought, whose feel for the game enabled him to influence play from his position in goals, it was Vries who initiated many of the teams attacking moves.

Bergara lives and breathes football, quietly planning his sessions, always with a coffee at his side. These type of habits have earned him the label 'bohemian'. Those who know him reveal he is loyal beyond the bounds of what is normal in this world. He is an optimistic person, a joker, who unites and advises players, helping those who are left on the bench or miss some games through injury. Be it during work or during meals outside of work, he would talk about his experiences as a substitute goalkeeper during his career and motivate players to continue working so they're ready when the opportunity arises. In addition, some fondly remember how his English instructions were as funny as his jokes.

Bergara paid a very high price for his British adventure: his wife and daughters stayed in Bilbao. They understood that football is Iñaki's passion and he did not want to sacrifice the happiness of his family by dragging them along with him. However, the frequent visits and temporary stay of one of his daughters who studied in Britain made the experience easier to bear.

Rangel reveals that Bergara was not the first Spanish goalkeeping coach that came to Swansea: "Ignasi Madier came to try it out but did not stay. He had been with me the previous year in Terrassa. Roberto knew him. In fact, Ignasi told me that Roberto had come to see us play a game and Ignasi had spoken with him after the match."

The list of Spaniards at the Swans could have expanded yet further even back then: Mikel Alonso, the brother of the international Xabi Alonso, came to Swansea for a couple of weeks on trial before ending up at Tenerife in the Spanish

Second Division; and Francisco Sandaza -a burly forward with long hair who had spent time in Scotland and Brighton - and a left-back from Barcelona C called Joshua Fernandez were others who didn't quite make the grade.

Amazed by Elland Road

After losing 1-0 to Reading in the second round of the League Cup, they played three consecutive home games: a 1-2 defeat against Doncaster in League One with Bodde being sent off; a 3-2 victory against Milwall in the Johnstone's Paint Trophy; and a league victory of 2-1 against Carlisle United (with a late charge of two goals in the eighty-first and eighty-third minutes).

This was followed by two consecutive away games. In the first, which was played in Cheltenham, the Swans won 1-2, but in the second they were defeated (2-0) by one of their old rivals, Leeds United.

Bergara was impressed with everything about this last match: "I found myself in the fourth or fifth game playing at Elland Road. Playing against Leeds in front of thirty thousand fans with the stands singing as if it were a final of the Copa del Rey in Spain. It was truly amazing". Leeds achieved seven consecutive wins including their triumphant match against the Welsh club, but they were eighteenth in the league table because they had started the championship with a deficit of fifteen points due to an administrative penalty as a result of their debts.

Orlandi debuted that September 22nd in League One: "Elland Road is a charming stadium. There, I soon realised I'd arrived in the UK. I was pushed and shoved, it was very physical and dynamic football." Due to the pace of the game, he had to adapt his natural playing style and gain weight and speed. Little by little the fighting spirit and honesty of British football began to bewitch him. He also had to adjust to his own team's playing style, where some of his colleagues still played long passes. During his first months Orlandi thought it highly unusual that he almost never received short passes during the friendly games throughout training.

Orlandi did not debut as a Swans player until the seventh league day and tenth official match. He signed on the 31st

August just minutes before the transfer market closed, the last Spanish player to make up the payroll for that season. Bob recalls having seen him in action for the first time in the Barcelona B side, positioned in a 4-3-3 formation next to Bojan and Giovani Dos Santos. "He was at the same level as those two players," says the Gaffer, convinced that Orlandi was an important signing for the club.

Jordi Cruyff - Martínez's best friend and someone with whom Orlandi had a good relationship after having got to know each other at the Spanish club, Alavés and later Barcelona – played an important role in this regard: "He has an extraordinary talent, with a natural left foot," Jordi recounts. It was Jordi who brought about the possibility of a move to Swansea, a city and team of which Andrea Orlandi knew nothing at all at that time. "He fitted in easily with the style Roberto wanted. There was nobody better suited than someone who had played with Barça, and who also adheres to the same style of football," explains Jordi.

Orlandi made his debut in the First Division in Barcelona against Athletic Bilbao in San Mamés, an unforgettable moment for him, as it also was to train side by side with Ronaldinho, Samuel Eto'o and Messi and Deco. After taking advice from Johan Cruyff's son, Roberto encouraged him to visit Wales after seeing him play with the first team in the Copa Catalunya.

Orlandi was contracted to Barcelona B, and at the end of the season he had to return to Alavés. "I accepted the invitation to visit the facilities and the city without any kind of commitment. I stayed in Swansea a couple of days with my father and Roberto showed us the people, the stadium ... everything," recalls Orlandi, who liked the way Martínez spoke to him and liked what he saw. However, he was aware on the other hand, that the change would be a dramatic one, although he had a lot of time to think about it after that visit in June, because his contract kept him in Vitoria.

After finishing preseason with the Basque side, which was immersed in insolvency law, the club announced that it would be implementing the expediente de regulación de Empleo (ERE) a redundancy plan and, in addition, the manager Josu Uribe told him that they had no room for him in their plans a week before the start of the League. He then had an offer from

Aris F.C., but he did not trust the Greek interest, which reached him via a dubious route through a Spanish agent. He was also influenced by footballers playing in Greece who warned him of the financial difficulties he may face.

When all seemed to be lost, he reapplied to Roberto, whose plans, for Swansea, convinced him, despite the Swans contract being financially worse than that offered by Artis. Orlandi recalls how the final signing was carried out: "I signed at an opticians in Barcelona which belonged to a friend of my mother and where there was a fax machine. I sent Roberto a fax at 23:00 p.m. on August 31st. The next day I was in Swansea. If I hadn't had that opportunity, I would have stayed in Alava adhering to the ERE, and sunk in recession which unfortunately has been the case for many people in Spain."

The Spanish-Italian Orlandi is polite, attentive, talkative and fond of children. The latter is made apparent through the devotion he felt for Spanish footballer Gorka Pintado's daughter whilst they were neighbours. On the pitch, the first thing that draws attention is his magic left foot, but Bauzá emphasizes that this should not detract from his work ability and vision of the game. Albert Serrán is his daughter's godfather, Jordi Gómez is his brother-in-law and Àngel Rangel has been a great friend of his in Swansea.

When Bauzá left the flat he shared with Rangel to live with his girlfriend, Orlandi and Rangel began to share many afternoons filled with milky coffee and chocolate muffins. The former would joke about the time when he 'nutmegged' the other in a Barça B - Terrassa match and the latter would respond by reminding him of the great volley goal he shot from thirty-five meters during one of their matches. This friendly rivalry continued with Play Station games.

Rangel and Orlandi were first-team players in the next event on the calendar, against Brighton, in the fiftieth match played at the Liberty stadium. Orlandi, on his League One debut, was dubbed 'star man' of the match by the Western Mail newspaper. Bauzá was substituted in his place in the ninetieth minute, which prevented the new 'Three Amigos' from playing together on the same pitch.

Swansea had thirteen shots on goal (eight of them on target), but the match ended with a goalless draw that fuelled the first murmurs of impatience among fans. A single victory in the first four games at the Liberty Stadium was a poor return, they needed to at least reach the top six. They were situated in tenth position, two points from sixth, four from second and eight points from top, with eleven out of a possible twenty-four points.

Re-educating some disgruntled fans

"We were trying to gradually change the philosophy, be more conservative and improve possession of the ball. It took us several months to understand the new tactics, and the first home games were difficult", acknowledges Roberto Martínez. In short, the stylistic changes meant -as Huw Lake points out - the need to re-educate the fans.

In 2007 the belief that playing with two forwards and keeping the ball within the opponent's half was the only way to win matches, especially within the lower leagues, was still widely held in the UK. The 4-4-2 formation, along with a few other very archaic football concepts, was considered so quintessentially British that - Martínez explains - even the FA defended it for years, though they are currently considering fundamental changes. It is no coincidence, therefore, that the name of the UK's main football magazine is 'FourFourTwo'.

The author David Winner argues that football in the United Kingdom was not developed as a form of entertainment, but to deter teenagers from sexual adventure and masturbation. The practice of the sport, according to this thinking, is that it should be painful and exhausting enough to expend teenagers' energy. This, according to Winner, is where British lack of confidence in ability and 'pretty' styles of play stems from - qualities which are associated with femininity. In this vein, a rugged player was considered more macho, whereas the skilful player was seen as effeminate.

At the beginning of October, the murmurs had escalated to 'boos'. The public demanded a more direct game and criticized the team for the few goal-scoring opportunities they created. After the goalless draw in Brighton, Roberto claimed he accepted such a reaction by the crowd, but added that no one was more disappointed than the managerial staff and the team.

He himself was not satisfied with the first half and recognized that the team needed to improve and aspire to reach the top six in the league. He therefore asked the fans to show their support during the ninety minutes and to freely express their emotions only after each final whistle.

Leon Britton, Swansea City's latest style icon, confirms that fans – unfamiliar with a close-passing style of play - requested at the start of the season that they adopt the long ball technique until they produced good results and until the new playing style was working effectively. Each one of the Spanish players has their own theory about this.

Guillermo Bauzá, for example, recalls that the fans did not know when they had to be positive: "When the fans see a typically British football match, they know what they must do. The largest standing ovations occur when a forward jumps for a ball launched up-field; when a defender makes a tackle to steal the ball; when there is a corner ... we made it difficult for them to know if they should applaud because we had made a short pass without losing it or because we had made a backward pass".

Iñaki Bergara also refers to the underlying feelings of doubt, nerves and impatience invoked in response to new ideas: "Even with the first pass the fans were already extremely flustered, they became impatient about a backward pass to restart the game or a follow-up with a centre pass, I can't tell you if a lot of the impatience was directed at our goalkeeper. We had a fantastic goalkeeper who played with his feet."

When Óscar Brau joined Swansea, the murmurs had died down, a little, but he had his own theory behind the reasons for the initial negative reaction to implementing the new philosophy: "Many fans see football as they do rugby: attack, attack, high long balls. They still like the fighter who is not afraid of making a grand entrance and bulldozing ahead. But in football you can also sit back and wait for an opportunity to pass the ball and strike back".

In this context, Roberto Martínez had to assume a pedagogical role, and grabbed every opportunity to convince everyone that they could still play attack football without using the usual techniques or systems: "It was via talks with the press, through football programs, and open meetings with fans in which I explained to them the reason for our change and what we were trying to do." These sessions are held several times a season in many British clubs to bring the players closer to their fans: a hundred selected fans can bombard the manager or the club's representative at these type of events.

The fans are at the heart of football in Britain. Everything starts with them and everything is done with them in mind: the season schedule with dates and times set since the summer; family-suitable hours; official publications of each club; merchandise or various social events that promote the coexistence of the club with their fans. Only Germany can match this aspect of British football.

Swansea is no exception. Some players remember a game where the referee delayed kick-off because a problem with the turnstiles was slowing down the fans' entry into the Liberty stadium. The club is only too well aware that it would be nothing without the fans, and that is also how the players see it. "You get paid thanks to them buying shirts or whichever club products. So, when we sign the football programmes, they ask you please, but you do it because you know that there will be two thousand supporters who want to see your photo signed in their programmes. It's easy to make them happy and it's one of the great pleasures of being a professional footballer," explains Bauzá.

A large part of these supporters are made up of entire families, wearing the official shirt and other merchandise, they enliven the stadium hours before kick-off. They might grab a lunch of fish & chips, perhaps make some bets on the game, and almost all will have the programme. This is because football in the United Kingdom is a ritual and a family day-out. In addition, each fan will only be devoted to the team of their town or city exclusively, to which they will lend their support even during the most painful defeats and regardless of what league the team is in.

Roberto Martínez believes that the arrogance that characterizes the British is why it is very difficult to make them change their mind in any way at all. Football, obviously, is no exception. Nowadays they accept and even call for other formats. The former England manager Graham Taylor said in mid-2012 that the selection process will never improve playing

4-4-2 and suggested a change in football culture. The Uruguayan manager Gustavo Poyet did not think it would be a simple task: "It is not just an issue of tactics, it is, above all, about being technically and mentally capable. British technique is better than what people say."

Swansea had suffered a number of injuries at the start of the season, including the one sustained by Britton, who was to miss three consecutive games. Under these circumstances, the Jacks were tested in a home game just three days after those first significant criticisms. Rangel was the only Spaniard of the eleven to play both halves. The home team scored in the twenty-first minute, Swindon equalled in the seventieth minute, casting shadows of doubt for the 240 seconds it took Feeney in scoring the final goal with a 2-1 final score. Despite the fact that his team was sixth in the Championship and five points away from the nineteen held by the league leaders Leyton Orient - their next opponents - Roberto was not at all satisfied with their results.

Turning Point

The first boost to Swansea's position in the league table that season would take place on October 6th, in an away game against the leaders at that time. A resounding 0-5 win, with four goals scored in the second half, sent a message to even the most sceptical and helped to inspire confidence in the dressing room as well as mitigate criticism. A brace scored by Butler, a goal by Pratley, another by Anderson and the last by Feeney in extra time, propelled Swansea into fourth position in the table, just two points away from Leyton Orient and Tranmere. Then, Leeds United produced an amazing run of nine wins and a tie in those first ten games, though the penalty of fifteen points, imposed at the start of the season, left them in twelfth position.

October brought with it a flurry of victories. Following the wins against Swindon and Leyton Orient, was the 2-0 win against Wycombe Wanderers (with the first goal by Bussy, who was now firmly a first-team player along with Orlandi) in the second round of the Johnstone's Paint Trophy. Following this they produced an exhibition match with a 1-4 victory in Bournemouth, which lifted Swansea City to the top of the table for the first time, although they were on level-pegging with twenty points with Tranmere and Leyton Orient. To conclude the successful month, the team defeated Yeovil 1-2 in the third consecutive victory away from the Liberty stadium. The team had worked so well together the previous day that Britton, by then recovered from his injury, hardly played the last eight minutes.

Bauzá was not surprised about the sweeping victories: "I didn't experience the old style, but it all flowed very naturally, little by little, towards the game that Roberto wanted us to play". According to him, the team finally managed to implement one of his manager's plans, a plan to control the games through possession of the ball and to try to turn the crazy intensity of British football around to their favour. "They had built a stadium sufficiently large and impressive to do just that", he admits.

November presented a fixture list of eight games ahead, exceeded only in January and March, with fixtures of nine games each. The team's winning streak would screech to a halt with two consecutive draws: firstly a 1-1 draw at home against Gillingham, playing with ten men from the twenty-third minute, and then a 2-2 draw at the Den against Millwall. In both games, Anderson rescued a point in the seventy-ninth minute.

Swansea sat at fourth place in the table, having played eight games without losing and another two without being defeated, albeit not in League One. Bauzá's double crushed Billericay Town in the FA Cup 1-2, and another goal from the Spanish striker meant that Swansea picked up a 1-0 win against Yeovil in the Johnstone's Paint Trophy. Bussy began to specialize in decisive goals, although in the next league challenge he had to wait for his opportunity on the bench.

The run of ten undefeated matches was curtailed on November 16th, with a 0-1 defeat to Huddersfield at the Liberty, who had fifty-three percent possession. Eight days later, an own goal from Tranmere granted them a narrow victory at Prenton Park. Rangel played in the first team again, sharing the pitch for a few minutes with his two compatriots, Bauzá and Orlandi, who came on in the second half. Swansea remained fourth, three points from Leyton Orient, although the leading side had a game in hand.

November 27: the first 4-3-3

The countdown to a decisive change was very much on Roberto's mind: "Little by little we grew in terms of possession football. But the change to reach the standard sustained right up until present day – Swansea City's hallmark of possession football – was implemented halfway through my first complete season as manager".

The boldness of the Spanish technique adopted in a League One team, plying their trade in the UK, is praised even today. Among the experts who speak highly of the beginning of Martínez's vision is one of his successors at Swansea City. Brendan Rodgers recognizes that Arsene Wenger was the first person who orchestrated English football to have more possession. "However, what Roberto did very well was to take possession to lower divisions, something very difficult, because in these leagues players weren't used to that style of football," he says. Rodgers admits that teams such as Liverpool or Manchester United had always played fantastic football but, according to him, the games were invariably transitional: "You have the ball, you attack; the rival team has it, they attack".

The Northern Irishman clarifies that Swansea City had played well in the past, though they had never adopted the 4-3-3 formation before Roberto's appointment as manager: "I had players who could understand the philosophy and apply it. The process began, in a very similar way to what Johan Cruyff did at Barcelona. Lee Trundle's departure months before was significant in the change of style, Lee's presence forced the use of the classic and rigid 4-4-2 and the striker had previously been heavily marked which limited his ability to be able to play. In the attack zone, Jason Scotland's abilities favoured the formation of two wingers and a centre forward".

November 27th was a momentous date for Swansea as it was the day Roberto Martínez would showcase the 4-3-3 formation that would come to characterise the club. The manager remembers the date well and even retains it, to this very day, amongst his personal notes on his iPad, a testament to that important decision and a milestone in Swansea's progression. "Opponents complicated games for us by closing down our attack, so, against Hartlepool I decided to change the system." Subsequently, the coach applied a variation of it with Bussy playing in varying positions during some away games.

The Welsh team, were positioned at the top of the leader board level with Leyton Orient on thirty-one points, who they thrashed 0-5 some weeks before. Possession was favourable for Swansea (fifty-four percent) with the match-winning goal scored by Rangel, with a pass from Bauzá, in the eighty-second minute. It was the right wing-back's first goal as a Jack. The eleven thousand four hundred and twenty supporters who attended the Swansea 1-0 Hartlepool match witnessed Leon Britton joining Ferrie Bodde and Darren Pratley in a line-up of three midfielders, without beginning to imagine just how important that new configuration would become in the future.

"When I arrived, Roberto told me that Leon would play in front of me, that he could play equally well with both feet, inside or outside. From what he said, I thought he was Maradona," says Rangel. With the new format, Britton's new position would become one of the most influential decisions in the future of Swansea in the coming seasons. "I don't know if it was because we didn't have that necessary football connection between two teammates or because a midfielder was needed that liked to control the play," adds the right wing-back from Sant Carles de la Ràpita.

Bauzá, one of the eight new faces to make up the First eleven, would resume his winning streak in the Cup tournaments, scoring in the 1-1 draw against Horsham in the FA Cup. In the replay of this second round tie, Swansea triumphed with a win of 6-2 in the opening competitive game at the new Liberty. It was one of the five victories achieved by the team in December. Those triumphs, all home games, reaffirmed Roberto Martínez's conviction in the effectiveness of that line-up: "In December I saw in Swansea a winning team, that month the change of style was finally accepted."

The successful run, the second since October, would conclude with two 3-0 wins, against Northampton and Southend, a 4-1 against Cheltenham and a valiant 3-2 victory against Leeds United on December 29th. It was a great end to 2007 which saw the Welsh team catapulted to the top of the table, achieving forty-three points in twenty-one games, ahead of two renowned clubs: Nottingham Forest, with thirty-eight points in twenty games, and even Leeds, with thirty-seven points in twenty-three games, despite their imposed penalty sanction.

"We started the season with a defeat and a draw, we had a hard time winning games during the first two months, but the results were finally beginning to show and we went into the winter games, winning a game against Leeds which was managed by Dennis Wise with Gustavo Poyet as assistant manager," says Rangel proudly.

New Year in the leadership

Swansea City had little time to celebrate their top position, because on the very first day of 2008 they attempted to maintain their lead in League One with the first of nine matches that the team would have to play in January. The Swans paid a visit to Swindon with some variation to their line-up on New Year's Day, and they managed to maintain their pole position despite drawing 1-1 in a match that they controlled up until the twentieth minute, with a great statistic of sixty-three percent possession. A goal in the eighty-seventh minute scored by Butler was equalized in the ninety-seventh minute by a home goal.

Four days later at the Liberty Stadium, Havant and Waterlooville also managed a draw with a goal in the final minutes of the FA Cup match (1-1). The marathon of matches resumed on the eighth of January, when Swansea City secured their place in the Johnstone's Paint Trophy final with a 1-0 home win against Brighton with the three Spaniards playing in the first team. Rangel and Bauzá would remain there for the next encounter, a first division game in Luton Town stadium, where Bussy scored to secure the 1-3 victory in which Roberto Martínez opted for the 4-4-2 formation.

He reapplied this formula, albeit with a worse result (defeat of 4-2), in the FA Cup replay against non-league side Havant and Waterlooville, who surprisingly prevailed over Swansea, despite Bauzá scoring yet again. January concluded with four more league games: three consecutive victories (2-0 against Port Vale, 2-1 against Crewe and 0-4 against Doncaster, with another goal from Bussy in this home thrashing) and a goalless draw at Nottingham Forest. Swansea City increased their lead and ended January with a ten-point advantage over second-place Doncaster Rovers, who had one game in hand. Nonetheless, the recent past ensured level heads and prudence as there were still nineteen games and three more competitive months ahead.

In the first game of February, Swansea marched on at the top of the league with a 2-1 against Oldham in the opening match of the season. Later, Swansea squandered a two-goal advantage in the last eight minutes against Crewe, drawing 2-2. A possession rate of around fifty-five percent was now almost considered the norm for each competitive fixture. The Swans subsequently went on to win three consecutive games: 1-0 against Walsall (the third victory throughout the course of 2007-08), 0-2 against Port Vale and 1-0 to Luton Town.

In the latter part of that month, Swansea faced two legs of the Johnstone's Paint Trophy against MK Dons. They lost 0-1 at the Liberty despite having more possession, and won 0-1 in Milton Keynes, but lost the match on penalty shootouts. Jason Scotland, who had scored the equalizing goal from precisely eleven metres, failed to score the penalty and Swansea lost their place in the final. However, this was one less distraction for the Welsh side from League One, they had a fourteen-point advantage over second-in-position – Doncaster – and had a schedule of eight games to play in March.

Record within Reach and the Arrival of Brau

The triumphant 0-1 against Huddersfield meant they had a club record within arm's reach. If Swansea were to win against Millwall on March 7th, they would outdo their best unbeaten spell in a league tournament, won thirty-seven years before: nineteen games without defeat. Perhaps that record, being within reach, caused some match day nerves. Before the first minute was up, the visitors had already advanced on the scoreboard. The final score at the Liberty was 1-2, preventing the Swans from achieving a historical run of games unbeaten.

Added to this setback was the draw with Tranmere Rovers, who scored the equalizing goal (1-1) in the ninety-first minute (again the Swans lost points in the very last moments of a game), and another defeat against Northampton Town (4-2). The Swans didn't let their heads drop, after those three bad results, they still remained six points ahead of the second-placed side.

That was when Óscar Brau would join the team, originally on a week's trial, – the sixth Spaniard. Roberto Martínez offered him a chance to stay until the end of the season after just three days. The masseur, who was not a member of any side, accepted the proposal, considering it an interesting experience. Óscar's brother, Juanjo Brau, is the physiotherapist at Barcelona FC. He didn't know Martínez on a personal level, but explains how the opportunity came about via a former Real Zaragoza player: "I had a good relationship with Xavi Aguado. I told him that I wasn't in any team and he told me he would call a friend of his who was in Swansea, who was going to have a look at the English Second Division, to see if they needed anyone". The Spanish manager was interested in dealing with another compatriot, therefore Óscar was in the right place at the right time.

He arrived with less than a month and a half of the Championship to go. The idea was to see how the club performed and to start, with them, next season in the Championship if Martínez agreed. Brau won Martínez over completely: "He had some unique qualities as a masseur. We gave him the nickname Magic Hands". Serrán gives very graphic details of the reasons for this nickname: "You tell him that something hurts and he puts his hands on you, his elbows or fists to leave your muscles relaxed". As a person, he is described as sincere, hardworking and funny, with more than a touch of insanity.

The competition proceeded with two home victories (0-2 against Bristol Rovers and 1-3 at Victoria Park against Hartlepool United) and two draws: 1-1 at Southend United Football Club and 2-2 in the second match against Bristol Rovers in less than a week, with Scotland scoring a brace, rescuing a point in the eighty-fourth minute, coming back after being behind earlier in the game with a 0-2 win. The Swans finished March with eighty-two points in forty matches. Carlisle

United had seventy-five points with thirty-nine rounds in the competition.

The situation was made far more complicated for Roberto Martínez's side in the next two games. Firstly, they lost 1-2 against Bournemouth, with both goals scored in extra time, and they drew in a goalless game at Brunton Park, Carlisle United FC's stadium, against whom they had an advantage of four points with four games left. Swansea had two games left to play at the Liberty and two away-games. Their leading position was at risk though their promotion wasn't under threat as they were still in first place with a ten-point lead over the third placed side. Doncaster were better placed in the league, who along with Southend United, Nottingham Forest and Leeds United were in contention to qualify for the playoffs (from third to sixth place).

Bussy, Hero of the Promotion

On the 12th April 2008 Bauzá earned himself the nickname 'Promotional Hero' by scoring twice in the 1-2 victory at Gillingham's Priestfield Stadium. Gillingham's goal was countered by the Mallorcan player's two consecutive goals in the forty-fourth and forty-seventh minutes. Bauzá was opportunistic from the outset, firing the ball into the net before the goalie could save it and, barely a minute later, he scored again as he controlled a cross with his chest and angled the ball into the net.

Predictably, the final whistle sent the pitch and the stands into raptures. The player who secured the two decisive goals shouted "Come on!" into one of the television cameras as he ran around the pitch. Bussy believes that he was merely lucky in winning the crowd's admiration, remaining grounded despite the crowd singing his praises and chanting his name: "Football, I think, is sometimes very cruel. The goal scorer is always remembered, but it is a team effort. And I was the scorer, on the day, thanks to the team. But for the fans, who are always very grateful for a result, they stop me in the street and sometimes even bow!"

One thousand five hundred Jack supporters turned out in Kent dressed in black and white checked hats or Welsh flags, and the Liberty Stadium opened its doors to another thousand seven hundred fans, all of whom witnessed the fabulous ninety minutes which sealed Swansea City's promotion to the Championship, for which they had had to wait twenty-four years. It was made possible courtesy of the ten-point advantage over third-division Doncaster, whilst Carlisle found themselves positioned seven points below in second place. Three games remained to seal their title as Champions.

Huw Jenkins, Swansea City's chairman, was looking further ahead when, even that celebrated day, he announced to the media that Swansea would have the chance to reach the Premiership soon enough. An ebullient Roberto Martínez confirmed that he would stay at the club for as long as they wanted him. Specifically, he said that they had had to throw him out as a player and that they would have to do the same to him as manager. These remarks would come back to bite him a year later.

The following Saturday, April 19th, Swansea welcomed Yeovil Town, who took advantage of the Jacks local euphoria to clinch a 1-2 win. Even then, the Welsh team were technically proclaimed Champions due to a last-minute defeat for Carlisle United– a team for which future Swans forward, Danny Graham played – against Southend United (1-2) and which secured their place in the playoff. These results meant that the eighteen thousand fans attending the Liberty Stadium were able to celebrate the title together with the Swans players and the backroom staff.

The celebrations would continue seven days later with a 4-1 thrashing against Leyton Orient, with a hat-trick from Bauzà before half-time. Guillermo was living the dream having scored twice, previously, on the day of the promotion and the three goals the day they celebrated becoming League One Champions. They did not celebrate with a trophy however given that they were still waiting for the outcome of the Leeds United tribunal regarding their appeal against the fifteen-point deduction they were dealt at the start of the season.

Promotion and...Champions?

During the promotional celebrations, no cup was presented to Swansea due to Leeds United ongoing arbitration hearing, but some players, Orlandi was one, held aloft cardboard replicas. They did actually receive a gold medal as a reward. All the Spanish players, joined their teammates on the 18th of April 2008, for a celebratory open-top bus journey from the old Vetch Field to one of the emblematic buildings of Swansea City, the Guildhall.

From the top of the bus, the very same used in 1981 when the club climbed to the First Division with Toshack, Roberto was the first to address the fans, whom he told must be very proud of Swansea City. Afterwards, he passed the microphone to Rangel, who entertained the thousands of surrounding fans with a typically Spanish chant: "Olé, olé, olé, olé". Bauzá was the fifth to speak, and made a brave attempt at singing in English ("And now you're gonna believe us…").

Finally, Leeds United lost their legal battle on the first of May. However, Swansea's 0-1 victory against Brighton in the final match of League One 2007-08 played on the third of May would have kept them in the lead regardless, reaching the end of the season sixteen points clear of Leeds. Rangel recalls the furore: "We knew that we were going to be promoted anyway and we celebrated without the trophy."

Nottingham Forest were also promoted together with the Welsh Swans after finishing second with eighty-two points, and, the team in third place, Doncaster Rovers FC, clinched the final promotional position after winning the playoffs.

On the third of May 2003, a few months after Roberto's arrival as a player, Swansea City had salvaged their professional place in the football league, securing their place in the fourth tier of British football by the skin of their teeth, it went to the wire, the very last game, winning 4-2 to Hull City. Five years later, also on the third of May, the team played their last match of another historic season.

Six Spaniards - Roberto Martínez, Iñaki Bergara, Óscar Brau, Àngel Rangel, Guillermo Bauzá and Andrea Orlandi—formed part of Swansea City in that unforgettable season, during which the Welsh club were crowned Champions with ninety-two points, a record in League One. For a return to the Championship, for which they had waited twenty-four long years, the fourteen away victories (on top of the thirteen home games) were fundamental. Neither the elimination from the FA

Cup nor the penalty defeat in the Johnstone's Paint Trophy tarnished their fourth big league win in the club's history. The Jacks were back on track!

On Balance

Swansea City managed to surpass an average of six hundred passes during the 2007-08 season in League One, a record, it served as an example for other clubs within the Championship, League One and League Two, who have subsequently tried to implement the style which Jordi Cruyff refers to as 'sexy football'.

Apart from that, the passing game is now so ingrained at the Liberty that it would be impossible to change: "The fans love the passing game. If a new manager wanted long passes, people wouldn't be happy. Therefore, the club always brings in players who like that style of football," Leon Britton says matter-of-factly. Roberto Martínez, the architect of the transformation, agrees: "Changes in football are very difficult, but once achieved, they are permanent. If a coach attempted to play now with a 4-4-2 formation and more directly, or tried percentage football, they would find it impossible."

Roberto admits that this promotion, with the Swans, is one of those moments which make all the stresses and pressures of football, particularly all the dark days endured by the club, immensely worthwhile. He remembers the records set throughout the season, but he also considers the way in which the team embraced the possession style of football to be equally special.

No plan, no matter how marvellous it might be, is worth it if it goes unaccompanied by victories. Bauzá recognises that, despite the fact that there is more patience in British football, they had the ability, quality or luck to achieve results that helped the fans to accept the new philosophy: "Without them, behind you, any coach can leave or any idea can be changed for another, simpler one". Furthermore, Guillermo is of the opinion that ball control compensated for the physical shortfalls they had in comparison with other teams, and it allowed them to display stronger defensive tactics than otherwise might have been the case.

Though the predominant characteristics of League One did not often favour Orlandi, he cherishes the beginnings of his adventure. Roberto encouraged him and gave him time to adapt. Andrea highlights the fact that British football is very honest, with footballers that give their all and leave nothing on the field. When he became more involved within the team, he had some bad luck in the form of an injury: "I broke my knee and you could say that the season went down the drain for me". Orlandi, at least, was lucky in finding Ultracomida, a delicatessen specialising in typical Spanish foods based in Narberth, a town some sixty-five kilometres from Swansea. In his worst moments, he would seek solace with fuet, chorizo, jamón or cheese.

Off the pitch, Iñaki Bergara's mother became ill and they had to give her medical treatment, circumstances that did not stop him remembering with nostalgia: "Along with my brother, she followed all the Swansea games via the internet, and even met Leon Britton and other players toward the end". On a sporting level, that first year Bergara was faced with many surprises, such as how well structured he found League One to be. Never had he imagined that the third tier in British football – which for him was competitive and beautiful – would exhibit such professional behaviour and would draw in so many fans to the stadiums. Swansea City had a loyal following of between seven hundred and three thousand fans that travelled to watch away games.

Despite the fact that it rains almost daily, Bergara saw only blue skies, because it was all smiles for him, to have been involved with a fantastic team of players, in both personal and professional capacities, and to have secured a promotion playing against champions from European competitions such as Leeds United and Nottingham Forest. However, he gives due credit to the successful style of play rather than to any contribution he might have made: "Swansea broke all the moulds in a totally physical aggressive league, you are expected to run a marathon each match, and if you don't the fans will let you know. But they were very generous in allowing our more honest style of play to develop".

Óscar Brau admits that he experienced things differently because the side already had a wide point's margin when he arrived. That is not to say that he wasn't aware, after a month and a half in the city, that the promotion was significant, given the great number of people which accompanied them on the open-top bus tour. Nobody, according to the masseur, could have foretold the near future of a club that had encountered quite a few problems in the recent past.

Once the season ended, Rangel had to undergo an operation for a groin injury he sustained in its wake, which would prevent him from playing the next stage. Despite this mishap, he describes his first year as an unforgettable and a unique experience, ever since a fan recognized him in a restaurant near the stadium on his second day in Swansea. It was the first time that he heard his name pronounced in a British accent.

The right back feels that all the players enjoyed that time, as well as a great team performance, he emphasises that it was one of his best seasons personally: "I played fifty-two games in all of the competitions, I assisted many times, we finished champions and I was nominated best winger in League One". For this reason, he attended a gala in London with Xavi Cruz, in which they were asked to award trophies to the best players in all four professional categories: "I had the honour of meeting Cristiano Ronaldo, Cesc Fàbregas and Fernando Torres".

Along with him, another four players from Swansea City featured in the Professional Footballers' Association League One Team 2007/08: Garry Monk in defence, midfielders Andy Robinson and Ferrie Bodde, and the forward Jason Scotland. The new players had been skilfully chosen given that three of them were included in the Team of the Year. The coach himself was acclaimed manager of the season in that category. It was a great climax to a great season and the winners' collective efforts.

Roberto Martínez considered this recognition a great honour which extended to everyone connected to Swansea City: "It represents the players' hard work and how much we have progressed as a club". Months later he would say that they had created something special and that they would continue to pursue their dream of reaching the Premiership. Some of the British media prominently featured these heartfelt statements, accompanied by a question raised by Martínez: "Why not aspire to be the best?"

But Roberto was about to receive an equal or greater recognition: an offer on the table from Sir Alex Ferguson himself to become assistant manager at Manchester United. Who would have thought that of the Balaguerian when, in 1999, he accompanied his close friend Jordi Cruyff to the UEFA Champions League dinner in Barcelona in which the Mancunian side celebrated their win at Camp Nou. "There were definitely rumours circulating about interest from Ferguson," Jordi acknowledged some time later.

At that time, Huw Jenkins, Swansea City's chairman, denied that it was a real possibility. However, Catalonian journalist Guillem Balagué, who had worked in the UK for over two decades, now sheds some light on the situation: "When Ferguson called him to be his number two, Roberto was a week late in returning the call, because he hadn't listened to the message. This is because he only uses his mobile one hour a day so as not to be a slave to the telephone".

The Spaniard's reply was negative as he wanted to continue his career as head coach. Since then, the relationship between Martínez and Sir Alex Ferguson appears to have had its ups and downs. In 2009, Roberto denied allegations that he'd criticized the Scotsman's overweening power in British football. At the start of 2011, Roberto would go as far as to claim that they had never been close.

CHAPTER 6

2008-09: SEASON FOR CONSOLIDATION

If the club had had one of the seven lowest budgets of League One in the previous football year, financial difficulties in 2008 - 2009 would be even worse. They had one of the lowest budgets within the Championship, which was around £4 million. With the Premiership drawing ever nearer, there was a temptation to sign new players, though this would put the club's economic viability in danger. The Club and Roberto Martínez opted to maintain a sound budgetary position and scrupulously plan for the next season.

The New Category

In May, Ashley Williams completed his permanent move to Swansea for a sum just short of £500,000, after being released from Stockport County F.C. a couple of months previously. He would help to rebuild the team's decimated defence in the last five weeks of the 2007-08 season. Later, Mark Gower, came aboard, signing on a free transfer. More recruitment would take place in the summer of 2008, amongst them the signing of four Spanish players: Jordi Gómez (released by RCD Espanyol),

Gorka Pintado (in exchange for around £100,000), the Argentine Fede Bessone (free) and Albert Serrán (for €100,000). Midseason, in January, Southampton released Nathan Dyer, who was subsequently signed by Swansea for a sum in excess of £400,000.

The pre-season kicked off with a week of physical tests in Swansea. The Welsh team then took a trip to Sweden again that year, specifically Ostersund (the usual venue for Martínez's pre-season tours), where they would continue their preparations with three daily training sessions. After another phase of testing in Swansea, the schedule for that summer would culminate in Spain with an intensive training course near Palamós.

There, the team played four friendlies in four days against Espanyol (a defeat of 4-0), Peralada (a win of 0-2), Palamós themselves (winning 0-1) and Barcelona B (3-3). On their return to Wales, after defeating Chester 2-3, the Swans played another two games to close the pre-season before the official competition began: a goalless draw against West Bromwich Albion and a 1-0 win over Dutch team Ado Den Haag - which is twinned with Swansea - with Orlandi scoring the winning goal. Bauzá was the top scorer, with ten goals in eleven friendly matches, whilst Pintado scored two hat-tricks.

To bolster daily training, particularly among the players who participated less in the league, Roberto introduced the Champions League Points. This internal competition consisted of allocating points to each player in each training session with a view to winning practice games or carrying out different individual and collective exercises. The motivation, besides friendly competition between peers, was that the two best players would qualify for the Champions League Final.

The side's Spanish players approached this new leg of the competition with curiosity and a certain degree of respect. On evaluation of the list of rivals, some seemed to be renowned players, with Premiership experience. Óscar Brau had heard the clubs Coventry and Sheffield being casually mentioned in Spain. Albert Serrán knew barely anything about the Championship, but had been informed by his teammates that it was an incredibly competitive league and trusted their judgement.

This second competitive tier in British football is a league with a large following, magnificent fans and a higher budget than the Spanish Segunda División. Orlandi laments that there are sometimes empty stadiums despite quality footballers that were capable of playing in any of the higher British categories.

Bauzá remained confident and convinced that Swansea wouldn't be worried by the change in division and believed that they would potentially feel more comfortable: according to him, the fact that there were larger stadiums and playing grounds in better condition would suit the Welsh team both home and away.

Risk of Distrust

More Castilian was spoken in the changing rooms at Swansea than ever before, with seven Hispanic footballers and members of the backroom staff. In fact, there were more Hispanic players than Welsh. This risked sparking distrust from the other players about compatriotic preferential treatment.

This did not go unnoticed by Leon Britton, one of the team's British players: "Perhaps initially you are a little worried, but at the same time you have to believe that you are good enough. If you are, and you adapt to the right style of play, the manager won't care if you're from Britain, Spain or Holland. If you play badly, you could be worried by the fact that the manager has introduced Spanish players." Orlandi saw things differently and believed that they would be first to find themselves in hot water if they didn't produce results.

Besides the fact that the Spaniards were less expensive than players from the British market, the tremendous results from the previous season were a confirmation of the buying policy, according to Roberto Martínez: "The Three amigos, were treated like heroes for contributing to the promotion and elevating the general skills level of the team".

Bauzá believes that a similar situation arises in many clubs that bring in a foreign manager. "Someone Dutch will confide in Dutch players, or an Argentinian in footballers from his own country. That way, they can more effectively express their ideas." Everyone will remember, in this sense, Barcelona at the end of the last century, who in the 1999-2000 season had a dozen Dutch players and technical staff amongst their ranks.

All the Spaniards knew one another more or less, therefore, in their first conversations they recalled the clashes between them in the Segunda División B or their past anecdotes as teammates in the subsidiaries of Barcelona and Espanyol.

It was inevitable that the language, those already existing friendships and other factors would lead to the formation of a clique in Swansea's changing rooms. They were more extrovert, and traditions had an influence. "The British eat fast and go home quickly, whilst we, the Spanish, eat slowly, we have a little coffee and we play cards, which could isolate our group a little," Bauzá explains.

To avoid divisions within the team and to encourage bonding of the entire group, the coaching team imposed rules. One rule was not to talk in Spanish during lunches and dinners. The players sometimes attempted to defy this and avoid the ban, though they quickly returned to English when they saw that the assistant manager was approaching to establish some order and sometimes impose fines. Furthermore, three players of the same nationality were not allowed to gather together on the one table. These were two methods used to encourage everyone to settle in and to improve their language skills.

A debut with defeat

In the first league game of the season, Swansea lost 2-0 at Charlton Athletic, giving away goals in the third and eighty-fifth minute from two set pieces. Roberto Martínez opted for a 4-5-1 formation: Britton, Bodde and Pratley formed the defensive midfield trio, accompanied by Gower and Butler, whilst Bauzá played upfront, with Scotland awaiting his opportunity on the bench. Along with the Majorcan attacker, the only other Spanish player to play that first Championship game was Jordi Gómez, who made his debut in the last ten minutes.

Among the absentees was the injured Rangel, who despite being unable to make it that day, points out the reasons behind the defeat: "We gave them too much respect. In Charlton, we debuted very timidly and we fell quite easily." Swansea started in the penultimate position in the table after their debut. It was the 9th August and they had practically nine months of lengthy competition, with another forty-three encounters ahead.

The next fixture was the first round of the League Cup. There were many variations in the first team, six Spaniards played in the triumphant 2-0 win against Brentford: Serrán, Bessone, Jordi Gómez and Orlandi started as first-team players, they were joined by Rangel and Bauzá during the second half. None of them featured in the first team four days later, in the league opener at the Liberty Stadium, though Roberto selected three of them as substitutions. Firstly Rangel, then Pintado – who in under twenty minutes scored his first official goal – and later Jordi Gómez went on to contribute to the 3-1- victory against Nottingham Forest.

As recognition for the good performance, Roberto Martínez called Pintado into his office to introduce him to John Toshack. Furthermore, his trainer announced publicly that Pintado's true value was over £6 million. It was his reaction to the criticism he had received for spending so little money on acclaimed attackers, as the Championship's other big clubs had done.

Owain Tudur Jones wasn't going to let Pintado forget that statement, and presented Gorka with a gigantic cheque for the value of £7 million, during a 'Secret Santa' session, a bit of fun that the players participated in every Christmas (until the arrival of Brendan Rogers). Tudur Jones was both funny and generous with his presents, which often tended to take advantage of any of his colleagues' distinguishing features. He presented Orlandi with hair products; Rangel with fake ears; Bessone a stuffed toucan; Bauzá some crazy wigs. He even dared to do the same with his manager: Roberto, who had just published his autobiography, received a commemorative plate with the inscription 'Most boring book of the year'.

Gorka Pintado, El Vasco (Spanish for 'The Basque') for some, is unassuming, humble, a joker with character. By mid-August he had already earned himself the nickname El Toro (Spanish for 'The Bull'). Leon Britton emphasizes his strength and his skill on the field and rates him as having a similar style to many British footballers. Pintado himself admits that his talents fitted perfectly with the Championship: "I could compete with the central defenders in the air. Many fouls go unpunished in British football. They push you, they hold you, they put their hands on your head and the referee doesn't blow his whistle. It may surprise you, at first, but you soon adapt if you like that style of play."

Jordi Gómez, who did not know Gorka very well, formed a very good impression of him during their first few months as teammates: "He was like Ronaldo. He was a physical forward and was guaranteed to score many goals." Roberto Martínez had always admired Pintado and saw in him a forward with great potential, scoring ability and experience. This was the ideal profile to make the most of the playing formation of using two wingers as per the manager's plan, and to keep Scotland on his toes if he wanted to keep his first team position.

The previous year, when he served in Gramanet, some agents from Sabadell had already contacted him, and the forward had even travelled to view the stadium and get a feel for the workings of the club. By contrast, the Welsh club's offer, still in League One, was insufficient at first, and when it was decided that they raise the sum, Pintado had already been signed by Granada. But they continued to observe him, and after Swansea's promotion to the Championship, negotiations resumed. A chat with Roberto was enough of an incentive for him to terminate his contract as Pintado appreciated that the Welsh offer was financially, and on a sporting level, better than staying at Granada CF.

Rangel, starting as a first team player, and both Jordi Gómez and Pintado coming off the bench contributed to the 0-1 league victory in Plymouth, where Swansea gained sixty percent possession despite their 'away' status. Rangel was positioned on the right side again after having been absent for practically the entire season. He worked hard at his recovery in Swansea, and within just two months he was training with the team again.

Three days later, on Tuesday 26th of April, Premiership side Hull City was the Swans opponents in the second round of the League Cup. Swansea passed the qualifying phase with a penalty scored by Jordi Gómez. A goal by Pintado had allowed for extra time at the Liberty Stadium. It had been twenty-six years since the Welsh club had reached the third round of the competition, and it was achieved with four Spaniards in the first team (Serrán, Orlandi, Jordi Gómez and Bauzá) and two more as substitutes in the second half (Rangel and Pintado). The

Spanish players were gaining more and more prominence at the club.

The following four fixtures of the Championship resulted in three home draws (1-1 against Sheffield Wednesday, Derby County and Burnley) and a defeat of 2-0 at Crystal Palace, the Eagles first victory of the season. Swansea were twelfth after seven days, with nine points, two beneath the playoff positions and four above the relegation spots in League One.

The Nutty English Professor and Settling in

Roberto Martínez would speak to the Spanish players in English if there were any other players around and in Castilian during personal conversations. However, he made sure that all of his compatriots started to receive English lessons four hours a week, Wednesdays and some Fridays, in a room at the stadium.

The teacher was Andrew Goss, a man who spoke English, Welsh, Spanish, French and Italian. When his wife passed away, his son wanted to cheer him up by inviting him to attend a Swansea City match. He had never watched a football match from the stands before, but from that first day he was converted and became a fanatical fan. It wasn't a typical game: it was the famous Swansea-Hull match in 2003. Who would have imagined that, in the near future, he would be giving classes to his side's various star players? Due to his admiration for the team, he decided to offer his services free of charge, with the occasional free pass to a match in return.

Some of the Spanish players also attended an academy, in Swansea, and others continued to have private tuition at Andrew's home. The atmosphere of the classes in the stadium was relaxed, with lots of joking about and with football dominating the conversation. Goss recalls how the players swore a lot, although he adds that they were also very enthusiastic and soon progressed to the construction of phrases.

The Swans remember Andrew – who called himself the 'nutty professor' – as energetic, talkative and a Swansea fanatic, and they also recall his Castilian skills. He had lived in Spain, which accounted for his knowledge of regional jargon and vulgar words.

Just as if he had been a student with an Erasmus grant, Bergara admits that he continues to have problems nowadays on account of the Castilian speakers who he spent time with on his British adventures. Jordi Gómez also experienced something unique to students – he believed his English skills were good as a result of his school studies, whilst realising that his limitations were largely due to the Welsh accent. Nonetheless, he started to gain confidence in the language used on the pitch, which was largely related to the technical aspects of the game: "On the playing field I used to speak Spanish with a Spanish player and English with an English player, to ask for the ball. Later, I started speaking in English to the Spanish player as well."

Besides the classes, to improve their language skills, they would – to varying degrees - listen to music, browse the internet, watch television with subtitles or read children's books. Orlandi read a lot of Harry Potter in English, and attributes his luck of getting to know the other Spaniards, especially Bussy, to the fact that his proficiency in English enabled him to become a translator for all his countrymen, over the years.

The Three Amigos had a season's advantage over the others. In fact, Bauzá, Orlandi and Rangel helped the other Spaniards settle in: "We had paved the way for the Spaniards who followed. They built on our experiences and adapted more smoothly than us three," says Bauzá. Despite that great support, there were some who faced some tough situations, like Bessone: "When I first met the assistant coach and he started to talk to me, I felt embarrassed because I didn't understand a single word he said and I didn't know how to respond."

Food was also an additional obstacle for the Spanish players, especially during the journeys to play away games. That season, the team didn't prepare food for the trips; instead the bus would stop at a service station: "You had to bring a Tupperware container with pasta or whichever food you had prepared to eat on the coach. This was very tough for me. And on arrival at the hotel, often after four or five hours travelling, instead of having a proper dinner, you had soup, cereal or a sandwich," Serrán explains.

The quality of the meat and fish they found in the supermarkets were good and allowed them to eat at home without any problems, but breakfast and lunch prior to training would be made at the club, where fried eggs, bacon, sausages and baked beans were often served. Gorka Pintado, who followed Spanish eating hours at home, never ceased to be amazed and used to exclaim: "How can we eat this?"

Roberto Martínez went through much of the same experiences in the nineties. The experience makes him assert how important it is to arrive with an open mind, to know you have other options and not to look for comparisons between what you do here every day with what you have in Spain. He has witnessed many cases where talented people who arrive from another country begin to miss the things that they no longer have on a human level. This affects them on the pitch, because only the ones who strive to adapt can bring out the best of themselves as a footballer.

In this sense, Martínez uses Rangel as a role model for integration, who in his debut season in the Championship met a Welsh girl from Cardiff who would become the mother of his children. Rivalry with the capital's side provoked little defensive quips from the neighbours of his in-laws, but the family became unwavering Swansea City supporters. Roberto Martínez thought that those who do not face the challenge with such an open mind, end up, sooner or later, returning to their native country.

Óscar Brau also met his partner in Wales: "Starting a family means you always have a connection with the city which you can never cut out of your life." Both Óscar and his wife searched for a name for their daughter that would sound the same in English, Castilian and Catalan, which also wouldn't be difficult to write or pronounce and that wouldn't have an unusual translation. The choice was Betsy.

The Welsh derby

On the 23rd of September, the anxiously awaited Swansea-Cardiff League Cup match took place, the first Welsh derby in almost a decade, with 17,500 spectators in the stands. Iñaki Bergara remembers the striking images of police and helicopters. On this occasion, certain information had come to light regarding altercations incited by Cardiff fans, who supposedly destroyed a service area near Swansea. But above all,

Bergara remembers that game as the first victory against Cardiff in nineteen years.

Joy erupted among the Jack Army with the triumphant goal, a free-kick by Jordi Gómez. The Spanish left-footer was the true hero of the match: he almost scored in the first half with an acrobatic effort, a surprising free-kick which went through the wall and McPhail was sent off, for the resulting foul, with a second yellow card.

He remembers it as his most special game as a Swansea player: "I was a first-team player, I scored the goal, we won and we qualified. The derby is like the Barça-Madrid of Wales. It is very important for people, so, from that moment, I felt very much appreciated." This was not least because he had been the great hero of an historic day, triumphing over arch rivals – who suffered their first defeat of the season – but also because the club qualified for the fourth round of the League Cup for the first time in thirty-two years. The following day, the Welsh media displayed the caption 'Gómez sinks Bluebirds as Swans take honours', and they noted how the Spanish intervention had played in Swansea's favour.

Bauzá had experienced some months previously just what it meant to be an idol of a British team. Bauzá was explaining by telephone to his close friends Bessone and Serrán everything that being the Promotion Hero entailed, and they suspected that their friend was exaggerating.

Later, they realised that he was being quite truthful. Bessone corroborates that Bauzá was often asked for photos and autographs in the street or in any restaurant they visited in the months following the promotion, and, on one random night at a party, everyone referred to him as a hero. The supporters even dedicated chants to him, the content of which Serrán never quite managed to comprehend.

Jordi Gómez, the hero of that derby, had spent almost his entire football career in Barcelona, before arriving at Espanyol. The summer of 2008 he had to leave the blue and white team, which couldn't guarantee him enough playing time, and then Swansea City became an option. The agreement ended suddenly, overnight, at the end of May. When he received the call from his agent, Jordi didn't think twice about it, due to the great interest Bob showed, and, above all because he knew the team and the city well.

His brother-in-law, a certain Andrea Orlandi, had given him endless details throughout the entire previous season. It was pure coincidence that, a while after playing together at Barcelona, they would be reunited at Swansea. "I didn't go there because he spoke to them about me. It was Roberto who was interested and made it known to my agent. It's important that a manager likes you," explains Jordi. He had to leave Spain, this opportunity arose with Swansea and he jumped at the chance.

Roberto Martínez speaks highly of Jordi Gómez's technical skill and quality of passing, but above all, his mental strength, his winning spirit and his discipline. In 2009, he even suggested that he may even play for the national team before too long. Bergara believes that he is a player with distinct timing, whilst Rangel still remembers a Sant Andreu-Barça B match, in which the home team lost 0-3 on a very windy day with two goals from outside the box, courtesy of Jordi.

Timidity is his distinctive feature off the pitch. It's difficult to get to know him well, but Bauzá thinks that it is worth it: "When you manage to enter his innermost circle, his intelligence and sense of humour shines through." Jordi Gómez's reserved character gives a misleading first impression, as was the case with many of his teammates, who thought he was bland, dry and a little arrogant, before they really got to know him.

The Jordi Gómez-Scotland Double

Roberto Martínez's team quickly returned to reality, with a bump, in the same week as the derby. The euphoria and a poor start were the reasons for conceding goals during their visit to Reading (4-0), a game in which Bob amended the format, aligning Scotland and Pintado together up-front.

The team pulled together after that heavy defeat, winning 0-2 against Preston, with a penalty goal by Jordi Gómez. The Swans were fifteenth, with twelve points, and the following day they happened to welcome Wolves to Wales, who were leading by twenty-two points. Jordi scored a goal in the first minute, a great start which shocked the away team, who they defeated 3-1, with another two goals by Scotland.

The goal scorers began to form a partnership which would go on to please the Jacks very much. This is a true reflection of the globalization of football: a forward from Trinidad and Tobago and a Spanish midfielder were a fundamental component of a Welsh club, who competed in the English Second Division.

Following that great victory, Bob Martínez's pupils slightly stagnated with two consecutive draws: 2-2 at Ipswich Town (with another goal by Jordi Gómez) and 0-0 at the Liberty Stadium against Queens Park Rangers, despite the results the Swans enjoyed favourable possession in both games. Needless to say, the Spaniard would again score one of the goals in the triumphant 3-0 match against Southampton. The team then visited Wolverhampton, who they had defeated in the first encounter in October and whom they would face again in the last match of that same month.

The Welsh side reached seventh place, equal on points with Bristol City, who occupied the last qualifying spot for the promotional playoffs. Wolves, on the other hand, were no longer leading the pack, but had dropped to second in the table. A double goal by Ebans-Blake allowed the home side to get their revenge against the Jacks with a victory of 2-1.

November was the busiest month in the calendar that season, with seven official matches. Of the six corresponding to the league competition, Swansea recorded three draws, two victories and a defeat. The victories were against Watford (3-1 with a goal by Bauzá) and against Norwich (2-3). A goal from Jordi Gómez in the second minute wasn't enough to prevent Roberto Martínez's team's first home defeat in the Championship: Birmingham triumphed 2-3. The three draws were played at Doncaster (0-0), Coventry City (1-1 with a goal by Jordi Gómez), and the hundredth Welsh derby took place at the Liberty, as had the preceding Carling one.

Pintado's Swim Away

Gorka Pintado was the scorer in the definitive 2-2 against Cardiff, in a performance that he will never forget due to the special significance of the match against their arch rivals. When celebrating his goal on that crisp day, 30th November 2008, he controversially won the fans' support, but was on the verge of being sanctioned and fined: "The Welsh Federation believed that there had been a provocation. But in the end, nothing came of it." The forward had mock-swam, a gesture that originates from a story dating back to September 1988, when three dozen Cardiff fans, cornered by a greater number from the opposing team, had to swim to escape the umpteenth fight between both sets of fans. When the Swansea fans commemorate that episode with their chants, Cardiff respond: "In the Swansea slums, they look in the dustbin for something to eat, they find a dead rat and they think it's a treat. In the Swansea slums..."

After that last draw, the rivalry was fuelled further by a championship table clash with Cardiff in seventh position with thirty points, and Swansea in eighth position with twenty-nine points. November ended with Swansea knocked out of the League Cup. Watford won 0-1, barely two days after having lost 3-1 against the Welsh side on the same playing field in the league fixture.

Swansea finished the year with eight consecutive draws, six of which were played in December: three goalless draws, at Bristol City and Birmingham football grounds, as well as the home game against Coventry City; two games with 1-1 on the scoreboard, against Sheffield United at the Liberty Stadium and an away game at Blackpool; and a 2-2 result in a home game against Barnsley. Jason Scotland notched up the four goals scored in those six games. 2008 concluded with Swansea in eleventh position in the table, with thirty-five points, six away from sixth position after twenty-six matches.

2009 kicked off to a good start. In the Championship, Swansea racked up three victories and one draw. Another two goals by Scotland saw them win 0-2 at Burnley, where Nathan Dyer, who originally came from Southampton, debuted in the last twenty-five minutes. The winger would play for the first-team at the Liberty Stadium in a match against Reading, an encounter in which Swansea had seventy-five percent possession and culminated in another winning 2-0; with another goal from Scotland and one from Orlandi, who hadn't played in a league tournament since October.

Among the Spanish Swans, Rangel and Jordi Gómez were the only ones who were a permanent fixture in the first eleven at that time in the season. With both playing from the outset and with the participation of Bauzá and Pintado (Orlandi and Serrán remained on the bench), the team scored 4-1 against Preston; Jordi Gómez scored the first goal in the second minute and Guillermo secured the third goal in the sixty-ninth minute. The Spanish players were even more instrumental during the following game, with Jordi Gómez and Pintado scoring in the 2-2 draw at Southampton. Orlandi and Rangel played, whilst Serrán and Bauzá were brought on as substitutes, so Bessone was the only one not to take part.

Fede Bessone had been released during the previous season to Nàstic, since he wasn't able to play for Espanyol, with whom he had signed for two years, as a result of not yet acquiring Spanish nationality. He would finally obtain nationality in December when he was with the Tarragona team, which had aspirations to climb into the Spanish Premier Division. The left-back started playing, but an injury and subsequent change of trainer had a negative impact on his form. The new coach, César Ferrando, told him that he couldn't rely on him, Espanyol would later make the same decision, despite Bessone having another year left to run on his contract.

The Argentine decided he wanted to leave Spain, therefore, when the opportunity arose to play in another country, he didn't hesitate. His agent, a friend of Roberto Martínez, initiated negotiations with Swansea. The presence of one of his best friends at the Jacks was a significant factor in his final decision: "Bauzá had told me that, given my skillset, I would have opportunities to play. If he hadn't been there, I wouldn't have been signed." In fact, they both shared Fede's first journey to his new destination in Wales. One Sunday morning his car followed Bauzá's all the way from Barcelona to The Village hotel in Swansea. "I turned on the sat navigation and we drove for eighteen hours," explains Bessone.

His new manager chose the Argentine because he was a very experienced left-back, someone Óscar Brau ascertains is a physical powerhouse, a very quick player and hardworking. Off the pitch, Bessone is happy and funny; he sings all day long and can whistle impressively. But if he's an expert in something, it's hurling breadcrumbs at the other diners, just ask Orlandi: "he throws them with brutal speed and precision."

Roberto's other facet

Guillem Balagué has worked as a sports journalist in the United Kingdom since 1991. Firstly as a correspondent for several Spanish media outlets, amongst them the old magazine Don Balón, and later as a member of Sky Sports, where he has presented the Revista de la Liga for years. The satellite television station had to find a journalist who was familiar with this tournament and who spoke English: "There were very few of us Spaniards back then."

One of the regular guests to feature on this weekly programme has been Roberto Martínez. Guillem saw in him a great aptitude for analysing football, and didn't hesitate in contacting him whilst he was still a player, informing him that they had the same requirements for guests as they did presenters: a great deal of knowledge about the Spanish La Liga and a good command of English. "He expressed himself better than many of the English coaches, and from the beginning it was clear that he had the capacity to coach and understood the concepts of the club environment," says Balagué. The journalist adds that he realised that his compatriot had a very good relationship with Jordi Cruyff, Iván Campo and the circle of footballers in Manchester. That was how these two Catalonians began to build a friendship, the journalist from Horta and the professional footballer from Balaguer. The friendship grew to such an extent that they became the voices – as narrator and commentator – chosen for the videogame Pro Evolution Soccer, in both the second and third versions.

Roberto Martínez was always willing to be on set whenever asked. On one occasion he even left Scotland during the Motherwell leg to make it to the studio on time. "He also gained the benefits of building his public profile through his work with Sky TV," Balagué points out.

During the programme Roberto became serious, and in perfect English he would analyse or address some matter related to La Liga, with which he was very familiar despite living away from Spain for years. In stark contrast, before going live, he had time for the most laid-back of atmospheres and jokes. "There were two Roberto's, one before the programme and another when we went live on air," recalls the sport journalist.

Besides his television experience for Sky, Roberto has made multiple appearances on the quintessentially British football programme, Match of the Day on the BBC. His broadcasting experience also includes being an analyst for ESPN and ITV in the coverage of the 2010 World Cup in South Africa and during the 2012 European Championships in Poland and Ukraine.

Although face-to-face it is possible to maintain a flowing and varied conversation with Roberto, Guillem Balagué notes that, at times, a certain moment is reached where you can't help but notice that he has his mind on other things. It is the same sensation that he felt with Pep Guardiola, and he attributes it to the fact that many managers are unable to switch off from football.

Roberto Martínez rarely uses his mobile phone, though he is very thoughtful when it comes to people he knows - even on the most complicated days of his career as a manager. During the week of the 2013 FA Cup semi-final, in which Roberto's Wigan faced Kenny Jackett's Millwall, Guillem Balagué's programme was broadcast live with a studio audience. "Our friend Rob Palmer, whose son is tetraplegic, has a fundraising organisation. Roberto, who is also a friend of Rob's, had the opportunity to get involved. He travelled for an hour, he arrived with a three-day beard and accompanied us for half an hour," Balagué recalls.

His television appearances and tireless work for charity have contributed to building Roberto Martínez's reputation in Britain, who, as Balagué recalls, is known as Spanish born but a British manager through and through.

The FA Cup Dream

Although everyone believed that it would be a transitional season, the team began to push themselves to make the next step, even when they were on top. The results and their good form went hand in hand, both at the Liberty and during away games. Pintado thinks that it was fundamental that they soon realised that they were a special team. "We won matches playing with skill and rivals began to show us respect." Rangel remembers that it was during the second round whilst he was in the dressing room that they began realising that the playoff was an attainable objective.

Besides the league matches, in January Swansea made it through two elimination rounds of the FA Cup. On Tuesday the 13th they won 1-2 in front of 2,800 spectators at Bridge Road, Histon's stadium (also known as the Glassworld stadium), against whom Bauzá and Pintado scored. Two Saturdays after, the Welsh side would be the protagonists of the great surprise of the fourth round of the FA Cup which, for some, is still considered the best Cup competition in the world.

Dyer and Scotland's goals —penalties— eliminated the reigning champions, Portsmouth, in a home game. That 24th of January put the region firmly on the map, for fans from all over the world. Roberto Martínez recognized the extent of the feat and felt that the players had thoroughly earned all the praise that they received following the result.

The Spanish manager believes that the League Cup is more financially driven whilst the FA Cup has more history and prestige. In fact, it is the oldest football tournament in the world. It is a competition that uniquely engenders a great many encounters between both professional and amateur footballers, with televised games and opportunities for the smaller clubs to claim a scalp by toppling one of the big teams and earn the title 'high-flyers'. Bob thinks that therein lies the charm of the FA Cup - a modest club can secure a budget for the next six years, as well as create interesting stories for the media.

Many want to imitate the heroic deeds of teams which, despite sitting in a lower category, clinch the coveted Wembley trophy. A good example of this was on the 5th of May 1973, when Sunderland, in the Second Division, triumphed over the powerful Leeds, managed by Don Revie. The television commentator said at the end of the game that the 1-0 victory for the Black Cats constituted, "probably the most surprising result ever at Wembley." This is precisely what happened when Swansea's arch rivals, their next door neighbours, Cardiff, were on the verge of causing a tremendous stir in 2008, when despite being in the Championship, knocked on the door of glory only to fall at the final hurdle losing 1-0 to Portsmouth in the final. Ironically, Swansea later avenged their rivals after eliminating Pompey.

The Cup dream concluded in February against Fulham, who were made to sweat in winning that fifth round tie. On Saint Valentine's Day, the Liberty Stadium very nearly set the scene for another great win against another premier side after Swansea equalized (1-1) in a match which saw an own goal by Monk countered by Scotland with his twelfth goal in the last twelve encounters.

The Cup tie was to be decided with a replay at Craven Cottage, a stadium which dates back to 1896. The home side saw their home playing field as a distinct advantage in taking on Manchester United in the quarter finals. And that was how it went: Fulham won 2-1, though they went through the wringer in achieving the win. Scotland brought the Jacks into the lead (it was his fourteenth goal in the past fifteen games), which kept hopes alive and kicking right up until the end of the game, when Dempsey and Zamora flipped the scoreboard by scoring in the seventy-seventh and eighty-first minutes. A landmark was reached that 24th of February, given that Roberto achieved his second anniversary as manager of the club.

Orlandi's performance during the fifteen minutes as a right winger in the first encounter against Fulham wasn't his best. Frustrations boiled over with his friend Rangel in a couple of games and both exchanged heated words. After that, Orlandi wasn't chosen to play in many of the following matches, including the second Cup game, therefore he requested that he be released. Roberto Martínez refused his request because he considered him to be an important part of the team. The Spanish-Italian player did not believe him, on account of the very few minutes he had played, but the coach left him speechless with a response that Andrea still remembers all these years later: "Listen, if you had played the day of the Fulham match, instead of quarrelling with Àngel, the club would now be playing the most important game in its history, against Manchester United."

The Challenge of the Playoffs

Roberto Martínez quickly looked for the positive side of the cup elimination. "We're interested in the league, we haven't played at this level for twenty-four years and we must continue to grow.

To see how we have adapted and how we can compete has been an important step," he expressed in an interview given with Efe Radio. As well as this, he was confident that his players would reach the playoffs, which is why he was so uncompromising: "In football, you have to dream big, because, if you don't, something will fail. But we must be realistic, since we are playing against sides which have been in the Premiership and have higher budgets than us." Roberto was happy to let the fans delude themselves and made the most of the inertia after the previous season's great glory to keep building.

At this period of the year, Óscar Brau's work was very important because, in British football, there is no masseur, normally the physiotherapist fulfils this role. The Swansea team was limited in terms of personnel, and Brau played a key part in the recuperation of some players who were suffering in the wake of a demanding schedule of sixty matches. All of them, including Bauzá, appreciated it: "We had peace of mind being able to ask him for a massage when needed. He had enough time to be able to do it."

He plays down the importance of his work and the nickname he earned, asserting that anyone could be 'Magic Hands' when they endeavour to do their job well and put their heart and soul into it. Brau recognizes that years of experience enable you to pick up little techniques and discover new details that produce results. Then there are those players who respond better to somewhat aggressive treatment, and do not protest, in contrast to others who are far more sensitive. With regards to the latter, treatment is less effective, since it does not penetrate so deeply.

His career within the football world is plentiful and varied. On a club level, he has been a member of the Grasshoppers, Wigan, Swansea and Poli Ejido. He has also collaborated with a selection of international teams from Andorra, Romania (during the 2000 Euro Cup) and the Ivory Coast (in the pre-World Cup South African stages). During this last venture, he became good friends with Didier Drogba and Kolo Touré. In addition to his extensive background in football is his experience in the tennis world. He has worked, to some extent, with brother and sister Arancha and Emilio Sánchez Vicario; the Russian Svetlana

Kuznetsova; Rafa Nadal; Carlos Moyà; Albert Costa and Carlos Costa, amongst others.

As if that weren't enough, he has networked extensively with numerous footballers, thanks to the sports material distributor Brau Sports. He introduced many English goods to Spain, designed specifically for children and students, but his star products are shin guards made from Italian carbon, which are personalized for each player. Many Swansea footballers ordered them. Rangel requested some new ones on the birth of his daughter, creating the design and adding her name to the existing inscription.

These shin guards were also the first of their kind to be sold in Spain. Though they are used by many League players, Brau created a bit of a furore when news leaked out about one of his clients in particular: "Without naming names, I can say that the world's number one footballer has been wearing them for four years. That means that they work. He wears them when he plays and more will be made for him when he needs them." Indeed, he was talking about Leo Messi.

Before the FA Cup game against Fulham, Swansea won 3 - 0 against Ipswich, with a goal from a free-kick by Jordi Gómez and two by Scotland, the first goal after a move by Serrán. The defender debuted in that game in the Championship, which, years later, he remembers as being his most special wearing a Swans shirt: "I played as a right winger in a great match and, in the third minute I ran down the wing, and helped to create the goal."

His position as a winger was due to a sanction imposed on Rangel, who listened to the beginning of that game from the radio in his car in the Liberty's car park. Later, he entered the stands which Albert had secretly given him access to: "I was very pleased to see him play, because he deserved it. He worked well but Monk and Williams were untouchable centre backs."

Serrán believes that joining the team so late affected the way he settled on and off the pitch. Roberto Martínez had confidence in a reduced group of players and hardly made any changes to the line-up, which is why the defender had to wait for injuries and bans to be able to play.

Rangel and Serrán, despite the occasional squabble during card games, held each other in high esteem, which, in part, was the result of being pre-match roommates. Years previously they had been rivals in the Spanish Segunda B matches, when Rangel's impression of Serrán was very different to what it is now: "I saw him as an argumentative person on the playing field, he used to always defend his teammates and was always looking for a fight. When I met him in Swansea, I was amazed, because he really is a softie at heart."

Gorka Pintado also had some disputes with Serrán in Segunda B games: "I knew him from having received a few knocks from him in some games, though it wasn't a big deal. He hit me, I hit him back, but at the end we shook hands. In a nutshell, it's better to have him as a teammate." Bergara underlines that above all else he is a professional, whilst Brau admired his tremendous marking of opponents: "A true marker. If there is a foot and it touches the ball, it's Serrán's foot." Leon Britton adds ruefully: "He sure likes to tackle."

Albert Serrán's time with the club had been guaranteed since mid-June. His agent had mentioned the possibility of an offer from Britain. It wouldn't be until the final months of the season that he established contact with the Swansea manager. The defender had never contemplated playing in British football, but he decided, with his girlfriend's encouragement, to take the plunge. It would be a good experience thanks to the presence of various friends from Spain playing in the UK. He had talked to Bussy, Fede and Jordi Gómez, with whom he had already established a friendship before meeting in Wales. He would later bond with the others and become godfather to Orlandi's daughter.

According to his teammates, he is a very gentle person, and is one of those players who quickly form bonds in the changing room. He always gives a hundred percent, whether he plays or not. In fact, Serrán did not stop working during those periods in which he was not part of the first-team. Albert remembers how Roberto Martínez had requested he be patient despite rarely playing.

He travelled, he was devoted to the team, but he mostly watched the games from the stand: "He told me that I had to keep going, to keep focused so that I was prepared when my moment arrived, as I was going to be important in the last third of the Championship. He was very sincere," recalls Serrán.

Eventually, he played nine consecutive matches, and notched up a total of twenty, between league and cup games.

A Team with Trust

Doubts regarding possible misgivings between the tight group of Spaniards and the other players dissipated naturally with the passing of time. Roberto Martínez did not give priority to the Spanish footballers, he continued to pick the team based on form and whoever was playing well got the jersey regardless of nationality. This is corroborated by the amount of time each teammate played over the season, many of his fellow countrymen did not feature consistently in the line-up.

Day-to-day relations were normal amongst the teammates, according to Bauzá: "We were lucky to have a group of open-minded players. It's easy to joke about Spanish players on one side, English on the other and Welsh on another, but these are little details which don't really matter."

The away trips played a fundamental role in establishing good relations between the diverse nationalities. The long bus journeys brought the players closer together with many a round of pocha (a Spanish card game) played in teams of two or three British players against two or three Spaniards. The former would practice their Spanish ("me pido dos", "me pido siete"...) and the latter their English ("you did it right", "you did it wrong"...). Those card games helped to bond the team, on both a sporting and social level.

Serrán believes it's only natural that, at the dinner table, the Spaniards would speak Spanish especially after the English speakers had retired to their bedrooms, although he could understand if some teammates felt offended by the constant jokes between them in their own language. Pintado was grateful for the rules established at the team dinners: "Some, like myself, who didn't know any English, always tried to avoid it. But necessity forces you to learn more."

All of the Spanish players, according to Orlandi, respected the new culture at all times, learnt the language quickly and made an effort to adapt. In that respect they all did their own bit. Bergara initially did not like the fact that the shops closed early and that the games were played at three in the afternoon, although he understood the reasons behind it: "It is one of the best times of the day, in the UK, it's clearer and sunnier."

The Final Stage of the Season

Mid-February, Swansea had fifteen Championship encounters ahead of them, practically a third of those played in the Cup tournament. The Welsh side won 3-1 against Doncaster, with two goals by Jordi Gómez and another by Scotland. These two players then went on to reverse their goal-scoring roles in a triumphant match against Ipswich. Before that, they had lost 2-0 against Watford; the team which had knocked them out of the League Cup had also broken their run of sixteen undefeated matches in all competitions.

The elimination from the FA Cup was followed by three consecutive league draws: at the Liberty against Charlton (1-1), away games against Derby County (2-2, after recovering from a 2-0 with goals scored by Rangel and Pintado) and Nottingham Forest (1-1). With ten match days to go, the Jacks were eighth in the table, two points less than Preston, who were sixth with one game in hand.

After winning against Plymouth 1-0 and moving to sixth position, which would qualify them to play in the playoffs, Swansea City weakened their chances of securing two promotions on the bounce, by securing only two points from the following twelve. Pintado's goal did nothing in the 1-3 defeat against Crystal Palace, played after the Swans lost 1-0 at Loftus Road against Queens Park Rangers and after a goalless draw at Sheffield Wednesday. The Wednesday match preceded another Welsh derby.

On the 5th April, in Cardiff, the score was 2-2, the same result as some months previous at the Liberty stadium, though the comeback was reversed from the previous encounter with a heart-stopping climax. The 1-2 goals scored by Joe Allen in the eighty-eighth minute seemed to deliver the verdict, but in extra time the home team scored a penalty that kept them in sixth place with sixty-four points in thirty-nine encounters, whilst Swansea totalled fifty-nine points with forty-one games played.

The last derby at the old stadium of the Welsh capital city was heated, again with almost as many police in attendance as supporters. Rangel caught some of the incidents: "Near to me, they started to throw coins. In the final minutes, when we were leading 1-2, the referee awarded them a controversial penalty." After the encounter, the Swansea players had to wait for over an hour on the pitch, whilst rumours circulated that Cardiff fans had thrown stones at Swansea fans, even at families and small children.

When reaching the playoffs felt like an almost impossible task, Swansea secured three consecutive wins: a 2-1 against Norwich City following two goals scored by Scotland; the striker from Trinidad and Tobago scored again against Barnsley (1-3), a match in which Jordi Gómez also scored; and the following match, Monk scored from a corner initiated by Orlandi to win 1-0 against Bristol City. This run of nine points placed Roberto Martínez's team in seventh place, with sixty-eight points, only one less than Burnley, though the club which had fallen from prime position in the league had one game more than Swansea yet to play.

It was the moment of truth. After twenty-four years out of the Championship, and during a so-called consolidation season, the Jacks aspired at the end of April to continue aiming high despite the fact that their team was only recently promoted. On the 25th of that month they planned on paying Sheffield United a visit and, on the third of May, their football season came to an end, in a match against Blackpool in front of their home crowd. Lamentably, the two matches ended with defeats of 1-0 and Swansea finished the season eighth with seventy-four points, behind Cardiff, who also eventually missed out despite reaching the same seventy-eight points as sixth-in-the-table, Preston.

Summary

On balance, despite not reaching the top six, the club was in a very positive position. Various Spanish Swans continued to express pride for having been signed during, what was regarded, as the best season in the history of the club up until that point. Without detracting from league action, the highlights that season were: Cardiff's elimination from the League Cup and getting so close to the quarter finals of the FA Cup after having crushed the reigning champions (Peter Crouch and Kanu's Portsmouth).

Iñaki Bergara believes that, during that season, they played boldly and uncompromisingly, despite having only a small budget, although he remarks that they drew quite often because they failed to go full throttle in some games. Some players also think that fatigue took its toll on a team low on players, in which the first eleven played almost continuously from August until May.

Óscar Brau credits the team on their recent promotion especially as they were battling with such a small squad. This disadvantage, according to him, did not prevent the players from earning the respect of everyone involved in the league nor did it prevent them from winning a lot of matches. However, he does acknowledge that in some of the final games, fatigue had set in and they slipped off playing the Swansea way, also the players did not think that they could truly win.

Guillermo Bauzá remained eager to play more, after starting the pre-season so well and was keen to repay the managers confidence in him. Nonetheless, he understood that there were new signings and teammates who deserved to play. With regards to his experience in the three lower divisions in British football, the Majorcan considers physical intensity, honour, and the dogged fight until the very last minute to be the common denominator. However, he does notice differences: "In the Championship, teams are more solid. In League One, the attack and defence tend to break loose a little bit. And, in League Two, I did indeed witness the more traditional style of British play, with less possession, more long passes and high crosses."

Andrea Orlandi personally laments the lack of confidence and opportunities, with the exception of the final part of the season. He acknowledges that it is only logical that a coach makes his decisions, but he is convinced that he would have responded effectively to having played more frequently.

Àngel Rangel, in contrast, was a constant feature in the line-up, playing some forty-six official encounters in each competition, even when he was injured. At the end of the season, he sustained inflammation to his tendon which didn't improve nor could it be operated on: "Roberto told me that he would rather have me play half-limping, so I played anyway and I gave it my all as I saw that he had confidence in me. I ended up in some pain." Rangel began the season, according to him, with too much respect for the new league, though his confidence grew alongside that of the team.

Jordi Gómez's memories of his unique season with the Welsh cub are unbeatable, due to the support from the fans, the collective effort and his individual performances. He played close to fifty games in all of the competitions; he scored fourteen goals; he was nominated player of the year, and featured alongside Scotland in the eleven top players of the season in that league. Away from the pitch, he paid little attention to any negative issues, possibly because he had his brother-in-law, Orlandi, nearby: "When I was in Barça B I introduced Andrea to the sister of my fiancé, who I had been dating for over ten years. They have also now been dating for over seven years."

Pintado, contrastingly, remembers that neither he nor his family adapted to British traditions. He defines his period in Wales as a job or just another experience in his career. Yes, he felt at home in a purely football-related basis and he believes that he played enough during his first time abroad, although he was impeded for a month and a half as a result of an injury sustained to the pelvic area. It started to bother him in December, he intended to avoid operating on it, but in February he finally travelled to Germany to undergo surgery. Following his recovery, he mostly played in the second halves of matches and found it difficult to prove his worth, though he admits that he can't complain.

Bessone looks back fondly on his debut season, during which he participated in approximately sixteen games. In his opinion the team, had a very strong line-up, playing at a good level and with a distinctive football style, despite failing to qualify for the playoffs. The Argentinian blames his injury problems on the drastic changes in diet. Everything seemed to be interconnected. Having to play and get up early forced him to take food at midday: "I was accustomed to eating at two and playing at six or seven. The quality of the food isn't the same as in Spain either."

Serrán's first year was quite hard. He's a player that needs to express himself on the field, talking a lot, communicating and directing from defence which he found difficult to do initially. Furthermore, he had to adapt to a defensive system which was different to what he was accustomed to. In Espanyol everyone knew the moves they had to make, for example, to stay together or to mark. He doesn't think that such stability in defence existed in Swansea, back then, each player tended to go their own way.

Roberto Martínez is aware of the fundamental role his compatriots played in his two complete seasons managing the Welsh side, but he adds that Swansea's collective mentality was primordial: "The seven Spanish players were great ambassadors for our football in Britain. They generated a lot of interest, though teamwork as a whole outshone any individual performances."

Many of the Spanish players agree that it was a somewhat unusual season on a collective level, during which the team lost some points due to inexperience and lack of playing time but also adapted and competed in a superior league. Likewise, Roberto Martínez praises the extraordinary progression in possession football: "The team played with great confidence, something very unique. We competed against great teams like Norwich, Sheffield United and Reading, who had come from the Premiership. We were able to keep the ball, notching up figures of six hundred or six hundred and fifty passes per game, something never before experienced."

All of this, what was achieved and the approach taken to reach that level, did not go unnoticed by the British football community. The name Roberto Martínez became part of the agenda for some clubs.

CHAPTER 7

2009-10 Swansea, 2.0.The Post Roberto Era

In June 2009, many doubts were beginning to circulate around Swansea regarding the possible departure of Roberto Martínez. On the fourth day of that month, the most popular opinion was that the Spaniard would stay on the Welsh bench. Forty-six percent of fans held this view, against thirty-two percent who thought that he would go to Celtic and twenty-three percent believed that his destination was Wigan. A few days later, the club accepted its loss and the search for a new manager began with some vigour.

Departure of Roberto

The former captain and the person responsible for elevating the team into League One had abandoned ship. The supporters were dumbfounded. The initial disbelief soon turned to indignation and Roberto Martínez became villain almost as fast as he had previously been made a hero. Judas was the most frequent term used over the coming weeks, it was in stark contrast to the adulation that Roberto had previously enjoyed. Fans had waited twenty-four long years for the triumphant moment that Martínez had finally delivered. It's no surprise that there were offers from bigger clubs, but at the end of the day it was his own decision to leave. Bob stated through the local press that the fans needed to stop viewing him as a Swan and instead see him as they would a player who leaves the team. This had happened only a year before the euphoric victory over Gillingham, putting them into the next league. Roberto had left the Swans then as a player only to return as manager. Twelve months later he had perfected the project with the reliable support of Huw Jenkins and all at the club, his relationship with the fans was very close and on a personal level he also felt very close to Wales. He showed no interest in Celtic's offers from Glasgow or from the other powerful Championship clubs. He had even rejected offers from Sir Alex Ferguson at Manchester United.

What had changed since the celebrations at Gillingham? What were the reasons that pushed him to abandon his plans to take Swansea into the Premiership? Neither the money nor the challenge of leading a premier league team were the factors behind his decision. The reason, he said, came one day, after a phone call from his big friend Dave Whelan, chairman of Wigan where he had started his English adventure: the club where he had proudly worn the shirt for six seasons. Whelan was a visionary and in the nineties set about changing the pace of a modest Third Division Club. The first Spanish players in the league started there, a move that was widely praised. Wigan Athletic F.C., the Latics (a suffix of Athletic, although an 'a' has replaced the 'e'. It refers both to Wigan Athletic F.C. and Oldham Athletic A.F.C.) were now firmly involved with the Spanish football market and it completely recharged the team.

Almost half a century before he appeared at the Wigan stadium (now the DW Stadium), Whelan was a professional football player, although his success had come more from business. It all started when he bought an Angling and Sports Shop that had been growing for three decades and now had hundreds of shops. The name JJB relates to the initials of the previous owners and was worn on Wigan's shirts. Roberto Martínez, Isidro Diaz and Jesús Seba wore these shirts in their inaugural season and sport them in the famous photograph, The Three Amigos.

In 2009, Dave Whelan's thoughts began to turn to Roberto Martínez, Bob, to give Wigan a new sense of purpose, a new vibe, but this time not as a player but as manager. "When Dave presented me with the project, it was a very difficult decision, but I couldn't say no to the challenge. He wanted to bring together a new group and to work in a different way from what he had done previously. It was a new start, which was exactly the situation with Swansea two and a half years previously. The call had come from Wigan, a club of real sentimental value for me. It seemed impossible that anything could have broken the bond, Martínez -Swansea. Nothing, except for Martínez –Wigan."

The skills mastered and perfected in Balaguer once again returned to the city near Manchester and more Spaniards were soon to follow. Iñaki Bergara, Óscar Brau, and Jordi Gómez, who had returned to Spain after his time at Swansea. They all made the almost 300km journey from Swansea to Wigan. "Going to the Premier League was exciting," Bergara recalls. "But there were conflicting feelings. It was sad to leave Swansea without finishing our aims. Yet, it was great to leave Swansea when the club was doing so well."

The growth of the club, on and off the field, as both a football team and financially meant a lot for the four men who left Swansea for Wigan, and the Championship for the Premiership. Óscar Brau realized that he had a lot to lose: "I find the fans very different. Fans in Swansea are fantastic; they deserve to be in the Premiership just for their enthusiasm. In Wigan you can have a thousand people on a Tuesday or Saturday but in Swansea there can be up to four or five thousand."

There were also fears that Àngel Rangel would join the expedition to Wigan. He surprised people by not making the journey: "They told me that without me the team would collapse." Martínez always understood Rangel's feelings towards Swansea and never applied pressure on him to do something against his wishes. But Graeme Jones and head of scouting, Kevin Reeves had already packed their bags. The anger in the hearts of the Jack Army was even greater when it was confirmed that Jason Scotland, the team's top goal scorer over the previous seasons had also signed with the Latics.

Being sentimental for his old club was a cert, but there was another reason, which Martínez could not reveal publically at the time. Swansea's financial situation wasn't bad but it did need a financial boost and the club needed a new star to take it to the next level. When Roberto left on the 15th of June, the club received £2 million (more than €2.3 million) double the amount received for Lee Trundle when he was sold to Bristol City. The transfer of Jason Scotland, who was around thirty years of age at the time gained another million. Martínez remembers how difficult and emotional it was and that the fans didn't understand the true reasons at the time. He felt that the club needed new life so this coincided well with his departure.

Swansea's budget, according to Roberto had practically doubled for the challenges ahead. Nevertheless the uncertainty provoked by the loss of the teams inspiration, back room staff and the two best players wasn't very good compensation in the eyes of most fans.

Uncertainty among the Spanish Swans

The departure of Roberto Martínez took place in the middle of June and had been delayed by an agreement being reached between Swansea and Wigan. They also needed to wait for Dave Whelan to return from his holidays in Mallorca. Swansea, in a last ditch attempt to keep Martinez had offered to double his salary. It had no effect and the chairman of the Welsh contingent, Huw Jenkins, accepted what was happening graciously. It was always a risk when dealing with professional players and managers especially ambitious ones. He understood that Roberto couldn't reject a call from the Premiership. "As a manager he led us in the right direction. He's a great man," he recognized later.

Whilst the directors of Swansea remained calm and received more than a hundred offers for a replacement, the Jack's supporters didn't hide their feelings and Spanish footballers spent many days of uncertainty wondering what the future held. "There was a definite fear," admits Bessone.

However there were others who accepted things more calmly: "In football, it is normal that one trainer goes and another comes. If you show your loyalty, you'll play the same with one as with any other."

Despite the worry, they understood that their former guardian wanted to grow professionally. Rangel believed that he had done the correct thing because it was not every day you had the opportunity to go to a Premier League Club. Everyone associated with football understood the decision.

The calendar for the 2009-10 games was already known ahead of any new manager being appointed. There was concern in certain quarters that the new manager would shift the club's philosophy and undo all the great work established by Roberto Martínez, who had always strived for the best results whilst playing attractive football. Guillem Bauzá shared the same values and vision. "There was a shared vision amongst the players and the club and no one wanted this to be tampered with. The team's structure and design, playing the Swansea way, worked well on the pitch."

Huw Jenkins explained that Swansea's style of playing was not negotiable, regardless of how many players were brought in. Roberto's substitute could not just be anyone. All the club's achievements and their future expectations could not be jeopardized. The new leader, in the words of Jenkins, would need to be an enthusiastic, young, brilliant manager, a visionary with great contacts in the world of football.

The substitute

Many names had been considered, including the Uruguayan Gustavo Poyet and Gary Speed. The €590,000 that Swansea needed to pay Sheffield United was an obvious obstacle. Poyet would very much have liked the opportunity to manage Swansea: "Swansea seemed an ideal choice. A wonderful team that had been developed by a fellow Spanish speaker, it was perfect. Unfortunately it wasn't to be."

In truth there were undoubtable similarities between Martínez and Poyet. Both had started their careers as players, both had First League experience where they had developed their respective philosophy's of playing, which were not dissimilar. Poyet later said, "Roberto was very good. This gave me the strength to carry on, to know that it was possible and I think it enabled me to convince the people at Brighton."

Swansea's choice was Paolo Sousa from Portugal, a double European champion footballer, who had gained an excellent reputation as a coach, even though his experience had only been with local Portuguese sides and a short period at Queens Park Rangers. Nevertheless he had extensive experience playing in the Italian, Portuguese, German, Greek and Spanish Leagues. There was celebration in Swansea, who were pleased to have another European who could continue from where Roberto had left off without the need to introduce any radical new plans. Bauzá commented: "He was an excellent player and will no doubt enrich my knowledge and teach me many new things."

Paolo Sousa was inaugurated on the 23rd of June 2009. The twelfth manager in fourteen years. "I am the right man," he said. Sousa also wanted to carry on the work of Roberto Martínez, using his ideas and visions. Money wasn't the most important thing. It couldn't compare with success, nor the journey or passion required. He knew also, that he had to maximise his time, and that high expectations were being placed upon him. Huw Jenkins reminded him that the ambition was to reach the Premier League, but also to remain financially prudent. English football had always been a favourite for Sousa. He considered it the best environment to develop the skills required for top flight management. When he arrived in Wales; the Championship was considered the fifth best league in the world. For some fans securing a Portuguese coach was a great result, everyone was aware of the 'special one's' success at Chelsea, now Swansea had their own 'Mourinho'.

Of all the people who'd contributed to his success, the greatest influence was Sven Gőran Eriksson. Eriksson had spent a lot of time with him off the pitch, giving him good advice and helping to build his confidence. He had also advised Sousa to play in the midfield position. Sven encouraged and nurtured his talents. Paolo Sousa was always considered an elegant part of any team he played for. Grey was the colour of the Swansea team's tracksuits, but there was nothing grey about Sousa's presence.

Albert Serrán remembers the first time he met him face to face, "He was very thin, but had a powerful voice." Andrea Orlando was also impressed with the way he carried himself: "He spoke perfect Spanish. He had class and looked you in the eye when he spoke. You quickly realised that he was a great person." For Orlandi, a passionate football player and fan, and a keen follower of teams such as Juventus and Turin, the Portuguese are legends. If he could display the same vigour and passion that Sousa had regarding the game, then he hoped to be able to move into the central position as an attacking midfielder.

Planning and the eleventh Spaniard

Roberto Martínez had gone and plans were being made for the season ahead, that included some games at the end of July in Spain in Catalonia, playing Spain B, the Palamos, Gymnastic de Tarragona, and Sabadell. The rest of the games would be against Trofense, a Portuguese side, the Dutch side Twente, the Scottish side Kilmarnock, and the Welsh sides Neath and Port Talbot.

The club had made it perfectly clear that they weren't going to spend a fortune on contracts. They would pay for two. David Cotterill, who cost €675,000 and Craig Beattie, another forward, who came from West Bromwich Albion, cost just under €1,000,000.

Before leaving the way clear for Wigan to negotiate the transfer of Roberto Martínez, the club also successfully acquired Nathan Dyer along with the arrival of Stephen Dobbie from Queens Park Rangers. Swansea didn't need to pay anything for either player. Dobbie had scored twenty-four goals in the Scottish league and was considered a good acquisition. Later came the arrival of the Trinidad and Tobago player Radanfah Abu Bakr and the midfielder Jordi López.

In the preseason Paolo Sousa had admitted that he wanted to find a striker with a different profile to the ones he already had on the books. Dobbie and Bauzá were both carrying injuries which made the situation extremely pressing. Initial talks with the Spanish striker Pablo Conuago had fizzled out. The Swans finally managed to acquire Cedric van der Gunn from Holland and Besian Idrizaj from Austria. Lee Trundle also

returned on loan. Shefki Kuqi, from Finland, arrived in January during the mid-season.
The Spanish Jacks had lost four of their best payers. The six remaining (Rangel, Orlandi, Bauzà, Serrán, Pintado and Bessone) were joined by Jordi López who became the eleventh Spaniard in the history of the Welsh team. Paolo Sousa had coached at Queens Park Rangers and knew the ex-Seville, Mallorca, and Santander Racing player, and therefore was confident that he would fit into Swansea's style of play. Lopez had also played in both youth teams for Barcelona and Real Madrid. This and the title he had gained with Madrid caused a great deal of excitement amongst the fans. "We were curious to find out what sort of person he was. From that moment on, we saw that he was a person who never stopped making you laugh," said Bauzà.

López was the victim of certain mishaps during his early period at Swansea. The team were waiting at El Prat Airport, Barcelona, to fly to London, just having completed pre-season training in the Montanyà, a hotel complex situated half an hour from the city centre. Bauzà, Serrán, Bessone and Jordi López missed the plane with all their equipment already on board. "We couldn't believe it," Bessone recalled. "Bauzà said that the plane had been delayed for half an hour and that there was plenty of time for coffee. I'll never forget that."

Whilst his friends saw the whole incident as slightly funny, Jordi wasn't too happy, as he had just arrived at the club and this was considered his trial period. Fortunately Paolo Sousa didn't mention it. The trio had to pay to get on a plane departing an hour later. They sometimes make reference to Bussy's scatterbrain but on this occasion he defends his mistake. "There were two flights around the same time going to London. One was delayed, obviously not ours."

The Karaoke fear

Jordi López also had to consider the importance of fitting into his new team. He had a few sleepless nights worrying over his singing initiation. Nothing could free him from standing up and singing in front of all his teammates on his first trip with them. Some had done it in Sweden, others in Leeds or near Walsall. Wherever they are, when the winning team toast each other with glasses of water over dessert, every new player is only too well aware that the anxious moment has come to get up from his chair and pretend to have a microphone by using a spoon.

We know that Roberto Martínez chose 'Beauty and the Beast' when he was a player and 'It's a Heartache' by the Welsh singer Bonnie Tyler when he returned as manager. As for the rest of the Swans, five of them endured the ordeal in the 2007-2008 season. Bauzà went for the classic 'Hey Jude' by the Beatles. Orlandi showed loyalty to his nation with 'Nel blu dipinto blu' (more popularly known as Volare), by Domenico Modungo. Rangel had planned 'La Bamba' but Ignasi Madier sang it first so he improvised with 'La cucaracha', with moves and music akin to Michael Jackson. La Bamba was heard again months later by Brau, near the end of the season.

This tradition provided some great times. The funniest moment was thanks to Bergara, who gets very embarrassed by these situations. He knows little English and laughs as he recalls his interpretation of 'Love is all Around' by Wet Wet Wet, the song that became a hit thanks to the film Four Weddings and a Funeral. The night before playing in Walsall, Roberto Martínez wrote the lyrics along with how to pronounce each word. The squad were all surprised when they heard Iñaki's almost faultless English pronunciation. There was even more of a shock when they discovered his method. Iñaki said, "I see that document as a sort of treasure, a beautiful treasure that I must savour. Thinking like that really helps me."

In the second season, Bessone attempted 'Three Little Birds' by Bob Marley, an artist that made another squad appearance with 'No Woman, No Cry' sung by Jordi Gómez. Serrán wanted to imitate Ottis Redding singing, 'On the Dock of the Bay'. Pintado surprised his teammates by singing the 'chiki-chiki dance' the controversial song by Rodolfo Chikilicuatre who represented Spain in Eurovision 2008. The following season, Jordi López performed the 'Macarena' by Los del Rio.

Bad start

The press and the betting shops had no faith in Swansea staying up. They were written off before the season had even begun. From the outside it seemed a failing team now that Roberto Martínez, Jordi Gómez and Jason Scotland had gone. The predications were seemingly proved correct in August, Swansea was bottom of the league after losing their first two games. The 2-1 blow at Leicester was followed by the worst defeat in two years at the Liberty, a 0-3, against Middlesbrough.

The journalists in the Welsh press were already commenting on the signings. Orlandi was also thinking about it. "We started with problems because we hadn't signed enough players and we also had to get used to the new coach's methods." Orlandi and Pintado played in an opening game with the other Spaniards on the bench. Rangel was the only Spaniard to play in both league games. Bessone, Jordi López and Bauzá enjoyed their first taste of victory with a 3-0 against Brighton in the Football League Cup. Serrán couldn't participate in this game because of a sprained ankle picked up two days previously. The injury kept him out of action for the next two and a half months.

In August, Swansea controversially finished their participation in the Carling Cup, with a 1-2 defeat to Scunthorpe. The game was a fiery and bad tempered affair, and Scunthorpe clinched the win with a penalty. Furthermore Swansea had to finish the match with only seven players on the pitch. Besian Idrizaj wanted to carry on playing whilst injured. Boddie had also been injured. Monk, Pintado and Rangel had been sent off.

Scunthorpe's coach later commented that the players discharged had left the referee little option, "the lack of discipline has cost them dearly. They are a fantastic passing team and we are really pleased that we defended well against them. The referee had no choice but to send their players off as they seemed to lose their composure." Paolo Sousa was very critical of the referee's decisions and went public even taking his complaints to the FA: "We didn't want to lose the game. There were very bad events that happened. Of course I don't appreciate it. We have an opportunity to write to the FA about the referee's performance. I never wanted the match abandoned, Idrizaj should not have gone back on the field but as we were down to only six players the referee put pressure on us to get him back on. I don't appreciate it." He went on to commend the extreme efforts of his team when playing seven against eleven. Idrizaj had cardiac problems and the saddest part of this story is that he died in 2010 of heart failure. He is fondly remembered by his teammates.

The team went on to secure two draws at home followed by a 2-0 win which encouraged the fans to believe that the playing style of Roberto Martínez had at last returned to the club. Although the Portuguese manager had his own style and was trying to stamp his authority on the team. Many commentators thought that the team was less creative and not as free as it was under Roberto but everyone was in agreement that the Swans looked a more solid side. "We were vulnerable in defence and he was the ideal man to combat this problem," said Rangel.

The victory in September was followed by a defeat of 2-0 to Preston North End and a triumph of 2-1 against Sheffield United. Lee Trundle celebrated his first goal of the season on the 26th of September. Swansea were sixteenth in the League, with eleven points in just ten days.

Craig Beattie scored three of the six recorded goals, in the following five games of the championship that contributed to two draws and three wins. The forward, who came on board during the final part of the signing window was considered single-handedly responsible for the two home wins. The 0-2 win against Scunthorpe led to a match against his old club West Bromwich Albion.

The Welsh Press was becoming convinced that Swansea was on the right path but it would take time to make an assault on the upper reaches of the league. Paulo Sousa was sure that the team was on track and that victories would follow. The Portuguese manager had bedded in and the players were receptive to his ideas, so receptive that in October they rose up to eleventh position in the league. The team had put themselves in a great position with a tally of twenty-two points only two points away from the playoffs.

The derby that strengthened feelings

The 7th of November duly arrived, a date that many Jacks had been eagerly anticipating. Swansea arrived under the guidance of Sousa, a new era had begun. Dyer and Pratley advanced the Swans' cause in the first quarter of an hour but the game was a 2-2 draw and the scoreboard seemed destined to remain at that. But another goal by Pratley allowed the fans to celebrate a double win against their biggest rivals that took them to third in the division.

Sousa believed that, whilst it was important to have the recognition of the Press, the fans and also other managers for their good form, the triumph in the derby was extra special because it reinforced the player's belief that all the day to day work was finally paying dividends.

"Since I started here, I've said that there is only one way to play and I believe that victory doesn't only inspire confidence but also the conviction and confidence that we need to progress," expressed the Portuguese manager at a Press conference at the Liberty.

In the month of November, with two further League games, there was a win against Derby County, with a single goal in the eighty-first minute by Fede Bessone. "It was one of my happiest moments as footballer. When the fans saw me score, they were overjoyed, it was an indescribable emotion." During the move Swansea had kept possession for over two minutes, Bessone received the ball between the centre and the back going on to score the vital goal. This goal was the accumulation of a run of eleven consecutive wins securing the Swans third place in the table.

It was an excellent position to be in considering nobody had given the team much hope at the start of the season. Nobody could have predicted the convincing 3-0 win (the first three shots before the first half-an-hour had even been played) against Newcastle at St James's Park. The Newcastle coach, Chris Hughton, said afterward that Swansea were a class apart from any other team in the division, and that other teams needed to up their game and skill levels when facing them.

The pattern of play that characterized the Swansea of Sousa led certain fans to refer to the games as being akin to a chess match. Sousa seemed to be influenced a great deal by his past as a player in Italy and sought to introduce that style of play. Bauzá remembers being encouraged to take control of the ball at speed, not allowing the opposite team to gain any advantage.

During the last month of 2009, Swansea scored six goals (three from Trundle and another three from Pratley) the deficit was four goals conceded, with a balance of one win, three draws and one lost (0-1 at the Liberty against Nottingham Forest). In one of the victories (0-2 against Sheffield Wednesday at Hillsborough), the performances of both Rangel and Orlandi were singled out for particular praise with many pundits predicting that they would be named amongst the top eleven players in the entire division. Over the space of a year Paolo Sousa's team was now in sixth position, with two more points than Sheffield Wednesday, who were seventh.

On the 2nd of January 2010, Swansea was eliminated from the FA cup losing their game against Leicester City. Six first team regulars, Rangel, Williams, Bessone, Britton, Orlandi and Dyer started, the Spaniards among them were Serrán, Jordi López and Pintado. Only Bauzá was missing. Thanks to Cotterill, Swansea were ahead at the start of the game but in the eighty-ninth minute conceded. The 2-1 reverse pushed them out of the tournament. Some detractors thought that Paolo Sousa didn't take the cup seriously. Sousa defended his decision to make changes to the side, and reaffirmed his commitment to the tournament: "The FA cup gives great prestige and money to the club that wins so naturally I am very happy to participate. I want to win every game."

The club could now concentrate solely on the league, where there was the no small matter of over twenty games ahead. It did seem that the Championship would stretch into eternity. Two weeks after the disappointment at the Liberty with Leicester, the Swans were back on top form, with a goal by Pintado. "It was very emotional for me because it had been such a long time since I had scored," recalled Gorka, who had endured a lean spell. The Toro (The Bull) also scored in the following match, the 1-1 draw at the Riverside Stadium in Middlesbrough. It was a less rewarding goal but still a great shot from Pintado's boot into the top corner. It was partly due to this goal that he was included in the fans best eleven players in the division for that month. They were to be his first two goals of the season, but they were also to be his last.

There was yet another draw when Coventry came to Wales. In this match, the last of January's fixtures, almost half the team were made up of Spanish players – Rangel, Bessone, Jordi López, Orlandi and Pintado. They were only missing Serrán and Bauzá to make the team complete.

Question of Injuries

The absence of Óscar Brau led to the question of injuries being raised, which had been particularly affecting the team, especially amongst the Spanish players.

Àngel Rangel had finished the previous season with an inflamed tendon. Sousa ordered him not to join the pre-season training. Rangel went to visit an expert insole fitter, to help with his ongoing foot problems. Since the start of the 2009-10 season he managed to play without any problems in his heels due to the special mould installed in his boots. The Swans were carrying other injuries too.

Guillermo Bauzà had been injured during the first round of games. Against Brighton, he picked up an injury just two minutes after he came on to replace Jordi López Felpeto. He had broken the meniscus, a fibro cartilaginous structure that partly divides a joint, without realising it. He still went on to help Dobbie win Swansea's three goals on that 11th of August. In the celebrations that followed the goals, Bussy was concerned about his knee and he mentioned it to Bessone. Fede wanted his friend to be substituted. Bauzà, then said that he couldn't leave the field now, not when they were playing so well, so he continued.

It's amazing that Bauzà spent so much time on the pitch, with such an injury. Why did Bauzá want to risk so much? "I knew this was my chance. The other matches, I had just been discarded and today I was winning." Bauzá felt that without his performance in that game, he would not have stayed at Swansea. Bessone also felt that there was no other option for Bauzá, he needed a big game. After speaking with Paolo Sousa, he decided that he didn't want to transfer to another club. The team was doing well and he felt a part of that. But Bussy found it harder to become involved with the team after his injury as he had to convince the trainer that he was fit and able to contribute. Bussy desperately wanted to be a part of the team's ascension to the premiership.

The person who had the worst luck among the Spanish players was Albert Serrán, of whom Orlandi said, was the best player with the worst luck that he had ever known. Serrán injured his ankle and this caused major problems for Paolo Sousa. Serrán and Darren Pratley also both became ill with mumps. "They were weak, with fever and their faces were a bit swollen," recalled Orlandi. These weren't the only health problems they had. They both had to miss two months from February onward due to hamstring injuries all this happened during Sousa's time. Serrán remains grateful to Sousa for his support during this difficult period: "Sousa put his confidence in me. He put me in defence. However, because of my injuries, I couldn't take part in any of the games."

Jordi López not only received a significant injury to the ankle at the end of January 2010 but also didn't have very pleasant memories of his initial period in joining Swansea. López thought he had a lot of obstacles to overcome in being accepted. It seemed that there was some reticence in certain quarters, some said it was akin to spending money on what they had already seen before and he had a lot to prove. But López was very excited to be joining the team. Jordi remembers that he wanted to run a week before the training was due to start, despite the fact that he had a twisted ankle: "I was on crutches for five weeks. I had a hematoma bigger than my hand, but they told me not to worry as this was normal and a lot depended on people's skin."

When he came back to Wales, he was quite the specialist on those types of injury. Fede Bessone wasn't playing either. He'd injured his knee. It was a few days after Jordi López had picked up his injury, on the 13th February, in the game against leaders Newcastle. "I was slightly worried during the last part of the game. I hadn't trained all week and was injured after five minutes," he recalls. The game against the Magpies (Newcastle) and the following game against Plymouth were both draws, of 1-1. It went on to be a successful month for Swansea with two good victories, 2-0 against Preston North End and 0-1 against Crystal Palace. These results were followed by a further two victories against Derby County, 0-1, and Peterborough, 1-0. Fede Bessone was later diagnosed with torn ligaments and a damaged cartilage. He was ordered to rest for six months and would not be able to play as normal until the next season.

Swansea Legend

One of the great Swansea legends, John Toshack, ended his second spell as Wales manager, that had started in 2004, leaving by mutual consent after nearly six years at the helm following an opening qualifying defeat in Montenegro.

The names being touted as possible contenders for the vacant position were Kenny Jacket, Bryan Flynn, Ryan Giggs, Chris Coleman, Tony Pulis and John Hartson. Eventually the chosen person was Garry Speed. Curiously, in 2004, Speed had threatened to leave if Mark Hughes was replaced by Toshack. Speed was unhappy with the criticism that Toshack had made against Hughes and the other players during a game against England.

A striker with Liverpool in the 1970s, forming a prolific partnership with Kevin Keegan, Toshack first became a player-manager with the Swans in 1978, leading the Jacks from England's fourth tier to the top division. He has subsequently accumulated vast experience at club level in Portugal, Turkey, France and Spain, where he coached Real Madrid to the 1989-90 league title. Toshack recalls that many people couldn't understand why he stopped playing at a top European club such as Liverpool and settled for a team in the fourth division. It is even more surprising when we consider he was born in Cardiff, the Jacks bitter rivals. But he was well received by the Swansea faithful and generally considered a good choice for player/coach. Although, his bad injuries hampered him from continuing with the same vigour on the pitch that he had previously displayed at Liverpool.

In the official program of Tasha's first game, the then president Malcolm Struel explained the motives behind his decision, "It's the moment of a man with great calibre." He also commented on the incorrect and unjustified statements made in the South Wales Evening Post, "Swansea has full confidence in Toshack." He admitted that Toshack was a beginner, but he trusted that he had been trained by Bill Shankly and Bob Paisley. Paisley later commented that Toshack had made a few mistakes, but was confident that during the two remaining months of competition The Swans would climb into the next league and he asked the fans to support Toshack in his new venture.

Toshack believes that his experience as both manager and player at Swansea was the most rewarding in his career, "I put myself on the bench so that I could get a perspective and could see where I could help." Swansea is a very special club for Toshack. He felt very proud that he had raised them from a fourth division club to a first in only a few years. It has never happened before or since in football history. Nevertheless, there had been a few problems along the way.

His worst memory at The Swans happened on the 25th April 1978 in the penultimate game of the season. That morning, his assistant Harry Griffiths, had gone to the changing rooms to help an injured player. Harry suddenly collapsed and died. It was a heart attack. They decided to carry on playing as this would have been Harry's wish. The team went out and won against Scunthorpe United 3-1. The following Saturday they beat Halifax Town 2-0 and clinched promotion to the Third Division. The joy of being in the new league faded after this tragedy.

Toshack had been joking with Griffiths some time before about him being the youngest manager in the football league, only just turning twenty-eight years old. The clubs ascent and Harry's death occurred within two months of each other. Toshack attributes the success of The Swans to Griffiths, acknowledging that despite his short life, he achieved great things. As a player, Harry made 421 appearances for Swansea, scored 72 goals, and was also capped for Wales. "Harry was a man who had done everything for the club. When they hired me, he was concerned that there would be no work for him. I told him I was there only to help. Nobody knew the club as well as he did. Swansea was his life. He had many roles during his years at Swansea: player, physio, coach, trainer, assistant manager and even gardener; he presided over four hundred games between 1949 and 1964 and was manager from 1975 – 1978. Harry was Swansea through and through."

In their second ascent to the league, the team also had to win the last game of the season. For the whole week, Toshack had problems with a muscle injury. It was decided that a substitute should be used. With only ten minutes left of the 1-1 game, Swansea had a chance to score. There was a problem on the left side and with only five minutes remaining a header resulted in a goal, making it 2-1. "I remember it as if it were yesterday. The crowd ran onto the pitch. We could hardly get into the dressing room, it was unforgettable, like a fairy tale," recalls Toshack.

In the following campaign, Swansea finished twelfth in the second division. It was in the 1980-81 season, when after finishing third, they succeeded in making the first division. The 1-3 victory at Preston North End gave the Swans the opportunity to enter the first division for the first time in their history. There was no promotion for Blackburn despite winning the same number of points.

Swansea beat all expectations. The club was mostly third in the division but often climbed into the top spot. Although after a barren run, losing five matches, they ended up in sixth position. Nevertheless, this was one of the best triumphs in the club's entire history.

Toshak admitted that it was all down to good blocking. "We had many youngsters who had risen up from the fourth division, three or four Welsh Internationals and we also signed up two Yugoslavians." It was during this period that, three members of Swansea's current technical staff returned to the club. Alan Curtis returned during the rise to the First Division after spending a year with Leeds, Colin Pascoe was eighteen when he joined in 1983 and Huw Lake featured in Swansea City's 1983-84 relegation battle.

They were the golden years, including three of their seven participations in the UEFA Winners' Cup, and are fondly remembered by the fans. Since 1984, Toshack's last year in Swansea, there have been several opportunities for a return. But other engagements kept him busy, "My time in Swansea was wonderful, but returning is a completely different proposition."

The distance between Sousa and the fans

Let's return to 2010. Six winning goals and two defeats allowed Swansea to accumulate fourteen points out of the possible eighteen in February. The players, even those who had initially taken against the new methods of working, were happy with the coach and admitted that they were improving on an individual level by following Paolo Sousa. However the situation with the fans was entirely different; they hadn't got used to the methods of the new Portuguese coach.

The discontentment was surprising because the team had accumulated twenty-four points in twelve consecutive games without losing in the league, from the 12th of December at the Liberty with the 0-1 win against Nottingham Forest, second in the League Table. Forest finally defeated the Swans in the Championship on the 6th of March, the only goal in the game arrived after ninety minutes and the fans at City Ground, in Robin Hood country, were overjoyed. On this day Rangel was the only Spaniard, and Bauzà the only compatriot who went into the Press Room after the game.

The Swans were on thirty-six points, twelve points separated them from entering the playoffs. They won against Watford at home, when Kuqi scored, and that made him forget the slip up against Forest, at least until the horror show against Blackpool where the Swans lost 5-1.

During the middle of March, a rethink was needed and Paolo Sousa stressed the importance of the fans behaviour: "We need our fans to be well mannered," he told media sources. He wasn't only referring to the task he'd had when replacing Roberto Martínez. Sousa believed it was important to teach the youngest fans how best to help the team because at times the fans seemed nervous. "They always want us to play well and win," Sousa continued. "They don't need to be nervous when watching the game, or create fear for our players. They should support the team as it's the footballers that get us the results."

Bauzá thought that the soured relationship between the players and the fans was because the fans were asking more of the team and not enjoying the games as much. Orlandi believed that there was no standoff between the players and the fans. He thought that Bauzá took to many things too heart: "Bauzá always dedicated himself entirely to his work, carefully monitoring every little detail to get the best results." Serrán thought that his effusive and temperamental manner sometimes worked against him, as it made him tense and obscured his outlook.

There was no denying Swansea were in a bit of a tail spin. From the 9th of March, the date of the win against Watford, to the 3rd of April they barely scored three goals and had no wins. There was a balance of three defeats and three draws, one was the woeful 5-1 against Blackpool and the 2-1 loss against Derby. The goal scorer that game was Orlandi who recalls it was not a happy period for the team.

The long championship

The three points attained out of a possible eighteen put Swansea fifth in the table with sixty-two points. Swansea's rough patch became smooth for a while on the 5th of April with a 3-0 win against Scunthorpe. However Scunthorpe played an excellent game, making the Swans work hard for the result, as did the teams who followed over the next few weeks.

The first game against Bristol was flawed from the beginning. Rangel had to be replaced in the seventh minute, due to an injury and the winning goal arrived in the last quarter in the eighty-fourth minute. This put Swansea in sixth place with Blackpool two points ahead.

A week later, Swansea overcame a major hurdle in the game against Barnsley. This comfortable 3-1 win, involved Serrán, who had been picked due to Rangel's injury. His action as a right winger earned him wide acclaim. Two more games were on the calendar waiting to be tackled. The 24th of April and the 2nd of May. Against Newcastle and West Bromwich Albion who had both ascended two places. Nottingham Forest and Cardiff were both determined to rise in the league in order to conquer Newcastle and West Bromwich for the playoffs.

Leicester City (with seventy points) and above all Swansea (with seventy-eight points) and Blackpool (with sixty-six points) had to avoid being the teams who lost out. Swansea needed to visit Sheffield Wednesday and welcome Doncaster Rovers to the Liberty. They weren't considered the worst of adversaries.

Other games were more in reach. They needed to play Peterborough United (fourth) and Bristol City (tenth). Unfortunately Swansea was on the receiving end of a fourth defeat, against Sheffield United. The United win was 2-0, Swansea didn't just need to rely on this win for the playoffs, because Blackpool had won 0-1 against Peterborough United. The Welsh side, who had only lost five league games since the start of March, had now been defeated six times.

Blackpool closed in on the playoffs with sixty-nine, Swansea were one point off the pace with sixty-eight. The second of May then arrived. Swansea's hopes were raised in the sixteenth minute, not because of what happened on the pitch, but for the goal that Bristol nicked at Bloomfield Road, the home of Blackpool. Swansea, however, needed to win. Everything was going well, after half an hour on the pitch. At the same time it was 1-1 between Blackpool and Bristol. The minutes were fast disappearing. Lee Trundle who had replaced Britton in the seventy-ninth minute, sent the ball into the net. A shot that would have sealed the playoff, if the goalie hadn't put his hand out to stop it. The dream drifted away. Blackpool were now also in sixth place.

Balance Sheet

Sousa's team gained thirteen points, with three wins, during the final thirteen days, having won twenty-four points, for example in the previous twelve. Pressure, reduced physical performance, bad luck, errors? What had been the cause of the slump at the end of the season?

One idea was that it was physical, and the players had not been prepared for such a long campaign. Àngel Rangel shared this idea: "Paolo wanted the players to be fresh, but there is also the need to maintain a general level of fitness when playing." The mental factor was also considered. Fede Bessone suggested that the tension of being in the premier position was a definite factor. There were general feelings of frustration and anger. Bauzá thought that Sousa's plan was quite good but it didn't succeed in the ultimate objective. However you could not be oblivious to the fact that this had been the best season for Swansea in over two decades, improving by one point the achievements of Roberto Martínez a year before.

Rangel was grateful to Sousa, although he did feel that he wasn't giving the players the same freedom as Martínez had done: "I didn't enjoy it. Every time I passed the ball, he said that I should use the tactic of going in front of a team member and passing the ball back to him. This isn't how I play football."

Orlandi only had words of gratitude for Sousa who had placed him back in the centre where he had not been for two years. He admitted that he had never worked with someone like him before. Serrán thought that the team was stronger, even if it had meant longer and more mundane training sessions. Serrán's only complaints were that his health problems had stopped him achieving his best, undermining the confidence Sousa had placed in him.

Pintado recognized that his season hadn't been very good in terms of the number of goals: "I didn't score many goals but I did try and turn things around during that time." Bessone was happy with the progress made, despite the difficulties and injuries that occurred at the beginning of the season. Bauzá at the beginning and Jordi López towards the end, had both lost half a season due to injuries. But he looked back fondly at the time that had passed. "We made history. Being almost in the playoffs was very disappointing, but we had to look at the bigger picture."

The chairman Huw Jenkins praised the 2009-10 football season, saying that Paolo Sousa had played a pivotal role at the club. When Martínez left, he was the ideal man. He knew the game inside out.

Roberto Martínez and Jordi Cruyff in a Barcelona-Zaragoza youth game (photo by Roberto Martínez/Y Lolfa).

The *brothers* Roberto Martínez and Jordi Cruyff (photo by Roberto Martínez/Y Lolfa).

Roberto Martínez with the captain's bracelet (photo by Roberto Martínez/Y Lolfa with the collaboration of Swansea City FC).

Roberto Martínez and Cyril the Swan, the Swans Mascot (photo by Roberto Martínez/Y Lolfa with the collaboration of Swansea City FC).

Roberto Martínez holds aloft the trophy of the FAW Premier Cup 2005-06 (photo by Roberto Martínez/Y Lolfa with the collaboration of Swansea City FC).

Roberto Martínez signs his contract alongside the chairman Huw Jenkins (photo by Roberto Martínez/Y Lolfa with the collaboration of Swansea City FC).

Àngel Rangel, Orlandi and Bauzá with the Champions Cup League One 2007-08 (photo by Guillermo Bauzá).

Rangel, Orlandi and Bauzá – 'The three amigos' – wear Mexican sombreros to celebrate their arrival at Swansea (photo by Swansea City).

Street celebration in Swansea on ascent to the Championship 2008 (photo by Roberto Martínez/Y Lolfa with the collaboration of Swansea City FC).

Huw Lake '*Lakie*' and Óscar Brau (photo by Óscar Brau).

Swansea's technical staff 2007 – 08, with Óscar Brau, Roberto Martínez, and Iñaki Bergara (photo by Óscar Brau).

Fabio Capello, former England manager, awards Roberto Martínez Best Manager for League One 2007-08 (photo by Roberto Martínez/Y Lolfa with the collaboration of Swansea City FC).

Àngel Rangel shares an evening with fans at the annual Bowling event (photo by Àngel Rangel).

Rangel shows his shin pads from Brau Sports at the Liberty Stadium (photo by Pablo Gómez).

Roberto Martínez and the seven Spanish Swans during 2008-09 pre-season (photo by Swansea City).

Fancy dress party: Serrán, Jordi Gómez, Bauzá and Bessone as the Four Ninja Turtles (photo by Guillermo Bauzá).

Serrán, Orlandi, Jordi Gómez and Bessone singing karaoke (photo by Albert Serrán).

Brendan Rogers in the small office at the Glamorgan Health and Racquet Club in Llandarcy used during his time as Swans manager (photo by Pablo Gómez).

Serrán and Orlandi in the changing rooms at Wembley Stadium, wearing shirts in memory of Besian Idrizaj, after promotion to the Premier League 2011 (photo by Albert Serrán).

Rangel receives a visit from his cousin Xavi Cruz, his father and two friends at a hotel prior to playing Chelsea in the 2011-12 season (photo by Àngel Rangel).

It's Chico time! Chico looks to succeed in the Premiership (photo by Swansea City).

'Nice to Michu' - Michu was on fire during the 2012-13 season and his goals won the affection of the Jack Army (photo by Swansea City).

Pablo Hernández became the most expensive signing in the history of Swansea City when he met up again with Danish coach Michael Laudrup (photo by Swansea City).

Rangel, Chico, Pablo Hernández, Óscar García and Michu on the pitch at Wembley, after winning the League Cup 2013 (photo by Óscar García).

The Swans celebrate after winning 0-5 against Bradford in the final of the League Cup (photo by Óscar García).

The Liberty Stadium, home of the Swans
(photo by Pablo Gómez).

Swansea fans observe a training session from the small road separating the training ground from the Glamorgan Health and Racquet Club in Llandarcy (photo by Pablo Gómez).

Orlandi, Serrán and Pintado (photo by Andrea Orlandi).

Jordi Gómez and Albert Serrán enjoy some free time after a pre-season meeting in Swansea (photo by Albert Serrán).

Albert Serrán and Fede Bessone, accompanied by their partners, build a snowman in Swansea (photo by Albert Serrán).

A trip out together in Swansea: Bauzá, Jordi Gómez, Bessone and Albert Serrán with their partners (photo by Albert Serrán).

CHAPTER 8

2010-2011: Swansea 3.0, a new ascent

Swansea had finished the previous season with a bad taste in their mouth: with one goal the dream of a playoff place had vanished, but this shouldn't take away from the fact that the team's performances had improved from those over the last twenty-seven years. The groundwork however was more than established to continue to see the club grow.

The tragedy of Idrizaj

Nevertheless, the season was going to kick off with the worst of news. On 15th May 2010 a tragic incident occurred, the likes of which have occasionally touched the world of football in recent years. Two weeks had passed since the end of the season when Besian Idrizaj, just twenty-two years old, died in his sleep at his family home in Linz, Austria. In an official press release, Swansea extended the clubs condolences to his family, friends and teammates but did not confirm the exact cause of death, although early indications suggested a heart attack.

Idrizaj was one of the great prospects of Austrian football and had been named Austria's Young Footballer of the Year in

2005. His performances did not go unnoticed by Liverpool scouts who came in for his transfer. Despite not making a single first-team start for the Reds, he enjoyed spells with Luton Town, Crystal Palace and Wacker Innsbruck. It was in fact, with that very Austrian side in February 2008 that Idrizaj collapsed whilst playing against Sturm Graz. At first it was thought to be down to a problem with his heart and there were concerns for his professional career, but in fact a virus was to be the original cause which enabled him to continue playing football.

From then on, he set out to succeed and put aside the scare, even though various clubs knew that his health proposed too high a risk making them unlikely to sign him. Swansea held no doubts after the Austrian passed all his medicals without problems. Paulo Sousa himself admitted that he had a lot of faith in Idrizaj. The Portuguese coach emphasised that Idrizaj had fought hard to achieve his dream and that everyone would recognise his talent. Sousa was convinced that the Austrian would get some game time that season.

Despite involvement in only three games during his first season as a Swan, Besian was well liked in the changing room and his death had a big impact on his teammates. Out of all the players, Shefki Kuqi of Finland had one of the closest relationships with Idrizaj as both players' families came from Kosovo. "It was the worst experience of my life," Kuqi grieved sometime after. "He was a fantastic lad and a great footballer," Rangel commented. Captain Garry Monk also offered his condolences to Idrizaj recalling that he always worked very hard in every training session to secure a place and that he always had a smile on his face.

The club decided to retire the number 40 shirt after his death and on 14th August, nearly three months after the tragedy, there was a breath-taking and respectful minute of silence in memory of the forward. Images of him were displayed on the stadium's video display with the date of his birth and death; 12-10-1987 and 14-05-2010. A year later, the fans were not going to forget about him in what was a very moving scene.

Departure of Sousa

At the same time Paulo Sousa and the Swansea directors were holding meetings. Sousa had been linked to clubs relegated from the Premiership such as Hull and Burnley, but he insisted that these meetings with club executives were to clarify the funds that the club was going to assign to strengthening the squad, never about his personal future.

In addition, the transfer bids and allure of other clubs for players like Leon Britton, Angel Rangel, Darren Pratley and Ashley Williams did not cease, all of whom were key to the Welsh club's setup. A lot of media outlets, particularly the BBC alluded to fraught relations between chairman Huw Jenkins and Paulo Sousa, in good part down to disagreements around the restricted budget for improving the squad. This appeared to have been the main reason why Sousa's contract with Swansea came to an abrupt end by way of mutual agreement.

In the official press release on 5th July Swansea thanked Sousa for his service to the club and wished him well for the future. Despite denying having made contact with Sousa two days previously, Leicester City officially announced on that very same day, 5th July that they were in talks with the Portuguese coach. Forty-eight hours later, he became their new manager taking on a supposedly long-term role.

However less than three months later, on the first of October, Sousa expressed shock at Leicester's decision to relieve him of his duties. "To be sacked after having been told there is a long-term club strategy is something I find very surprising," he said at the time. It was the sixth dismissal since Milan Mandarić took the reins of the club three and half years before. The directors praised Sousa and stated that the only issue was the bad run of results with only one win in nine in the Championship.

Two years later Sousa himself admitted that it was a big mistake to have left Swansea, this coincides with Jordi López's explanation: "The coach was demanding better conditions. The club had limited facilities: we would change in a gym and we just about had a training ground that was worn out."

Part of the fan base did not complain much about Sousa's departure as there was criticism over the style of play that he employed. Swansea had only conceded thirty-six goals managing twenty-four clean sheets. But on the other hand they had a tally of forty goals and were unable to score in eighteen of their forty-six league fixtures.

Swansea remained without a coach during pre-season, and although nearly all the Spanish players sensed Sousa's departure, they were less in doubt about it than the departure of Roberto a year before. Pintado was an exception; he was rather unfazed by the new change in the Swansea dugout: "Just another one for you. In football, one day you've one manager, the next you've someone different."

The new manager

Huw Jenkins for the second consecutive summer was faced with the challenge of finding someone for the Liberty's dugout who could pick things up where they were left off. To fit the bill the profile of the new manager seemed clear; someone decent, (reasonably) unknown and cheap. Although there wasn't much time to stir up rumours, the majority of the names that were coming up in the polls in the press met that description.

The Uruguayan in charge of Brighton, Gus Poyet and Welshman Gary Speed were being heavily linked. Joining them was Exeter manager Paul Tisdale; the Scunthorpe manager used to handling a modest budget Nigel Adkins; Gareth Southgate, Tony Mowbray and also Chris Coleman.

Some doors were closing. On July 8th Exeter announced that Tisdale had decided to continue managing the League One side, on July 12th Sheffield United refused Speed's departure by denying Swansea permission to enter into talks with him. Although options were running out and the start of the season was drawing ever closer, on July 13th Huw Jenkins claimed that his club were in no rush to appoint a substitute for Paulo Sousa. Jenkins confirmed that they had received rejections from the three official approaches made. One of those rejections could have been from Wigan who apparently blocked Graeme Jones' departure, assistant to Roberto Martínez during his time at Swansea.

The Welsh club asked its fans to show the same patience and calm as the directors, who were not willing to make any wrong moves, whilst they fully trusted Colin Pascoe and Alan Curtis to manage the team during the first days of pre-season.

By mid-July Nigel Adkins and Brendan Rodgers appeared to be the front runners with Gianfranco Zola and Steve Clarke as backup options. Then on July 16th, eleven days after the departure of Sousa, Swansea announced the name of its new manager. He was a young, ambitious professional (thirty-six years old), who was well worth the wait. Nevertheless it was only a one year deal.

"I'm very proud to become manager of Swansea City – a progressive club that plays the game the right way. My aim is to continue that philosophy and help the club progress. I want to play offensive, attacking football, but with discipline. I have inherited a wonderful group of players and, I can help them develop and improve," was the opening statement of Northern Irishman Brendan Rodgers as the new Swansea manager. It was a club that enabled him to show his qualities and achieve more in the game, "The groundwork is there but I can see that this can be built upon." Rodgers was reluctant to comment on promotion but gave assurances that the team would work hard to produce positive results.

In December 2009, after half a year in charge, Rodgers and Reading had parted company by mutual agreement. It was his second role as first team coach after his spell in charge of Watford. Though Rodgers already had big club experience from his time as part of José Mourinho's technical setup at Chelsea. Mourinho placed a lot of trust in Rodgers, so much that he placed him in charge of the reserves and recommended his move to Watford.

Rodgers was fond of Mourinho's ambitious and open character as well as his desire to learn and communicate. Nevertheless Rodgers sets himself apart from one of the biggest influencers on his career in other areas, "I learned a lot about football from José; mentality and psychology, but I am my own person. I like to win, but I like to win well and with style."

As a footballer a bad injury forced Rodgers to hang up his boots at just twenty years old. However he turned that setback around taking it as an opportunity to get into coaching, always trying to learn something new. For example, Rodgers never took issue with joining Swansea without his own technical staff;

instead he accepted being amongst Swansea's own such as Alan Curtis and Colin Pascoe who helped him settle in by getting to know the club better and quicker. Later, Rodgers needed to multitask within his role so as to not hamper the club. Faced with a shortage in staffing, he found himself needing to use his own network of contacts to close out transfer deals and deliver on scouting tasks. "Sometimes, less is more," declared the Northern Irishman.

Predictions and Departures

As soon as Brendan Rodgers joined the club, Swansea went on a training camp to Holland. From the offset one of the concepts which Rodgers put a special emphasis on was increasing aggression in the team's play.

The arrival of Rodgers alone, his career credentials and the squad available to him did little to assuage the doubters. Even before pre-season had begun the bookmakers, a fair share of journalists and fans did not believe in the project. Not only was the Welsh side not amongst the candidates for promotion to the Premiership but such was the lack of faith in the Swans that they found themselves tipped for relegation in the polls.

This prediction may well have taken into account the impact of Leon Britton's departure. A move that had been in the pipeline from the previous season despite attempts by the Welsh club to reach an agreement with Britton the talks had failed. In addition, the slight midfielder from England was annoyed by allegations made by Paolo Sousa in December 2009 in which Sousa had claimed that Britton turned down the best contract ever offered in the history of the club. "I am surprised and disappointed that the nature of my contract talks has been made public," admitted Britton.

In June 2010 his relationship with Swansea was weakening further, after some rumours linking him with Wigan whose interest perhaps sparked his desire to not renew his deal, surprisingly Britton ended up signing for Championship side Sheffield United. In a deal similar to the one which saw him originally arrive at Swansea; Britton moved on a free transfer. It was a sign from Britton that he needed a new challenge and his new coach satisfied him by assuring him that he was to be a key player in the transformation of Sheffield United's style of play and an important part of the teams plans to reach the Premiership.

But soon Britton was regretting his decision. The departure of Sousa and what he made of his new club were making him doubt the decision to leave Swansea. His time at Sheffield went by with manager changes and hard-fought matches with tough tackles and long passes looking for the second ball. "He spent six months watching the ball being passed over his head," explained Gorka Pintado.

In addition to Britton, two of the Spanish Swans whose contracts were expiring departed the club that summer. One of them was Fede Bessone who went to the legendary Leeds United. It was the departure of Sousa, who he played many games under, the emblematic status of Leeds and the financial package that he was offered that pushed the Argentine left back to make the decision.

His close friend Guillermo Bauzà's contract was also expiring that June. Paulo Sousa had told him he was going to be calling upon him less, so Buazá did not hold out for a renewed deal. "I did not know that he was going to leave. If I had have known, I would have held out because I had a good relationship with the club and the directors held me in high regard," bemoaned Bussy.

The forward thought that at his age, twenty-five, he should be getting more game time whilst his partner had just found a permanent job as a paediatrician in Oxfordshire. It was then that links with Charlton came about which would allow Bauzá to stay close to his girlfriend. Though no agreement was reached despite appearing in a few friendlies for the London club nor did trial periods with Dutch side Sparta Rotterdam or Spanish Second Division side Elche prove successful.

Although there were talks of returning to Swansea, he finally signed for League Two side Hereford United in mid-September. Dropping down two divisions could have seemed like a step backwards, but Bussy had other ambitions in life that did not revolve around footballing success, "Playing for Hereford meant I was only an hour and a half from Oxford and only an hour and a half from Swansea, so I could keep attending Swansea University."

His time with Hereford with which he scored on his debut (Match day 7: Bury 1-1 Hereford) came to an end in January. On March 11th he turned a new page and joined Northampton Town who were also in League Two at that time. Just a week after joining he was in the starting XI. Playing nine matches he scored four goals for his new club which was closer to Oxford. However being further from Wales he was unable to attend university during those months.

Later Buazá's priorities were to see him sign for Exeter City in the 2011-12 season. The city of Exeter is in southern England, two and half hours from Swansea and Oxford on the motorway, but is amongst the most culturally rich in the UK, with one of the best universities in the country and has an added attraction: its proximity to a number of ideal surfing spots.

In addition, the young coach Paul Tisdale who had been mentioned as a replacement for Paulo Sousa at Swansea, was easy-going with his players; he didn't make them live in Exeter for example. Wednesdays and Sundays were days off whilst sessions on Mondays and Thursdays began at 1pm.

For the first time in the last four pre-seasons, there was no Spanish signing for Swansea, and aside from the departures of Bessone and Buazá there was a danger of someone else's exit. Orlandi's contract was coming to an end in June 2010 but despite the Welsh side's desire to renew it Paulo Sousa told him to wait until he found a club that he could take Orlandi to with him. Orlandi was not convinced on going to Leicester City and therefore preferred to stay at Swansea. However his contract renewal was delayed as club chairman Huw Jenkins sought to consult with the new manager on the club's plans. As soon as Brendan Rodgers arrived and was given the go ahead, Orlandi signed a new deal with the Jacks.

The melodrama of the summer took shape in the form of another Spanish Swan. A big offer from newly promoted Premiership side Blackpool came in for Ángel Rangel. Brendan Rodgers having just arrived had promised him he would be allowed to leave if a Premiership side showed interest in him. However during the pre-season training camp in Holland neither the club chairman nor the manager allowed him to leave.

The promise had been broken and in a chat five minutes before a friendly game, Rangel reacted by refusing to play for fear of getting an injury that might cause the transfer deal to collapse. Instead of stepping out onto the pitch with his teammates that day or sticking around to watch, Rangel was around the hotel discussing what had happened with his brother-in-law Xavi Cruz. A few days later, Huw Jenkins asked for the wingback's patience telling him his transfer would go through. Although this could not be further from the truth, with the squad returning to Swansea with no deal agreed. As if that were not bad enough, Rangel was to suffer an injury that he personally thought was a result of the stress that the situation caused him. It was the second time he was denied the opportunity to realise his dream of playing in the Premiership, after Swansea had turned down an offer of over €1 million from Fulham earlier that year at the end of January.

Fifth poor consecutive debut

Rangel's absence due to injury gave an opportunity to Albert Serrán at right-back. Swansea opened their season on Saturday 7th August away to Hull City with a 2-0 defeat, their fifth consecutive opening league day loss. The Welsh side had more attempts on goal and fifty-one percent greater possession than their opponents. Surprisingly Brendan Rodgers' starting XI was as follows: De Vries in goal; Serrán, Monk, Williams and Tate at the back; Pratley, Jordi López and Gower in midfield and Dyer, Dobbie and Cotterill in attack. Two Spaniards started whilst the other two countrymen, Orlandi and Pintado had game time in the second half.

Pintado had to be taken off during the game due to a shoulder injury and was set to be out for the next three months of the league. "It's such a pity. In pre-season he was doing well, scoring goals," recalled Orlandi.

Swansea were to show no signs of struggling in terms of goals claiming two comfortable wins at the Liberty over the next seven days. On Tuesday 10ᵗth August, the Jacks defeated Barnet 3-0 in the League Cup before outdoing that performance with a 4-0 win over Preston North End the following Saturday.

Away from home, however, things were not improving and Swansea fell to three defeats in their next outings in the league; 2-0 against Norwich, 2-1 against Leeds and 3-1 against

Nottingham Forest. At least that poor string of results was compensated for by good performances at home; with a 1-0 win over Burnley, 2-0 over Coventry City and 2-0 over Scunthorpe, as well as victories in the league cup second and third rounds with consecutive 3-1 wins over Tranmere Rovers and Peterborough United. The poor away form at last came to an end on September 28th with a 3-2 win over Watford at Vicarage Road, their first away league win.

Swansea were eighth on fifteen points (as were the four clubs above them in the table) scoring twenty-three goals in all competitions, with eight of those courtesy of Scott Sinclair, four of which were in the League Cup. Sinclair was beginning to justify his £580,000 transfer fee, a deal which can be fully accredited to Brendan Rodgers. The Northern Irishman knew Sinclair well from his spell with Chelsea and was sure that he would bring the extra edge that he needed to Swansea.

Amongst the other new recruits who arrived on frees was the promising Neil Taylor (who Alan Curtis recommended and knew from the Welsh Under-21s), Congolese goalkeeper Makabu-Kalambay (from Scottish side Hibernian, who Rodgers knew from his time at Chelsea) and Dutch midfielder Kenny Agustien who came from AZ Alkmaar. What Agustien had to offer fitted in perfectly for both Swansea, in terms of his skill but also for the Premiership in terms of his physicality.

October saw the first two draws of the season, both goalless at the Liberty, one against Derby County and the other against Queens Park Rangers. Swansea also won three games that month with Sinclair scoring in each (2-0 at home to Leicester and 1-0 and 3-0 away to Reading and Crystal Palace respectively).

By this point in the football calendar two savoury clashes were served up; a visit to Wigan Athletic for the League Cup fourth round on October 26th and a trip to the Cardiff City Stadium for the first derby of the 2010-11 campaign. The first clash did not go their way with a 2-0 defeat to Roberto Martínez's side with Serrán who was playing centre back picking up an injury. The result however was not a true reflection of the match with the second goal coming in the ninety-third minute and a Beattie goal for Swansea wrongly disallowed.

As for the derby, things fell in favour of the Jacks with a 1-0 victory (the Swans enjoying fifty-one percent of the possession and thirteen attempts on goal). The goal scorer was Emnes who one week later finished his loan at Swansea. After match day fifteen of the division, Queens Park Rangers were top of the league with thirty-three points, followed by Cardiff on thirty-two and then Swansea on twenty-nine. In fourth place was Derby County with twenty-four points.

Swansea 3.0

Aside from the positive results, Swansea under Brendan Rodgers was beginning to show signs of a style more to the liking of the fans than displayed the previous season. "Our football was more attacking, we were creating chances, that was pleasing," noted Rangel.

Rodgers summed up his perfect team setup in three concepts: "Offense, creativity with tactical discipline." All rooted around the premise of controlling the play, always playing the ball out from the back patiently and stretching the play to use speed on the flanks with the aim of getting many men forward into the opposition's area. The Northern Irishman demanded a high tempo approach from his players, not just on the attacking side but also in their defensive duties; he considered aggression and high pressing as fundamental in this. "We went out onto the pitch to squeeze the opponent," points out Rangel. Rodgers wanted to see his team take the initiative as soon as possible as he is convinced that the best form of defence is keeping the ball.

All of the players had agreed on the evolution of the team with the succession of each manager, as Orlandi summed up "Roberto was attack-minded: score goals and score many. Sousa began with coverage at the back: once you have a clean sheet, go and win the game. And Brendan is a mix of the two: he wants to go and attack but defend in an organized manner."

Training sessions with Rodgers though they were not long they were very intensive. They were sessions based on possession and position exercises, often in confined spaces, that always kept in mind the hallmarks of the identity he wanted for his team. One of the dressing room heavyweights Garry Monk commended Rodgers' training sessions and also publically criticised Paulo Sousa for not making them work hard in every session and for not allowing them to put in extra sessions on their own.

Rodgers also put a lot of effort into ensuring his men researched their rivals, something that set him apart from Roberto Martínez. The Northern Irishman assigned the day before and hours leading up to each encounter to video analysis and talking tactics. He also possessed personality and charisma in leading the dressing room, without getting too close to the players; he would publically stand strongly by an individual or the collective group when the situation required it. At Swansea he maintained that the group; united both on and off the field, always came before any individual.

After the derby on November 7th, nothing else went well that month. Swansea lost two of the next three matches at the Liberty; 0-1 against Bristol City and 1-2 against Portsmouth. Between these they won 1-0 against Middlesbrough in front of the Jack Army and drew 1-1 away to Doncaster Rovers with a last-gasp strike from Rangel in the ninety-third minute. Then a 3-1 win away over Ipswich Town at the start of December covered up some of the blushes of the poor run of form, however it was only to continue in the next three clashes. Firstly, the 1-1 draw at home with Millwall (with another goal from Rangel), and then two consecutive defeats away; 1-0 against Leon Britton's Sheffield United and a 4-0 thrashing against Queens Park Rangers. "On Boxing Day we went to league-leaders QPR. They were four points ahead of us and put four goals past us. It was a hard defeat to take," recalls Rangel.

To sum up, four defeats, two draws and two wins since the Cardiff vs Swansea game up until the 26th December. After that match, Queens Park Rangers were top with forty-four points from twenty-two games, followed by Cardiff on forty points from twenty-two, then Leeds United with thirty-nine points from twenty-three and then Swansea in fourth place with thirty-seven points from twenty-three games.

But the Swans were going to see off 2010 and welcome in 2011 the best way possible. Swansea rose to second place in the table after two 1-0 victories at the Liberty against Barnsley on the 28th December and Reading on the first of January.

Winter Transfer Window

The Swans reached January and the opening of the transfer window with the winds of change blowing through the dressing room. Finnish attacker Shefki Kuqi and midfielder Jordi López were released by the Welsh outfit whilst various players left on loan, amongst them was striker Gorka Pintado.

With six months left on his contract, the departure of Jordi López was by mutual agreement. The midfielder had only played five matches under Brendan Rodgers and with the club needing funds to strengthen the squad it was seen as a positive move to part company with one of the highest wage earners in the squad. López however has his own version of events: "Swansea wanted to break away from all of Paulo Sousa's work because they ended on bad terms. As a result it is us the players that have to pay for it, as we were brought in under Sousa and now the club is set on making our lives impossible."

López, who gets called Felpeto due to his second surname, felt no shame in leaving "My memories were not good ones. It was perhaps the worst period in my footballing career. The day-to-day was tough what with injuries and performances on the pitch and this had an effect on my family." López was to end up until June at Dutch side Vitesse under Albert Ferrer, the former international right back who had played for Barcelona. Afterwards he would move on to Greek side OFI Creta before joining Ukrainian side Hoverla Uzhhorod where he played during the 2012-13 season.

Pintado had only played in the final minutes of Swansea's opening league match against Hull City in which he picked up an injury. Now his new destination on a loan deal, was AEK Larnaca. "I saw that there was no possibility of playing for Swansea. On return from injury, the team was doing well and there was no place for me," explained the forward. Jordi Cruyff who was the director of football at the Cypriot club, recalls that he had no doubts given the source of the recommendation, "I called Roberto Martínez to ask him about players of a certain profile and he advised me on some, one of which was Gorka. Sometimes we share this type of information."

In terms of arrivals, striker Luke Moore signed a two and a half year deal from West Bromwich Albion, though the star signing was Leon Britton. Yes, Britton was returning just half a year after having abandoned the Welsh outfit recognising the mistake he had made: "My style fits in at Swansea and Swansea's style is ideal for me. It's a perfect union." It was a return that was celebrated by the fans and by Brendan Rodgers himself who had previously revealed his disappointment in not having been able to work with Britton.

Swanselona

With the return of Britton to his team, Rodgers was asked about his midfield and his idea that their possession of the ball was a crucial concept: "Joe Allen and Leon Britton are our Xavi and Iniesta. They are of small build and not that tall but they have great minds. They are brave and always wanting the ball. Putting players of this sort into the midfield is something that is done by Barcelona, Swansea and no-one else."

Brendan Rodgers never hid his fondness for Barcelona. "My idea of football has been based on the Barcelona model from when I was a young coach. It was my passion, just like that of the old Dutch school." The Swansea coach must have thoroughly enjoyed each of the Barcelona training sessions that he went along to as a spectator, something he did especially during the Frank Rijkaard era at Barça. And so his two passions came together; his favourite team model led by a Dutch coach.

The typical British style never appealed to him as a player. He always refuted the notion of football as a so-called game of stats, the only statistic that was of real interest to him was possession, as when in possession it is clear that the opponent cannot score.

Rodgers aspires to coach at one of the big Spanish clubs one day; he loves the country, people and language. In fact he has mastered the language because he considers "the quality of your life is in the quality of your communication. The more possibilities you have to express yourself the better." Despite this however Rodgers was surprised to discover on arriving in Barcelona for the first time that Catalan was spoken there.

Rangel explained that Barcelona had always been an example for them from the beginning: "We tried to copy them in every way we could even though we were playing at a somewhat lower level." The style that Swansea had adopted since the departure of Roberto and progressed under the devotion of Rodgers was to result in the introduction of the nickname Swanselona during the season.

Brendan Rodgers usually talked about each Barcelona game with Andrea Orlandi who was enjoying that season's training sessions with lots of possession exercises as they were very similar to those employed in the Barça B team.

The coach was trying to fish more than Barcelona's ideas; he also attempted to sign Jonathan Soriano. The striker was playing in the B team although he had been brought up through the FC Espanyol youth academy. However a financial deal could not be struck and later in January 2012, Soriano would end up with Austrian side Red Bull Salzburg.

It would appear as paradoxical that such a devotee to the Barcelona academy system could strike up such a strong, understanding relationship with José Mourinho during their time at Chelsea. This leads us to suspect that, José Mourinho and Pep Guardiola have more in common than they let on, such as an appreciation for methodical and well-executed work.

Mid-Season

When Swansea had to travel to Leicester on the third of January 2011, they had already played twenty-nine games (twenty-five in the league and four in the League Cup). Though there was still half the season still ahead; no less than five months of demanding league action with twenty-one games on the horizon. No longer was Paolo Sousa in the Leicester dugout but in his place strangely enough was Sven Goran Eriksson, as recommended by Sousa. And it was the Swede that was the bringer of joy that Monday with a 2-1 win over the Jacks.

Swansea's next challenge came on January 8th in which Rodgers made their home advantage and superior standing count. Swansea's 4-0 thrashing of Colchester United who were mid-table in League One saw them through to the next round of the FA Cup. However the journey in the FA Cup was very brief that season. Despite the next challenge being a home tie against a side in the league below, on January 29th Swansea were eliminated from the competition by Leyton Orient who won the match 2-1.

All that remained was the Championship. Between the two FA cup rounds Swansea played two games, one was a 3-0 win against Crystal Palace (with a brace from Sinclair) and a 1-1 draw away to Barnsley (again Sinclair was the scorer). At that stage of the competition, QPR were top with forty-nine points, followed by Cardiff and Norwich who were both on forty-seven points. Swansea were in fourth also with forty-seven points but had played one game more. Joining Swansea in the playoff places were Leeds United on forty-five points and Nottingham Forest on forty-three. With forty-two points, both Watford and Reading were still in the chase for those coveted playoff spots.

In the busy month of February Swansea stepped on the gas and won five out of six of their games, four of them in succession. The fifteen points were a result of a 2-0 away win to Bristol City (with a brace from Pratley), 4-3 away to Middlesbrough (coming back from 3-1 down to win it in the ninety-fourth minute), 1-0 away to Coventry and two 3-0 wins at the Liberty against Doncaster and Leeds United with a brace from Sinclair in the latter.

The only sting in the month was on February 6th against the most hurtful opposition possible. Cardiff avenged their 0-1 defeat of the reverse fixture with a win at Swansea by the same margin. Defeat in the derby dampened the return of Britton who was making his home debut for the Jacks having only featured in previous away games against Bristol and Barnsley. The only goal of the game came in the eighty-fifth minute courtesy of Craig Bellamy. The Cardiff star confessed to Rangel after the match that he was the defender that gave him the most difficult time. The right back was the only Spaniard in the starting line-up whilst Serrán was on the bench although did not feature.

Serrán had begun the campaign getting plenty of game time due to Rangel being injured. Upon Rangel's return, Serrán's involvement was limited. "The season did not start well and therefore there were a number of changes, one of which was me. From here on the coach would use me as a fifth defender in the final minutes of a game to help if the team was under the cosh," explained Serrán.

Orlandi too was not having the best of times at that point. By January he had been involved in twenty-four matches, starting fourteen, but he did not enjoy the same confidence that Paolo Sousa had shown in him the season before. "I never quite had that feeling," complained the talented left-footer. Later in January he had the misfortune of getting injured twice: first his left thigh and then his right one. "I never made it into the team again," he added despondently.

Despite Serrán and Orlandi not playing as much as they would have liked, both were enjoying themselves off the pitch. Until the age of fourteen they had been teammates at Espanyol, and at Swansea, sharing a changing room again, they had strengthened their ties. Orlandi in fact chose Serrán as his daughter's godfather. Spending the majority of the time at home bored with the bad weather whilst most shops were closed resulted in some deep poetry. "He would send me poems in Spanish about what happened in training for example, and my girlfriend and I would laugh," recalled Serrán. With the focus being mainly on the team, Orlandi would pass his rhymes under the door of the hotel room which Albert was sharing with Rangel. Serrán too was brave enough to write his own poems to Orlandi which were just as funny although not as elaborate.

Automatic promotion fades away

The next two months of the Championship were to bring a bad spell of results for Swansea. Between Saturday 5th March and Saturday 23rd of April, Swansea tallied up two victories (3-2 away to Nottingham Forest and 3-0 against Norwich at the Liberty), three draws (two 1-1 draws at home against Watford and Hull City and a 0-0 draw at Portsmouth) and four defeats, all away from home (a 1-0 defeat against Scunthorpe and three 2-1 defeats against Derby County, Preston North End and Burnley). As a therapy to help deal with the bad batch of away outings, Rodgers brought the whole team to the luxurious Pennyhill Park Hotel in Surrey outside London for spa treatments. The team also went to see the musical Billy Elliot as a team building exercise. The manager was so concerned with the four consecutive away defeats that he also arranged for a talk with a psychologist.

Hardly nine points from a possible twenty-seven, scoring eleven goals (with just one from Sinclair) and conceding the same. During this period of the season Swansea went from second place, five points off top and one above third place, to fifth in the table thirteen points adrift of league leaders Queens Park Rangers and five points clear of sixth and seventh place (Nottingham Forest and Leeds United).

The role of striker Fabio Borini was becoming vitally important. In his debut against Forest, just two days after the sealing of his loan deal from Chelsea to Swansea, he scored twice. In the final two months of the league competition he scored six times including the two against Forest, bringing freshness to the Welsh side's attack at a decisive period in the season. Rangel believes that the temporary loans Rodgers struck were key in the final stretch of the Championship. Besides Borini, two other attackers bolstered the club: Welshman Jermaine Easter who played six games between the end of November and mid-January and Slovak-born Hungarian Tamas Priskin who played in four games from the end of March. "With Sousa, fitness caught up with us in the final months, but the team had an amazing freshness about it the following season," explained Rangel.

Swansea ended the league season full of team morale after comfortable victories in the last three contests with a 2-0 victory away to Millwall and two goal-filled wins at the Liberty Stadium (4-1 over Ipswich and 4-0 over Sheffield United in which Britton rounded off the win with a goal against his former teammates). It was May 7th and after forty-six unending league fixtures, Queens Park Rangers and Norwich won automatic promotion to the Premier League with eighty-eight and eighty-four points respectively.

Although Swansea were tied on eighty points with Cardiff, they led the four playoff places with Reading in fifth place on seventy-seven points and Nottingham Forest in sixth with seventy-five. Leeds United fell outside the playoff places in seventh with seventy-two points.

Both Welsh sides therefore would have the home advantage in the return fixture of the two-leg knockout, which always saw third place take on sixth and fourth playing fifth. Swansea were to visit Forest on Thursday 12th May and host them on Monday 16th, whilst Cardiff had to pay a visit to Reading on the 13th with the return leg in the Welsh capital on May 17th.

If Swansea were coming into the first leg on the back of a good run of results, Forest were coming into it in even better form with fifteen points from the last eighteen. For the first leg Brendan Rodgers selected De Vries in goal; Rangel, Williams, Tate and Taylor in defence; Allen and Britton in the centre with Dobbie playing ahead of them and Dyer and Sinclair joining on the wings and Borini in the centre forward role. Orlandi and Serrán had to contain their nerves from the bench.

Jack hopes suffered a blow within fifty-two seconds; that's all the time it took before Swansea were down to ten men following the sending off of left back Taylor. Pessimism set in for the Welsh side. They had to play a man down for eighty-nine minutes at the City ground where Forest had only lost twice in the league all season. "It seemed like a great season was about to fall apart," admitted Rangel. But Rodgers quickly made a move. He decided to sacrifice Dobbie for the introduction of Monk, going from a defensive 4-4-1 to an attacking 4-2-3 formation. The task was clear; to be organised and leave everything on the pitch.

The clock was ticking, Swansea were holding together and not only proving resilient to their opponent's onslaught but they overcame it in the first half. Swansea also had a few good chances thanks to Dyer's pace and attempts from Borini (who was taken off injured in the second half). Apart from a few chances, the Swans failed to create any danger and as the minutes passed they started to really feel the pressure. Monk cleared the ball off the line, and then there were calls for a penalty from the home fans for a Williams hand ball just before the referee confidently disallowed an Earnshaw goal. It seemed inevitable that the game would conclude in Forest's favour. But Swansea held out in heroic fashion and celebrated the 0-0 draw as if it were a win. Brendan Rodgers praised his players whom he said had been "tactically brilliant."

Despite the tiredness amongst the team, the Northern Irishman opted for the same formation in the return leg four days later with the forced introduction of Monk for the banned Taylor. Dobbie, who was the player sacrificed due to Taylor's dismissal was the only one who could not be excused as being fatigued. Orlandi and Serrán again took a place on the bench at the Liberty which was rammed with a crowd of nearly twenty thousand. No-one wanted to miss the historic date that could lead to a third trip to Wembley; the first was in 1994 when Swansea beat Huddersfield on penalties in the League Trophy (sponsored by Autoglass) and then in 1997 when they lost to Northampton Town in the Third Division playoff final.

The first goal of the semi-final against Forest perfectly defines the type of team Swansea is. After one hundred and seventeen minutes of playoff action the stands at the Liberty were not growing flustered or impatient as Dobbie took a short corner to Sinclair who returned it to him, before it was given to Britton at the corner of the eighteen yard box. A position that perhaps reminded him of his times playing on the wing, Britton lost his man with a dummy and dragged the ball back with his right foot on to his weaker left foot before releasing a fantastic curling effort from outside the box. Euphoria erupted amongst the Jack Army; 1-0 to the mighty Swans.

Less than five minutes later in the thirty-second minute, Dobbie found himself within space to receive a throw-in. Never was the Scotsman as quick and skilful as he was in those magical seconds. He executed a perfect one-two with Dyer, sprinted directly for the edge of the box going past one defender before nutmegging another to then unleash a low and angled drive from the edge of the D that just sneaked inside the opposition goalkeeper's left-hand post. The veterans in the squad that had fought through all the divisions below the Premier League, those such as Britton, could not believe their eyes; Swansea were 2-0 up.

The situation could not have been better for playing down the clock with patient passing triangles of possession. And so the semi-final continued until the seventy-ninth minute when Earnshaw got in behind the home defence and struck a low first-time shot to make it 2-1. The ex-Cardiff man was keeping Forest in reach of the Wembley Final.

Serrán came on for Sinclair in the eighty-eighth minute to help the team see the game out, "To go out there even for five minutes shows that the manager has faith in you," said the Spaniard. A possible 2-2 had been denied by the post with

Forest's siege resulting in a shot on goal in the ninety-second minute. Even though there were two more minutes of the referee's indicated injury time to go, Forest went for broke and brought everyone forward including goalkeeper Camp for a corner kick. The fists of De Vries were what rose highest that day. His clearance landed at the feet of a Forest player outside the box who slipped allowing the free ball to run for Pratley who did not hesitate to press forward. It seemed as if the whole stadium was reminding him with their shouts that the Forest goal was keeperless. As soon as he looked up just on the halfway line, Pratley struck the ball with everything he had in those final moments after what had been a very stressful season. The power was enough to carry the ball, after two bounces, into the back of the net.

The racing down the touchline of Brendan Rodgers', who celebrated with the first row of the stands with his arms held aloft, was a reflection of the ecstasy felt throughout the stadium as another unforgettable chapter was written in Swansea's history. There was only a day's wait to find out who the opponent would be with the Playoff Final to be scheduled for Monday 30th June. The first leg of Reading – Cardiff had finished goalless. The fan's off both Welsh clubs eagerly anticipated the return leg in Cardiff. The prospect of a Wembley derby between Swansea and Cardiff with a place in the Premier League at stake was beyond enticing. However surprisingly, Reading, formerly under Rodgers, prevailed 3-0 and therefore a high stakes clash between the arch rivals was avoided.

The Dutch Connection

Some four-hundred Dutch fans were not going to miss the historic date at Wembley to support the Swans. They were supporters of ADO Den Haag, a club with which Swansea holds a very special connection beyond the habitual pre-season friendly played each year. The creator of this connection is current Swansea director and one of the saviours of the club in the Tony Petty era, John van Zweden. Tickets for the Playoff final were quickly on sale from his business in The Hague and were snapped up in double quick time.

But how can this mysterious connection enable a Dutchman to have such a high level involvement with Wales' second city's football team? To understand it, one needs to track back three and a half decades to when an adolescent van Zweden decided to seek a pen pal through an ad in the Swansea City magazine. A fellow young supporter of the Jacks, David Morgan, was intrigued by the advert and curious enough to become his pen pal.

Choosing Swansea City was not by chance but it came about as a result of a coincidence. For John's sixteenth birthday, his father took him to watch Chelsea vs Manchester United. The game was an early kick-off allowing them time to go and watch another game nearby that afternoon, which turned out to be Fulham vs Swansea. It was from there that the passion for the Swans began since father and son always shouted for the underdogs.

From the end of the seventies, David would always write him detailed match reports of all the games which helped improve John's English and also engender strong feelings for a club, that were then battling in the fourth division. It was this passion that pushed him two years later to drive an Opel Ascona, adorned with a Swansea City sticker, all the way from The Hague to the Vetch Field in Wales. He keenly felt the need to experience the atmosphere of a match, first hand, of a team that had become a big part of his life.

A not so youthful John didn't hesitate many years later when on a Thursday night in 2002 he received a distress call from his friend David. The club was bankrupt and needed to gather a group of investors to financially re-float it and seize it from the hands of Tony Petty. The wallpaper company that Van Zweden ran in The Hague afforded him a healthy income, so after running it past his bank and without saying anything to his wife, John drove from his Dutch home to a Welsh court with a decisive cheque in his hand. With a further five local supporters, David Van Zweden, with the help of the Swans Trust, was intent on saving the club. Nowadays, Van Zweden describes that £50,000 as the best investment of his life. From there on he became a director of the club and initiated the link with ADO Den Haag from which Ferrie Bodde would later come.

Van Zweden's passion for the Swans is visible in the personal museum that he has created in his office at The Hague. On display there he has programmes from 1925 right up to present day all bound together by season, numerous jerseys, scarves, flags, photos and tickets. He preserves these and other Swansea City related items but also holds many unforgettable personal memories of his own. His favourite moment is Swansea's promotion to the Premier League and his favourite players are Alan Curtis and Leon Britton.

However he is not the only grand collector of Swans memorabilia, Welshman Gwyn Rees also possesses his own particular museum dedicated to the Jacks. His collection includes four thousand programmes, some two hundred pin badges, around two hundred various books, more than one hundred and fifty DVDs of matches, tens of jerseys, postcards from the 1920s, photos, fanzines and other items.

It all began in August 1964 when he went to his first match. It was a second division clash against Crystal Palace and he still remembers the atmosphere in the stands and the shouts of the hotdog and programme vendors. From that day onward when he bought his first programme, he could not resist the temptation to accumulate Swansea merchandise of any kind. Nowadays his favourites are the programmes that started off his collection and admits that the pre-war ones are the most difficult to find. All of them are stored in a folder with a colour for each decade but he also has them all in digital format.

Currently he handwrites articles for the programmes as well as working at the stadium on match days. He has accompanied the team on many away visits to the likes of Liverpool and Manchester United to Walsall and Shrewsbury to name a few. Amongst his favourite moments as a fan he also highlighted promotion to the Premier League as a polar opposite to the years of extreme financial difficulty. On the player's podium he is very clear about his choices; Ivor Allchurch, Alan Curtis and Lee Trundle.

Swansea left empty

Swansea had gone twenty-eight years outside the top division and there was only one game between them and reaching the

Premier League for the first time in the club's history. This opportunity arrived only eight years after the club was on the brink of permanent relegation from the football league, also in May in 2003. "You go into it with great enthusiasm but also a great sense of responsibility. It was a game that could change your life," expressed Orlandi in speaking about the 2011 playoff final.

Brendan Rodgers opted to stay in the hotel in which Blackpool had stayed the year before. A decision motivated by superstition as Blackpool had achieved promotion. The day before the match, Swansea trained at Arsenal's sports village where the Swansea players, who were used to their modest facilities, could get a taste of what could come with promotion and rub shoulders with the professional elite. There was also time that Sunday to visit Wembley.

The Reading-Swansea match was going to be held on the same pitch that Barcelona had schooled Manchester United 3-1 in the Champions League Final just forty-eight hours earlier. Was it another sign of fate that this would be a historic day for Swanselona?

On that Monday 30th May 2011 all the Welsh front pages led with the game. One of the headlines cited, "Last one out close the door," referring symbolically to the door of the city of Swansea whose inhabitants were going to London en-masse. Half of the eighty-six thousand spectators planning to fill Wembley were going to support the Swans in a match that was worth £90 million. That was the estimated amount for the winner based on £40 million in TV rights and another £48 million from various sources over the following four years; as if sporting glory was not enough.

The entrance ceremony of the two starting XIs led by their managers gave goose bumps. The colours of the stands, the atmosphere and the fireworks that were set off from the centre circle go to show how much the British love their football. Whilst automatic promotion avoids any potential suffering, to be part of this experience at Wembley is an unforgettable experience in the career of any footballer.

Even though he was no longer contracted by Swansea, Iñaki Bergara was still emotionally tied. In his Bilbao home, recovering from a knee operation, the goalkeeper trainer impatiently asked his daughters to put the game on the computer. He did not want to miss a second of it. "I would have paid any amount to have set foot in that stadium with those ninety thousand people," exclaimed Bergara.

The first chance of the match fell to Reading. Chaos in the box after various saves and the ball was finally cleared by Ashley Williams. After that scare, in the twelfth minute, the first tense moment of the final arrived. Reading defender Khizanishvili pushed Borini for having obstructed the goalkeeper's kick out even though the referee had already blown up for the free kick; both players received a yellow.

Khizanishvili was again to feature in the next bookable offense, taking down Dyer in the penalty area leading to Swansea's first goal. Scott Sinclair converted the spot kick in the twentieth minute with a low shot sending Federici the wrong way. Just seventy-five seconds later, before there was time for joy in one camp or sadness in the other, again Sinclair was celebrating in the same corner, now for his second goal. After a quick break down the right side from Dobbie, Sinclair was at the back post to guide the ball into a virtually open goal. Federici in goal got finger tips to the centred cross from the Scotsman but could not prevent it from falling to Sinclair who made it 2-0 which unleashed the Welsh euphoria.

From down the same right flank came a surprising third for Swansea in the thirty-ninth minute. Dyer at full speed pulled it back but the defender's block fell to the feet of Dobbie, who with a striker's instinct shot first time leaving the goalkeeper helpless. Half time arrived with a convincing 3-0 score line just after Reading star Shane Long failed to convert a goal mouth opportunity following an error from Swansea's centre backs and indecision from Dorus De Vries.

It seemed impossible that Swansea would allow promotion to slip away, but the setting changed dramatically with the second half just underway. The turning point was an own goal by Allen from a corner to make it 3-1. Even though forty-one minutes remained Rodgers made a conservative change introducing Pratley for Dobbie. The change however did not prevent Reading from creating far more chances than in the first half. From another corner, Matt Mills took advantage of

Swansea's aerial weakness with a towering header into the corner of the goal.

3-2 was leading many to fans to fear the worst, and just three minutes after their second goal, nerves reached fever pitch in the fifty-ninth minute when the post denied Reading an equaliser, just as it had done to Forest in the semi-final. Garry Monk also made a miraculous block from a follow up shot in the same move.

It is stomach-churning to think that after forty-six longwinded match days, more than four thousand minutes of league action, everything could have fallen apart if the woodwork had not been on their side at the right time in the playoffs. Rangel claimed that the luck of champions that they had lacked at key moments in previous seasons was now with them. 3-3 would have been decisive given the dynamic with which the game had turned. Reading was dominating Swansea, contrary to what had happened in the first half.

Guillermo Bauzá enthusiastically encouraged his friends from an Irish pub in Mallorca, hoping to see all his ex-teammates promoted, not just for the Spanish Swans but for himself too. He still felt very much part of the club's transformation process and promotion would be the culmination of many years of hard work.

The Jack Army's suffering went on until the seventy-ninth minute and was heightened by the enraged clairvoyant celebrations of Borini when referee Phil Dowd blew for a second penalty for a foul on the Italian by Griffin. Orlandi revealed a dressing room secret, "We know that this referee loves to award penalties and he's one we often take advantage of." Both fouls in the area were clear, although it is for sure that perhaps Borini played his part in getting it. As one would say, football is for the quick and the smart. Sinclair's second kick from the spot went the same way, though this time it was mid-height and the keeper went the right way but couldn't save it. The game was decided at 4-2. From then until the final whistle was only a matter of minutes, and just as they had done against Hull in 2003, Swansea won decisively 4-2, in the month of May having scored a hat-trick.

In the press room there were unexpected congratulations from the Reading manager, "Congratulations to Swansea from an ex-Cardiff player." Brian McDermott acknowledged Swansea's superiority in the first half and their excellent season. He also gave credit to the Welsh side's next steps by declaring his belief that they would play a big role in the Premier League.

Mark Gower, who came on for Britton before the penalty, and Luke Moore who replaced Allen at the death, completed the list of those privileged to have played in the historic final. Albert Serrán, the other Spaniard called upon, remained on the bench in hope, "It was great to experience it with the possibility of being involved. It is nerve-wracking but it is worth it in the end for the memories that you have."

Serrán endured the ninety minutes beside Orlandi who did not take it well that he had been left out of the squad, "I had been called up in recent games and was feeling good. I'd had a problem with my knee so had an injection to be able to be at Wembley. Not playing the final is hard to take for me, though I still felt involved due to the games I played in throughout the season." Meanwhile his brother-in-law Jordi Gómez was following every kick on the internet from Spain hoping to see his introduction.

The entire Swansea team paid an emotional tribute to Besian Idrizaj as they lifted the Trophy at Wembley by wearing t-shirts printed with his picture and name. "We wanted his family to know that we were there dedicating it to him. It was an extra motivation for us to achieve something special," Rangel said. The Swansea fans too were to commemorate Idrizaj just as his ex-teammates had done when in the fortieth minute (linked to his shirt number) they all stood, and destiny had it that it was to coincide with Dobbie's goal. It was a tribute that came just days after the first anniversary of his death which had fallen on the day before the playoff semi-final second leg against Forest.

Gorka Pintado who had returned from loan with AEK Larnaca was able to be at the final in Wembley. If Swansea were to be promoted to the Premier League, his contract was to improve however his main focus was not on this, "Your salary would depend on the number of games played. There were issues though, with the second choice keeper, although he was always in the squad, he never played a match and thus received nothing." Pintado of course was there at the dinner, on the bus and at the various celebrations. Though afterwards he would sign a deal to return to Larnaca where in 2013 he and other Spanish players including Serrán had to endure the days of bank deposit freezes that effected Cypriot football.

The other Spaniard that had left in the winter transfer window Jordi López found great pleasure in his ex-teammates achievement, wishing them well as he watched the game online during his holiday in Spain. However in the months leading up to it whilst he was in Holland he did not pay much attention to the ins and outs of Swansea. "I wanted a break from my time at Swansea as it was not an easy period for me," the midfielder pointed out.

Bergara had faith that Swansea would win the game even though he admits the two Reading goals were hard to take but his knee prevented him from externalising his joy and jumping up and down. He felt a lot of joy in seeing how the players had grown but more so especially for some of the club training staff, "I was so happy for the likes of Huw Lake and Suzan Eames who get on with everyone there at the club."

Club chairman Huw Jenkins made a pleasant gesture during a conversation with Guillermo Bauzá in which he told him that he was part of the success that the club had just achieved. Buazá (from the Balearic Islands) made a series of phone calls of congratulations as soon as they won promotion.

Post Wembley

Brendan Rodgers believed that promotion was totally deserved, "We played the best football in the Championship. We won the right to be in the Premier League." The manager highlighted the performance of his players despite the enormous pressure that they were under. Looking to the future, he was of the view that the priority was to improve the clubs facilities and down the line increase the stadium to a forty thousand capacity. He had aspirations of growing year on year, something that would be possible if the club managed to continue playing at the top level of English football.

After the Wembley celebrations there was the party in Swansea with an open top bus tour of the city to share the elation with the fans. Rangel and Orlandi were the only Spanish Swansea players to celebrate two promotions in three years and the only ones to have battled through the top three divisions of English football. The players' bus was followed by another identical one which was reserved for family members. Amongst them were Rangel's parents and brother-in-law who had returned from London by car with Baptist Minister Eirian Wyn the day of the final. Xavi Cruz recalls a brief exchange with John Toshack on leaving the stadium:

- How are you Mr. Toshack? – asked Cruz.
- Not too bad – replied the Welshman with a big smile

It could not have been a more appropriate moment as the club confirmed its return to the top-flight of English football, something that had not happened since the Toshack era.

For three members of the squad, promotion was very special as they had been part of the historic match in which they secured safety against Hull in 2003. Britton, Monk and Tate had battled in a Swans shirt in all the divisions of professional football. It was a dream come true, a reward for the hard work they had put in during their careers, as Britton puts it "If you had told me this was going to happen back in 2003, I would have thought you were mad. It is to the credit of each manager, the chairman and all the players." Something the midfielder would have missed out on if he had not returned from Sheffield.

And that's what happened to Bessone, who did not feel as involved in the team's success as he watched the final from Spain. At the time he regretted more than ever having left for Leeds, however he was delighted for his teammates and sent some of them messages of congratulations. In addition, as a fan, he was content to see a team with such a style of play enjoying success. "When I left Barça my mind was only set on playing that way," he explained.

Nobody including Bessone himself would have imagined that, two months later on 31st August, he would be going to seal his return to Swansea. At 1pm on the final day of the transfer window, his agent called him to tell him that Alan Tate was injured and that this opportunity had come. The call came whilst the left back was eating in Leeds with Luciano Bechio (his closest teammate at Leeds United) and his wife. One hour later the offer was secured and so he terminated his contract and by 4.30pm set off in the car at full speed for Swansea. He also had to pass a medical that day in Wales. In the end, he arrived on time by managing to reduce the nearly five hour journey by forty-five minutes. "If the police were to stop me, I would have been going straight to jail," emphasised the Argentine who was yet to absorb what was happening to him. To go from not being included in a Championship club to becoming a Premier League player, even more so for Swansea; at that time, he was the happiest man in the world.

Bessone was not going to see his Call of Duty online gaming friend Albert Serrán again. Before returning to Swansea, Serrán had left the club even though Brendan Rodgers had offered him another one year deal with the attraction of the Premier League. The manager regretted Serrán's departure saying, "He is a guy that you must have if you are going into battle. He is a strong and aggressive defender that knows how to play the game. Unfortunately he wanted more game time." Serrán understood that having been given little game time in the Championship there was little chance of getting more in the Premiership. "I gave it my all, but wasn't given the opportunities that I felt I had earned in training." His decision, after great thought was taken before the promotion.

Serrán fondly remembers a relaxed chat that he had with Rangel who had been his roommate throughout that season. It was in the form of a farewell on the day before the playoff final at Wembley. It was a moving conversation in which both reminisced the anecdotes and memories of their years together over a cup of tea which Serrán had made. Serrán later moved to AEK Larnaca,. The presence of Jordi Cruyff as club director at the Cypriot outfit was once again decisive.

As for Rangel, the future was not clear. Despite his contract coming to an end on June 30th, he advised his agent that he did not want to hear of any interest from other clubs during the playoffs. He did not rule out a return to Spanish football although he knew that the UK was right for him as he had been creating a name for himself there since day one. In the end he chose to renew his contract with Swansea; the club that had given him the opportunity to turn professional and now was enabling him to play in the Premier League. Rangel went from the Spanish Segunda División B to the English elite league in four years, the same four years which Roberto Martínez had spoken to him about when they first met.

From the ten Spanish Swans that happened to be at the club in the 08-09 season the Swans could only count three in the 11-12 campaign; Àngel Rangel, Andrea Orlandi and Fede Bessone. That summer the number could have increased however discussions came to nothing.

Regardless of the number of Spaniards in the squad, Brendan Rodgers still firmly believed in his football philosophy. Whether they were away at Old Trafford or Anfield facing Manchester United and Liverpool respectively, he believed in maintaining the philosophy which had brought about success. Chairman Huw Jenkins was also categorical in his views; the club were to remain faithful to their principles. The task, to dominant games and play possession football in the Premier League, was not going to be easy. The players could not be happier with their coach. One of the captains Garry Monk held no reservations in publically declaring that Rodgers had brought the team technically, physically and mentally to a whole new level, with no discredit to the previous managers he noted.

The Swansea brand was going global as was noted from a piece in the Australian Sunday Times that raised the question as to whether with the promotion of Swansea - the competition should now be renamed the English and Welsh Premier League. The effects were going to be immediate and well-known. Local politicians for example began to plan for the need to improve infrastructure, though not just in terms of increasing the stadium's capacity but also looking at access, transport, parking and other things. The city was preparing itself to deal with the extent of its sporting success.

CHAPTER 9

2011-12: Debut season in the Premier League, by Ángel Rangel

There is no-one better placed to recount first-hand this historic season than the Spaniard that pulled on the Jacks jersey most often. Rangel and Swansea were making their debut in the Premier League, and this chapter offers a unique opportunity to relive the emotions, thoughts, memories and assessments of the defender in a diary format from a viewpoint of each match day.

Match day 1 (15/08/2012): Manchester City 4 - Swansea 0

The Welsh side's Premier League Debut produced one of the worst possible outcomes against a talented Manchester City side who were strong candidates to lift the title. During that week, their manager Roberto Mancini insisted that argentines Tévez and Agüero were unfit. Despite this, when Agüero was introduced he scored a brace in a great solo performance. Orlandi remained on the bench for Swansea whilst Rangel, who found it hard to sleep the night before, played the full ninety minutes. It was not every day that you would make your debut in the Premier League never mind playing away at Manchester City's stadium.

- Manchester City: Hart, Richards, Kompany, Lescott, Clichy, Yaya Touré, De Jong (Agüero, 59), Barry, Silva (Milner, 82), Džeko, Johnson (Savić, 74).
- Swansea: Vorm, Rangel, Caulker, Williams, Tate, Britton (Allen, 65), Dobbie (Routledge, 65), Agustien, Dyer (Lita, 81), Graham, Sinclair.
- Goals: Džeko (57), Agüero (68), Silva (71), Agüero (90).

"Welcome to my Premier League diary. Today I will start by telling you about our first match, against Manchester City no less. It was a bittersweet debut, on the one hand I am happy to have played my first ninety minutes in the most competitive league in the world, but on the other, it was a heavy and painful defeat by the standards of any team. But in the end they had more firepower up top and the magic of Kun and David Silva put the game to bed. Despite everything though, I believe that we left there feeling reinforced having seen that we could compete with our style of football against a team of stars with a budget one-hundred times that of ours. With regards to the trip, the truth is it was very entertaining. The new guys had to stand on top of a chair and sing into a bottle as if it were a microphone in front of the whole team. And I can tell you there is some talent in this team; Wayne Routledge and Leroy Lita dazzled us with a golden hip hop performance. Things got a little complicated when goalkeeper Michel Vorm did 'Beat it' by Michael Jackson, but he was forgiven since he had a great game today. And that's it, I am writing this as we return home on the coach with my friend Orlandi who is righting the world's wrongs. We will arrive around 3am and tomorrow we will get up and think about Wigan."

Match day 2 (20/8/2011):
Swansea 0 - Wigan 0

The second match of the season was special for two reasons; the Premier League was coming to Wales for the first time and the manager of the visiting side was the architect of the Swansea project. Roberto Martínez's dream of seeing the Swans play in the Premier League at the Liberty Stadium had come true, even if it was from the visitor's dugout. "I felt proud as well as a mixture of other emotions. Brendan Rodgers had managed to strengthen and improve the whole group. It was a shame that we missed a penalty, but a draw was a good result as playing against Swansea at the Liberty is very difficult," recalls Martínez.

Wigan also had some former Swansea players; Jordi Gómez was in the starting XI and goalkeeping coach Iñaki Bergara was amongst the technical staff. The television coverage of the game in the early stages of the match, centred on Roberto, whose departure in mid-2009 was not well received by the Swansea faithful. In the days leading up to the game, Roberto stated that his former club would be the revelation of the season.

- Swansea: Vorm, Rangel, Caulker, Williams (captain),Taylor, Agustien, Britton (Allen, 74), Routledge (Dobbie,74), Dyer, Sinclair, Graham (Lita, 84).
- Wigan: Al-Habsi, Alcaraz (Stam, 37), McCarthy (McArthur, 64), Caldwell, Watson, Di Santo (Rodallega, 70), Moses, Jordi Gómez, Boyce, Diamé, Figueroa.

"So after a thrashing in the league debut against Manchester City, Saturday 20th August was our next game. This time it was our home debut in the Premier League at the Liberty Stadium. And it could not have been against any other team than the team whose manager scouted me; Roberto Martínez's Wigan Athletic. We started very strongly with our style of combining well, and right away we had our first chances. Wigan did not have the ball for the first thirty-five minutes, but we failed to open our account. At halftime the score remained 0-0.

The second half was much the same, we were lacking the necessary luck to score our first Premier League goal. Wigan improved their side with two changes and could have taken the game after hitting the post twice and having a penalty saved by the great Michel Vorm. Once again he showed why he is the Dutch number two goalkeeper. Final result 0-0. At least it is

Swansea's first point and with each game we are going to improve. And personally I am very happy for having played the full ninety minutes again.

The next game is against Sunderland back at the Liberty where we need to take the three points and grow in confidence. Before that though, we will travel away to Shrewsbury (a League Two side) in the League Cup second round, and that is the beauty of these competitions. There are ninety-two professional sides all in the mix and only one will emerge the victor. I will not travel for medical reasons but hope to have recovered for the next league game."

Match day 3 (27/8/2011): Swansea 0 - Sunderland 0

After losing 3-1 to Shrewsbury in the League Cup, another goalless draw began to provoke a sense of anxiety around the club and in the team itself due to the inability to score a single goal in three matches.

- Swansea: Vorm, Rangel, Caulker, Williams, Taylor, Agustien (Allen, 80), Britton, Routledge (Lita, 71), Dyer (Dobbie, 80), Sinclair, Graham.
- Sunderland: Mignolet, Bardsley, Gyan (Richardson, 77), Brown, Cattermole (Wickham, 70), Larsson (Elmohamady,70), Gardner, Colback, O'Shea, Sessègnon , Anton Ferdinand.

"It was the second consecutive home game, this time against Sunderland who are amongst the clubs that have brought in the most signings this season. Once again the Liberty was full (with a 20,000 crowd) and as against Wigan, we dominated the majority of play. We created many chances but did not manage to score to relieve the anxiety of scoring our first Premier League goal. The final score was 0-0 meaning we had two points from a possible nine, kept two clean sheets in the last two games and were growing bit by bit in a very strong and competitive league. I made a return to the team and played ninety minutes again.

Over the next weekend there is an International break and the following Saturday we travel to London to face Arsenal who are going through a difficult period but still have very good players and a great manager.

Match day 4 (10/9/2011):
Arsenal 1 - Swansea 0

Going to the Emirates, despite the doubts over Arsenal's performances, was not the ideal place to get a first Premier League goal and win. Swansea looked good but lost due to an unfortunate mix up between Dutch goalkeeper Vorm and Rangel which decided the game.

- Arsenal: Szczęsny, Sagna, Mertesacker, Koscielny, Arteta, Van Persie (Chamakh, 82), Walcott, Ramsey, Arshavin (Benayoun, 64), Frimpong (Coquelin, 76), Gibbs.
- Swansea: Vorm, Rangel, Caulker, Williams, Taylor, Agustien (Mark Gower, 65), Britton, Allen (Dobbie, 76), Dyer (Moore, 86), Sinclair, Graham.
- Goals: 1-0, Arshavin (41).

"This time we found ourselves in one of the most modern and beautiful stadiums in European football, Arsenal's Emirates Stadium. We travelled to London on Friday and stayed at one of the Meliá Hotels. It was like being back in Spain, everyone was Spanish. Also I was sharing a room with the third Spaniard of the team, the recently returned Fede Bessone. Fede had played with us for two seasons before going to Leeds. But now he was back and the truth is he was thrilled. And of course, he had to sing in front of the team. He was impressive, singing Bob Marley's legendary 'Everything is gonna be alright'. Andrea Orlandi, the other Spanish player had remained in Swansea injured.

We were up against a Champions League side with recent acquisitions such as Mikel Arteta (from Everton), Benayoun (from Chelsea) and Mertesacker (from Werder Bremen). It was an open game. Both teams had chances, but it was to be decided by some unfortunate play by our goalkeeper which Arshavin capitalised on scoring the only goal of the game and seeing out a 1-0 victory for the Gunners. I played another ninety minutes but we were still without our first Premier League goal. Though on the up side, we have only lost two games against Manchester City and Arsenal and I am sure that if we continue to play the football that we have shown in the first four league games, the results will come."

Match day 5 (17/9/2011): Swansea 3 - West Brom 0

We had to wait until the fifth league match for the first Jack victory thanks to the first three goals of the campaign for Brenden Rodgers' side. During the week, Rangel had told the press that they needed to turn possession into points. The Catalan defender returned to the starting XI and completed the most passes and featured in the "Team of the week" on both the MSN and WhoScored websites. Bessone also featured in the closing minutes.

- Swansea: Vorm; Rangel, Williams, Monk, Taylor (Bessone), Britton, Allen, Gower, Dyer (Routledge, 71), Lita (Moore, 71), Sinclair.
- WBA: Foster, Olsson, Shorey, Dawson, Reid, Mulumbu (Dorrans, 45), Morrison, Scharner (Cox, 68), Thomas (Brunt, 45), Odemwingie, Long.
- Goals: Sinclair (1-0, 14), Lita (2-0, 24), Dyer (3-0, 49).

"After what was a sad week with the passing of Brendan Rodgers' father due to cancer and the four Swansea miners who were trapped underground and lost their lives, we hosted West Bromwich Albion. After an emotional minute of silence, the team couldn't have been more motivated going into a match in search of our first Premier League goal and victory in front of 20,000 fans; and indeed we were. Scott Sinclair opened the scoring from a penalty, and then Leroy Lita scored before Nathan Dyer scored the final third goal. A 3-0 victory dedicated to the bereaved families and of course our manager. It was a comprehensive victory, and we have yet to concede a goal at the Liberty in our first three games. You could see a Swansea side that was again improving greatly, defensively and offensively, confidence is sky-high for travelling to London to take on another heavyweight; Chelsea at Stamford Bridge. Again I played the ninety minutes.

For the fans of football stats I would like to add that despite playing for a side below mid-table, I am the player with the most passes and touches of the ball in the first four fixtures in the Premier League. More than the greats like David Silva, Wayne Rooney, Frank Lampard or even defenders like Chelsea's Ashley Cole. Before match day five, I had made three-hundred and ninety-nine passes in four games, an average of one-hundred per game. In the most recent game I managed eighty-nine. This is a reflection of Swansea's style of combination football in which everyone is comfortable on the ball and enjoys it. It is a pleasure for me."

Match day 6 (24/9/2011):
Chelsea 4 - Swansea 1

A new visit to another of the great Premier League stadiums results in another thrashing despite the sending off of Fernando Torres in the thirty-ninth minute. Rangel led the stats for most tackles with seven.

- Chelsea: Čech, Bosingwa, Ivanović, Terry, A.Cole, Ramires, Meireles (McEachran, 83), Mikel, Anelka (Drogba, 79), Torres, Mata (Malouda, 60).
- Swansea: Vorm, Rangel, Monk, Williams, Taylor, Britton (Routledge, 45), Allen, Gower, Dyer (Dobbie, 72), Sinclair, Lita (Graham, 59).
- Goals: 1-0, Torres (28); 2-0, Ramires (35); 3-0 Ramires (76); 3-1, Williams (86); 4-1, Drogba (94).

"Another game against one of Europe's greats in one hell of a stadium, Stamford Bridge. I was very excited going into this game. That morning I received a visit from my father, brother-in-law and two friends that had come to see the game. They were motivated like me, and like me they knew that all the years of hard work were paying off by playing in great stadiums like this against top players such as Drogba, Torres, Anelka and

Mata. I had to mark Mata and I believe it was a great duel. After being involved in a few moves he was replaced by Malouda, but we met to exchange shirts afterwards.

Unfortunately the team lost 4-1. When Torres was sent off in the thirty-ninth minute for a rash challenge it was already 2-0. Even with the sending off and despite our best efforts right up until the final whistle, Chelsea secured a deserved victory albeit the score was a little flattering. Already in the tunnel was Juan Mata waiting to exchange jerseys. It is a major attribute of a great player and good person; when a footballer of his stature shows humility and personality like that. I would like to offer him my thanks. In addition, I had the honour of being able to speak before and after the game with another recent Chelsea arrival from Barcelona. Oriol Romeu, who comes from where I am from, he was rested that weekend after having played one hundred and twenty minutes in the Cup against Fulham mid-week. Aside from the result, they have been two days full of emotion what with seeing friends and family and also taking home the shirt of a player that is going to be one of the stars of the season."

Match day 7 (2/10/2011):
Swansea 2 - Stoke City 0

Premier League football returned to the Liberty Stadium with a clash of styles; the combination football of the home side against the preferred direct football of the visitors. Five points from the first six matches meant Swansea desperately needed the win.

- Swansea: Vorm, Rangel, Monk, Williams, Taylor, Allen, Gower, Routledge (Moore, 66), Dyer, Sinclair, Graham(Lita, 85).
- Stoke: Begović, Shawcross, Wilkinson, Woodgate, Whelan, Wilson (Huth, 33), Pennant (Shotton, 80), Whitehead, Delap (Jerome, 55), Walters, Crouch.
- Goals: 1-0, Sinclair (pen. 9); 2-0, Graham (85).

"A match at home to Stoke, a team that are also playing in the Europa League. A very physical outfit that focus on the long ball to target Peter Crouch, and use any throw-ins in the opposition half, corners and free kicks to launch the ball into the area and make chances. This is Stoke, they don't put three passes together. But our style prevailed and we controlled the game keeping the ball and made it very hard for the defence in the box with our full aggression. We won 2-0 with goals from Sinclair and the star signing that season, Danny Graham, who finally opened his account after seven games. I played the ninety minutes. The team are doing well; seven played, eight points and in mid-table (bearing in mind that we had not conceded a goal at home in our four games). However now it is time to improve our away form, we had lost three (against Manchester City, Arsenal and Chelsea). The next fixture is away to Norwich City after the international break."

Match day 8 (9/10/2011):
Norwich 3 - Swansea 1

"Our recent victory enabled us to come into the next two weeks with a greater sense of calm as there was to be another break for international obligations". Given that until now, Swansea had visited the Etihad Stadium, Emirates Stadium and Stamford Bridge, Norwich seemed like a team that Swansea could notch up their first away victory against. However, after just ten minutes everything was against the Jacks. Whilst writing this chapter Rangel had a fever, as at the time he came down with the flu due to the sudden drop in temperature of the weather.

- Swansea: Vorm, Rangel, Monk, Williams, Taylor (Richards, 74), Allen, Britton, Dyer (Lita, 69), Routledge(Dobbie, 60), Sinclair, Graham.
- Norwich: Ruddy; Naughton, Barnett, Martin, Tierney; Bennett, Fox, Johnson, Pilkington; Hoolahan (Crofts, 79), Morison (Holt, 67).
- Goals: 1-0, Pilkington (1); 2-0, Martin (10); 2-1, Graham (12); 3-1, Pilkington (64).

"Motivated by our recent victory it was time to visit Carrow Road and a team, just like us, that had been promoted from the Championship. Everybody knew the importance of the game; it was an opponent that we had to take maximum points from. We therefore travelled by private jet (a little thirty-five seater plane) accompanied by the club's executive board for group morale and to make the journey quicker. We seemed ready for the contest but that wasn't the case. After ten minutes we were 2-0 down due to a lack of concentration and organization on the pitch. Despite Danny Graham scoring to make it 2-1 and a few moments where we threatened an equaliser, Norwich in the end scored the decider from a corner to make it 3-1. It was a bad day. We have to turn the page and learn from our mistakes. Again I played the ninety minutes. Days like this show you that there are no easy games in the Premier League and that lapses in concentration will cost you heavily. Either way, we are mid-table and on Saturday we have another away game, against Wolverhampton, to show that we have learned our lesson and collect our first points on the road against another direct rival."

Match day 9 (22/10/2011):
Wolverhampton 2 - Swansea 2

Swansea finally picked up points away from the Liberty Stadium. As positive as that seems, the downside is Swansea held a 2-0 lead until Wolves equalised with two goals in two minutes in the final stages. Orlandi enjoyed his first minutes of game time at the elite level of English football. Rangel who was in the starting XI again, was involved in the second goal with a great pass leading to the assist. After the game, Rangel was the league's best defender in Yahoo's Fantasy Football league and ranked twenty-second overall. In addition, he was the player with the second most passes in the league behind Manchester City's Yaya Touré and featured in MSN UK's best eleven that week.

- Wolverhampton: Hennessey, Stearman, Johnson, Berra, Ward, Hammil (Milijaš, 68), Henry, O'Hara, Jarvis (Guédioura, 68), Doyle, Ebans-Blake (Vokes, 83).
- Swansea: Vorm, Rangel, Monk, Williams, Taylor, Britton (Orlandi, 75), Allen, Gower (Moras, 86), Dyer (Routledge, 83), Graham, Sinclair.

- Goals: 0-1, Graham (23); 0-2, Allen (34); 1-2, Doyle (84), 2-2, O'Hara (86).

"It was the second consecutive game away from the Liberty and was covered live on Sky Sports as well as Spain's subscription-based TV football channel Gol T. Once again my best footballer friend Andrea Orlandi travelled with the team after recovering from a lengthy knee injury, it was also his official Premier League debut coming on in the second half. We started the game with a lot of aggression and maintained possession although Wolves threatened first. We went 2-0 up in the first half thanks to goals from Danny Graham (making it 3 goals in 3 games), and Joe Allen. We were also playing some great football.

We started the second half strongly, though as the game went on we were giving away possession and we missed chances to kill off the game. It seemed like a sure win, but that is never the case in English football. With ten minutes to go Wolves made three changes, and once again the anxiety to take all three points weighed heavily on us. We dropped very deep and gave Wolves a lot of room which they took advantage of by bombarding us with balls into the area. Then they took a corner trying to narrow the gap, and finally two minutes later the inexplicable happened: they equalised due to the lack of defensive organization and aggression that is needed to hold a lead when away from home. Final score, 2-2 and a major disappointment. It was another lesson to be learned, but also our first point away from home to break the losing streak of four consecutive away defeats. We have nine points, three off the Europa spots and three ahead of Bolton who are in decline and have to come to the Liberty next Saturday. I played the ninety minutes."

Match 10 (29 October 2011):
Swansea 3 - Bolton 1

Swansea were able to win and impress in an important match, extinguishing the flame of another rival mounting a recovery. Rangel put in an impressive performance, attracting the attention of many in the British media. This match would be remembered for the fact that Britton completed one hundred percent of his passes (66), something that no other midfielder or forward had achieved in the previous six Premiership seasons.

- Swansea: Vorm, Rangel, Monk, Williams, Taylor, Dyer (Moore, 90), Gower, Britton, Allen, Sinclair, Graham.
- Bolton: Jääskeläinen, Steinsson, Cahill, Wheater, Gardner, Eagles, Reo-Coker, Pratley (Kakuta, 75), M. Davies, Petrov (Robinson, 52), N'Gog (Klasnić, 75).
- Goals: 1-0, Allen (49); 2-0, Sinclair (57); 2-1, Graham (own goal, 73); 3-1, Graham (93).

"After a week of much reflection and analysis of the draw suffered at Wolverhampton we hosted Bolton Wanderers, another team destined to have to fight to avoid relegation. In a packed out Liberty Stadium on a humid afternoon, and with the desire to beat a direct rival, the big match began. With the same starting XI as the previous week, we began to control the match, although there weren't any shots on goal in the first half. At the half time whistle the score remained 0-0. However the second half was a different story. We pushed harder and a foul on Nathan Dyer saw Bolton left-winger, Gardner, sent off for a second bookable offence. The resulting free kick paved the way for Joe Allen to break away and finish in the style of Andres Iniesta, going past three opponents and slotting the ball home with his right foot.

After the goal, the footballing performance really began. The whole team felt confident with the ball, so we opened up the pitch and had several chances on goal. The second goal came from a corner on the left. Dyer tried a shot on the goal but his attempt ended up at my feet. While controlling the ball in the area, former Swansea player Darren Pratley brought me down and the referee didn't hesitate in awarding a penalty. Scott Sinclair made neat work of the penalty to make it 2-0. Although we continued to make chances, ten-man Bolton found themselves a goal when Danny Graham put the ball in his own net with ten minutes to go. The whole stadium was probably thinking back to the match against Wolves, but this time it was different. With Bolton desperately on the attack, I took advantage of an interception to pass the ball to Danny Graham who, with only the keeper to beat, scored to make it 3-1.

My notes:

1. We demonstrated that we had learned the lesson of maintaining a lead.
2. Danny Graham scored four goals in as many games.
3. No team has scored against us in the first five matches at home – Graham's own goal was the only goal we have conceded.
4. I played the full ninety minutes again and I had won the penalty and made an assist.
5. We are in tenth place with 12 points, six places above the relegation zone and three away from Europe.
6. I have been named in the team of the week in the webpages of several media sites, such as ESPN, Eurosport, and Sky Sports etc."

Happy Hallowe'en 2011

"We celebrated Hallowe'en night. The truth is I don't even recall how it's celebrated in Spain, but in Wales they celebrate it like the Americans with the infamous trick or treat whereby people dress up as famous horror characters and go from house to house with a bag or a bucket asking for sweets. And so I took my two kids, Bailey – dressed as the Scream character – and Angel Noah – dressed as Spiderman – along with their cousins, along our street. It's not easy knocking on every door with six sugar-crazed children who were adamant that if someone refused to give them sweets they would pay them back with an egg in the face. Thankfully, nobody refused. The adults' Hallowe'en party was an entirely different affair, although it's common here for the adults to wear fancy dress too. People dress up and either go to house parties or nightclubs and follow the social tradition of drinking as much as they can handle."

Match day 11 (5 November 2011): Liverpool 0 - Swansea 0

November began with an important match, one of those that Swansea fans would have circled when the season fixture list was first released. It involved a visit to one of the UK's most revered football grounds – Anfield Road – to face Liverpool, a team that demands respect. It would be remembered as a well-earned draw and for the standing ovation that the Welsh side received from the Liverpool fans.

- Liverpool: Reina, Johnson, Škrtel, Agger, Jose Enrique, Henderson (Kuyt, 46), Lucas, Adam, Downing, Carroll (Bellamy, 74), Suárez.
- Swansea: Vorm, Rangel, Williams, Monk, Taylor, Britton, Allen, Gower (Agustien, 90), Routledge (Sinclair, 74), Graham, Dyer.

"After the home win against Bolton, we next went to Anfield Road. It's one of those grounds that I had always hoped to play at one day. With the stadium full and thousands of Swansea fans making more noise than the home fans, the match began with a clear chance for Liverpool. Andy Carroll hit the crossbar from six yards out with fifteen minutes on the clock. After that, we began to impose the Swansea style of play, dominating possession, passing the ball from one side of the pitch to the other and creating chances. Only whistles were heard at Anfield; Liverpool fans were used to seeing their team with the ball but that's not what was happening.

It was more of the same in the second half. We had most of the possession, although Liverpool had some dangerous moments courtesy of Adam and Suárez. Our best chances came with fifteen minutes to go, forcing Pepe Reina into several impressive saves against Danny Graham, Nathan Dyer and Mark Gower, who had the closest attempt of the match with a shot that sailed just over the goal from the penalty area after a great collective effort. Our keeper, Michel Vorm, showed his mettle at the end of the match, making three stunning saves and giving us a point in a match we initially thought we'd lose. A point feels like a win especially when the Liverpool fans give us a standing ovation at the end of the match. I had never experienced anything like it, and the truth is it filled me with pride to see the supporters of one of Europe's most famous teams applauding you for having given an experienced team at the top of the European profession a lesson in football.

My notes

1. I played the full ninety minutes.
2. First clean-sheet away from home, and the fifth clean sheet of the season – making us the side with the most games without conceding a goal in the Premier League. Swansea sits tenth in the table with 13 points.
3. My father, Angel, and brother-in-law, Xavi, along with two of my best friends, Mingo and Malio visited me and saw the ovation at Anfield in the flesh. After the match, they said it had been an incredible experience. We're now on the international break, but in the next two weeks we play at home against both Manchester United and Aston Villa,

Bowling Night

Every year, the team and the fans meet to play ten-pin bowling, with each player being assigned to play two games with a team of Swansea supporters. At the end of the two games, prizes are awarded to the highest scoring player, the lowest scoring and the team that includes the family with the best score. As with every year, many people came along to take part in what is a great chance for those close to the club to have a nice time with their footballing idols, have their photos taken and get players' autographs. The truth is the scores are not very impressive but it must be said that I had a great time with one family that takes part every year and which I've had the fortune to play with nearly every season since being with Swansea. I can never score higher than 130. The highest score was that of Portuguese goalkeeper José Moreira who came from Benfica, he was awarded a trophy for his score of 160. The worse score was that of young French player Darnel Situ who came from Lens with a score of 82 points. I imagine bowling isn't a very popular sport in France. I believe that this type of event over the years has helped strengthen the great relationship that the fans and players have had season after season."

Match day 12 (19/11/2011): Swansea 0 - Manchester United 1

After the two week break the Premier League returned with another important date for Swansea fans; Manchester United's visit to the Liberty. However everything went wrong early on in an unfortunate game which Rangel regrets. A rare error in his passing resulted in a Manchester United goal. It was one of the few mistakes he made given that he recorded a ninety percent pass completion rate from seventy-seven passes, a rate that saw him ranked first in terms of passing in the Premier League. Such a statistic led him to be involved in numerous interviews and the focus of reports in both the British and Spanish media. Manager Brendan Rodgers after the game asked that the Spanish defender wasn't held accountable as Rodgers himself accepted responsibility for the defeat. In addition, it was possibly one of the only few games that Rodgers changed the formation.

- Swansea: Vorm, Rangel, Monk, Williams, Taylor, Britton, Gower (Dobbie, 79), Routledge (Allen, 45), Sinclair, Dyer, Graham.
- Manchester United: De Gea, Jones, Vidić, Ferdinand, Evra (Fabio, 51), Carrick, Giggs (Fletcher, 76), Park, Nani, Rooney, Chicharito (Valencia, 84).
- Goals: 0-1, Chicharito (11).

"After another international break we returned to Premier League action, this time against current Premier League Champions and Champions League finalists Manchester United. Once again there wasn't a free seat inside the Liberty Stadium for what was the biggest game in the club's history. And of course, the fans did not want to see us lose such an important contest and we wanted to extend our unbeaten run at home by another week.

We started strongly with chances in and around their area but without any clinical edge. Then all of a sudden in the eleventh minute the unexpected happened, something uncharacteristic. I was building the play from the back and passed the ball to Leon Britton who was playing in a defensive-holding role. But Ryan Giggs intercepted it and quickly went on an attacking run which he ended with a low cross to Chicharito who made no mistake. United were 1-0 up having done nothing. But Swansea didn't give up and nor did I. Immediately we sought the equaliser and our best chance of the game arrived falling to Scott Sinclair, who from a Wayne Routledge cross couldn't finish in front of a gaping goalmouth. At half time it was 1-0. In the dressing room it was said that we needed to go and press high up the field, audaciously and fearlessly; and that's what we did. The second half was all us; we were attacking, we had chances and several corners but we couldn't capitalise and get the equaliser. 1-0 was the final result however it was very unfair.

My notes:

1. We went up against the second best team in Europe.
2. I believe as a team we were better and a draw would have been the right result.
3. My mistake stuck in the minds of all those that saw the game who have labelled me with the blame which I accept as I cost us the game.
4. However I'm not concerned because it was a one-off mistake in my passing, which I have shown to be a strong part of my game and the stats prove I'm one of the best passers in the league.
5. What's more is defensively I went home satisfied having marked Park Ji-Sung and kept him totally under control the whole match. He didn't go past me even once or have a chance on goal. Apart from the goal, they didn't create a single chance down my side. I played the ninety minutes.

I would like to finish by thanking all of those that left me messages of support on Twitter because even though I was content with my performance I was also very hurt for causing my team to lose and for letting down thousands of people with my stupid mistake. We learn from our mistakes, so now thoughts are on Aston Villa who visit the Liberty next Sunday and on setting things right."

Match day 13 (27/11/2011):
Swansea 0 - Aston Villa 0

The game played at the end of November at the Liberty was an emotional one due to the passing of Welsh national team coach Gary Speed hours before. The emotional scenes reached a climax during the minute of silence with Villa's goalkeeper Shay Given, who was a close friend of Gary Speed, in tears. The game itself ended in a goalless draw. After that week's game, Swansea had taken two points from a possible nine, but one must bear in mind the quality of their opposition in those three games.

- Swansea: Vorm, Rangel (Richards, 27), Monk, Williams, Taylor; Allen, Britton, Gower, Sinclair, Dyer (Routledge, 82), Graham (Lita, 54).
- Aston Villa: Given, Hutton, Warnock, Dunne, Collins, Herd, Delph (Bannan, 79), N'Zogbia, Agbonlahor, Heskey (Jenas, 69), Bent.

"We were already in the dressing room, just twenty minutes before going out to warm up, when we received the terrible news that Gary Speed, the Welsh National team manager, had passed away just hours before. It was a big shock for us all what with Welsh internationals like Joe Allen, Ashley Williams and Neil Taylor amongst us. In addition, Leon Britton had worked with him a few months back at Sheffield United. Across the board, the news struck at the hearts of all of us. In the Aston Villa side was one of the most effected by the news, the first choice goalkeeper Shay Given who was a very close friend.

Gary Speed was a man totally immersed in the world of football, a legend as a player having played for Newcastle and Leeds United amongst others and of course for Wales before becoming manager. In terms of management, he had been successful too with Wales starting to play more attractive passing football which was producing good results. After considering the option of postponing the game it was decided that it would go ahead to honour Gary and his family in addition to observing a minute's silence. The crowd could not contain their emotions and after a few seconds the whole Liberty began to sing, "There is only one Gary Speed, there is only one Gary Speed." It was truly emotional and painful for those that were close to him.

The game started with a high tempo with Swansea dominating and Aston Villa throwing themselves at every fifty-fifty ball though neither of us created chances. Twenty minutes in the unexpected happened; I slipped whilst we were on the attack and went over sharply on my ankle, however I tried to carry on. But the pain was getting worse and I was substituted for Jazz Richards.

It was a very open game right until the end with both teams enjoying chances. Although Leroy Lita had the clearest opportunity of the game, after turning his man his shot went just wide of the post. It was a goalless draw that brought us one point closer to safety and five above the drop zone. Once again we managed a clean sheet. Personally I was left with ligament damage to my ankle that will see me out of action for four weeks. I am positive and I know that I'll be back stronger than ever for the difficult Christmas period."

Match day 14 (3/12/2011): Blackburn 4 - Swansea 2

Away from home Swansea had only managed to claim two points, Blackburn was a fixture the Swans would have been targeting. However it is local striker Yakubu's day who nets all of Blackburn's goals. Rangel is out with injury, Bessone travels but doesn't feature and Orlandi doesn't make the team sheet. Allen is sent off collecting a second yellow on the eighty minute mark before Blackburn score their definitive fourth goal making it 4-2. The sending off would see him sit out the next game against Fulham.

- Blackburn: Robinson, Samba, Givet, Dann, Dunn (Petrović, 76), Formica, Pedersen, Lowe, Rochina (Vukčević, 40), Hoilett, Yakubu (Roberts, 87).

- Swansea: Vorm, Richards, Williams, Monk, Taylor, Britton, Allen, Gower (Moore, 61), Sinclair, Dyer (Routledge, 45), Lita.
- Goals: 1-0, Yakubu (20); 1-1, Lita (35); 2-1, Yakubu (47); 3-1, Yakubu (57); 3-2, Moore (66); 4-2, Yakubu (pen. 82).

"It was another peculiar feeling for me; not travelling with the team and having to listen to the game on the radio. The team lost 4-2 with four goals from Blackburn's Yakubu. Lita and Moore scored for Swansea. From what I heard on the radio and what teammates told me after the game, the team played well, with much more possession and we were set up better than our opponents. But it was just one of those days when every ball the other team's striker touches he scores. We conceded two goals from corners, a penalty and one from a move on the wing. Even with ten men and 3-2 down, the team did not throw in the towel and we had chances to equalise. Such a pity as the team deserved more out of the game. We have to keep learning from our mistakes and concentrate on the next game. The next will be against Fulham at home; a vital game.

On a personal level, it has been a peculiar week for me as I'm not used to six hours a day in the gym and seeing my teammates out training on the grass. Double daily sessions focused on direct treatment of my ankle with anti-inflammatory creams, Compex use and lots of ice. In the gym I have alternated cycling sessions with upper and lower core muscle work and lots of balance exercises. This was in addition to swimming which I was also doing daily. After those first seven days of rehabilitation I was already walking fine, barely noticing the pain and psychologically a lot more optimistic. There are only three weeks to go according to the medical advice but I'm sure I'll return sooner than predicted thanks to being surrounded by a great medical team that work with me every day."

Match day 15 (10/12/2011): Swansea 2 - Fulham 0

The recent run of results made a victory essential. A strong performance at the Liberty was an absolute requisite for Swansea given their poor returns on the road. With Rangel and Allen absent, a key performance from Dutch keeper Vorm helped the team claim three valuable points to place them comfortably in the table going into two consecutive away games.

- Swansea: Vorm, Richards, Caulker, Williams, Taylor, Britton, Gower, Routledge (Dyer, 89), Moore (Agustien, 69), Sinclair, Lita (Graham, 76).
- Fulham: Schwarzer, Kelly, Senderos, Hangeland, Riise, Davies (Orlando Sá, 79), Etuhu, Bryan Ruiz, Dembelé (Frei, 77), Dempsey, Johnson.
- Goals: 1-0, Sinclair (56); 2-0, Graham (90).

"It was another home game against a direct rival, Fulham. I nervously watched the game from the stands. In the first half, despite having a lot of possession we only had one chance. Fulham however did not even manage to approach our area. After the break things changed, we had more punch and found ourselves with a lucky goal from Scott Sinclair from a corner. It seemed as if it was going to be an easy afternoon to collect the three points but that wasn't the case. After the goal we dropped deep and Fulham began to play. Right away they were through one on one against our super keeper Michel Vorm who made a spectacular save, something he was to do again just a few minutes later. With Fulham launched forward in attack, we could have killed off the game with a clear chance that fell to Danny Graham, but the London defence sent the ball out for a corner. Five minutes to go the unexpected happened; penalty to Fulham. Everything was pointing to a draw, but no. Once again, super-Michel made the best save of the weekend from the Clint Dempsey penalty. Already in injury time, from another corner kick Danny Graham sealed a 2-0 win for a Swansea side that remains in mid-table and is on good form at home. Now we have two away games in a row against Newcastle and Everton.

Two teams from the north that will make things very difficult for us. But we are eager to get our first win away from the Liberty Stadium.

It has been a positive week in all other ways too. I am stepping out onto the training pitch to do some running in conjunction with my usual balance exercises to strengthen my ankle. Everything is going as planned, and I hope to be training by the end of this week or the start of next and be available for the Christmas period which will certainly not be easy.

Off the pitch it has been a week full of events. Like every year we had our calendar signing event when the whole squad sits in a room at the stadium and signs the new official Swansea City calendars for the hundreds of fans that attend. Also held at the stadium a few days later is a party for the kiddos with magicians, clowns and the like. We also make ourselves available to sign autographs and have our photos taken with the youngest ones and to wish them a happy Christmas. Like with the Bowling Night, these events further enhance the sense of community and strengthen the bond between the players and fans who are all committed and working hard to achieve the same goal.

When I say it was a positive week that's also in reference to Swansea City FC being nominated best sports team in Swansea and nationally throughout Wales. Luckily, due to my injury, I get to attend club events as a representative. I therefore had the honour of accepting one of the awards with two other injured teammates at one of the galas and speaking on behalf of the club and of course all those linked to it. It was not an easy task to speak in front of hundreds of important Welsh sports personalities in English, but just like the football, it's all part of the job. It's such an honour to be part of this club at the moment, in the best period of its history, with the ever-increasing recognition for having overcome our almost total disappearance from the English football league in less than a decade. A truly incredible achievement which awards like these recognise."

Match day 16 (17/12/2011): Newcastle 0 - Swansea 0

A point at Newcastle can't be considered a bad result. Allen returns to the starting XI however Rangel continues to recover from his injury. Swansea had fifty-one percent of the possession but just three attempts on goal (all off target) to Newcastle's twenty-two.

- Newcastle: Krul, Coloccini, Perch, Santon, Simpson, Obertan (Sammy Ameobi, 82), Tioté (Vučkić, 82), Cabaye, Jonás, Best (Shola Ameobi, 71), Demba Ba.
- Swansea: Vorm, Richards, Williams, Caulker, Taylor, Allen, Britton, Gower (Agustien, 45), Routledge, Sinclair, (Dyer, 77), Graham.

"Another game that I didn't make the squad due to injury, so obviously I didn't travel with the club. At least I could watch the game live online. It's not easy to play in stadiums like St. James' Park which is filled with forty-five thousand spectators nearly every game that make plenty of noise cheering on their team and pressurising the away side. In the first half Newcastle dominated and owned us, enjoying various chances. We went in at half time 0-0. Second half things changed and we came out a lot braver. They continued to cause us some trouble but we had more of the ball despite not managing a shot on the opposition goal. Newcastle struck the post a couple of times but the team defended well and Vorm continued his marvellous display of saves. In the final minutes of the game came our only chance which fell to Sinclair in the box, who having been put through one-on-one with a defender by a great Joe Allen pass, shot wide.

Final score 0-0. I believe it is a great point for Swansea that proves that away at the big clubs it's possible to get a result. I also want to highlight the tremendous effort that my teammates put in against a physically superior team. We slogged it out in the end and were rewarded with another point to add to our tally."

Match day 17 (21/12/2011): Everton 1 - Swansea 0

A second trip of the season to the city of Liverpool. Swansea search for a victory to avoid the danger zone. But a move from a dead-ball situation decides the game in which Swansea again has more possession (fifty-four percent) but also continue to struggle in front of goal (with only one of their five shots on target).

- Everton: Howard, Hibbert, Jagielka, Baines, Heitinga, Coleman (Gueye, 31), Drenthe (Cahill, 81), Osman, P.Neville, Fellaini, Saha (Stracqualursi, 75).
- Swansea: Vorm; Richards, Williams, Caulker, Taylor (Rangel, 45); Britton (Lita, 74), Allen, Gower (Agustien, 45); Routledge, Sinclair, Graham.
- Goals: 1-0, Osman (60).

"After just two training sessions with the team, the boss called me up to travel with the squad although knowing full well that I would be on the bench. We were going to another stadium up north, Goodison Park, where once again the crowd plays an important role in the match. Despite a good start and having more possession, the half-chances to score fell to Everton. Nonetheless we were still solid and comfortable.

In the forty-fourth minute our left back Neil Taylor took a heavy knock to his lower leg (between his shin and ankle) which forced him to come off in much pain. The only wingback available was me, so I had to come on without warming up. I went onto the right side as Jazz Richards moved to play on the left. Two minutes later half time arrived all square at 0-0.

After warming up for ten minutes the second half got under way. Neither team was managing to assert their dominance with a lot of play in the middle of the park and few chances created. I felt like I was just floating around, as having trained very little I lacked the sharpness needed to perform at this level. Though sticking with it as I do, bit by bit I began to get into the game, combining with Routledge and Allen who drifted more to my side.

Everton having done little found themselves with a more than dubious corner and scored the only goal of the game thanks to a header by Osman. We tried to react and had a good chance from another header by Graham but Howard was well placed to save it. In the end, it finished 1-0 to Everton. The team was very disheartened after the game having yet to win away from home, but I'm sure that in 2012 things will change and we'll collect many points. Aside from that negativity, you have to say that we are four points above the relegation zone, and on a personal note I'm very happy to be playing with my teammates again."

Match day 18 (27/12/2011): Swansea 1 - QPR 1

With the Christmas period comes a schedule packed with matches, however Swansea do not play until December 27th. They are fixtures that teams put extra effort into for the fans, especially the youngest ones who take advantage of the holiday season to go to the stadiums with their families. Queens Park Rangers, winners of the Championship in 2010-11 with direct promotion, are the penultimate opponents of the year for Swansea.

- Swansea: Vorm, Rangel (Moore, 57), Caulker, Williams, Richards, Agustien, Britton, Allen, Routledge (Dyer, 57), Sinclair, Graham.
- QPR: Kenny, Young, Hill, Hall, Traoré, Barton, Derry, Faurlín, Mackie, Taarabt, Helguson.
- Goals: Graham, 1-0 (14); Mackie, 1-1 (58).

"Back to the Liberty for one of those games that you know you have to win as it's against a direct rival, QPR. I was back in the starting XI after four weeks. I felt good with no pain in my ankle, and was adding depth to our right side with no issues at the back. We deservedly went ahead in the first fifteen minutes through Danny Graham who showed great control on the edge on the box and finished with a great low drive. We were comfortable, keeping the ball without any problems and working down the clock. Then just before half time, I took a bad knock to the same ankle that was previously injured, and the pain was such that I couldn't run properly. In the dressing room at half time the pain got worse so they changed my support bandage to see if I could continue. I was given ten minutes of the second half to see if it was better, but it wasn't and the boss took me off as a precaution.

Unfortunately, not having time to re-organise from the changes we failed to clear a long ball into the box which led to them equalising; 1-1. The team gave it their all for the last twenty minutes but it was one of those days where it was always going to end in a draw, and so it finished 1-1. Apart from feeling disappointed at having not won the match, we take the positive of collecting another point and maintaining our good run of form at home where we have only lost once this season."

Match day 19 (31/12/2011): Swansea 1 - Tottenham 1

As was the case with the majority of managers, Brendan Rodgers needed to make changes to his starting XI due to the high number of games in quick succession. Rangel put in a great performance in the second half despite still carrying an ankle knock.

- Swansea: Vorm, Richards (Rangel, 45'), Monk, Williams, Taylor, Allen, Gower (Agustien, 62'), Dobbie, Dyer, Sinclair, Moore (Graham, 69').
- Tottenham: Friedel, Walker, Gallas, Kaboul, Assou-Ekotto, Sandro, Van der Vaart (Defoe, 71'), Parker (Livermore, 72'), Modrić, Bale, Adebayor.
- Goals: Van der Vaart, 0-1 (44'); Sinclair, 1-1 (84').

"It was the final day of 2011 and the second consecutive game at home. On this occasion we are up against a team considered amongst the best in the league, and rightly so. Tottenham play attractive and effective football. I started the game on the bench to my surprise, as the day before I was still in a lot of pain with my ankle. But once again the boss showed the great faith that he has in me. As always at home we got off to a strong start keeping the ball and enjoying a couple of chances, but without making a break through. At least we were making the likes of Bale, Adebayor and Van de Vaart run around. It seemed like we were heading into the half time break all square before we were unfortunate to concede from a cross finished by Van de Vaart making it 1-0.

I was sent to warm up to be introduced at the start of the second half, but genuinely, I was a bit concerned about my ankle as I knew it wasn't one hundred percent. However the show of faith from the technical staff to ask me to play given the circumstances is something spectacular knowing that there are other better prepared players on the bench. It couldn't have gone any better. My introduction sought to add a more attacking element to the team, and with it came Sinclair's equaliser from my cross from the right wing. I also nearly scored my first goal of the season from a corner. The final score was a 1-1 draw. The team deserved something out of the game which we could have won, so I'm genuinely happy."

Match day 20 (2/1/2012): Aston Villa 0 - Swansea 2

2012 cannot begin any better for Swansea nor for the Spanish players; Swansea secured their first away victory and Rangel and Orlandi featured in the starting XI (just lacking the inclusion of Bessone to complete the Spanish contingent). An important win in terms of league standings and also on an emotional level it made having to travel on New Year's Day easier to take.

- Aston Villa: Guzan, Cuéllar (Hutton, 55), Collins, Dunne, Warnock, Agbonlahor, Petrov, Clark (Bannan, 85), N'Zogbia, Ireland (Albrighton, 69), Bent.
- Swansea: Vorm, Rangel, Caulker, Williams, Taylor, Britton, Agustien, Orlandi (Allen, 58), Dyer (Sinclair, 78),Routledge, Graham.
- Goals: Dyer, 0-1 (5); Routledge, 0-2 (47).

"After the Tottenham game we only had a brief time to celebrate the New Year with family. On the first of January we were already travelling to Birmingham to face Aston Villa the following day at Villa Park. What a stadium by the way. I returned to the starting XI and surprisingly so did one of my best friends in the world of football Andrea Orlandi in an attacking midfield role. Fortune was certainly shining on us after just four minutes when Nathan Dyer took advantage of a Villa mistake to open the scoring with a great finish. Despite Villa threatening from corners and free-kicks, we continued to create chances to go two or three goals up. However the second goal was evading us with the score 0-1 at half time.

Villa came out stronger, pressing us making it difficult for us to build from the back. But the second goal came from a great individual play by Wayne Routledge, who played a killer ball through to Graham who struck the post before Routledge converted the rebound. For Routledge it was a historic goal being his first in the Premier League after more than one hundred games with various clubs. 2-0 was the final score, the first win of 2012 and the first away from the Liberty. I have to say that Orlandi despite lacking match fitness, played very well for the seventy minutes he was involved. I'm very happy for him given that he hadn't played at all this season and yet he showed what an important player he is. I played the full ninety minutes and want to note that we have kept nine clean sheets this season."

FA Cup Third Round (07/01/2012): Barnsley 2 - Swansea 4

The Premier League is on hold for two weeks but the next game is five days later away to Championship side Barnsley in the third round of the FA Cup. The game produced a victory seeing Swansea through to the fourth round with a first goal of the season for Rangel. Orlandi played again.

- Barnsley: Steele, Hassell (Wiseman, 57), McEveley, Foster, McNulty, Addison, Done (Noble-Lazarus, 52), Perkins (Gray, 57), Drinkwater, Davies, Vaz Tê.
- Swansea: Tremmel, Rangel, Monk, Williams, Taylor, Britton, Agustien (Allen, 66), Orlandi (Sigurdsson, 58), Dyer (Sinclair, 78), Routledge, Graham.
- Goals: Vaz Tê, 1-0 (29); Rangel, 1-1 (30); Graham, 1-2 (46); Dyer, 1-3 (54); Vaz Tê, 2-3 (65); Graham, 2-4 (89).

"This time we were up against a Championship side at a difficult ground in adverse conditions; the cold, the wind and the playing surface. Despite this we still went all out. It was difficult to move the ball from side to side, transitional play was very slow and so we didn't create much of a threat. We knew that only by moving the ball quickly would we break down our opponents and this wasn't happening. Barnsley went ahead around the half hour mark after a counterattack, but a minute later I scored my first goal of the season. I was in a forward's position, Dyer played me a pass inside, and I turned and finished perfectly with a low drive across the goal. I honestly couldn't believe, being a full-back that I could score a goal that Romario or Salinas would be proud of. But yeah, it's always nice to score a great and important debut goal, above all for the reaction that you get from the team.

We went out in the second half and right away made it 2-1. With a strike from some thirty metres, taking advantage of the wind, Danny Graham caught out the home-side keeper. It was a screamer. We then went 3-1 up, with a goal created by Routledge and expertly dispatched by Dyer. Barnsley weren't going to give up and cut the deficit after a mistake at the back which Portuguese striker Vaz Te converted for his second goal of the afternoon. It seemed like the equaliser would come, but we showed great composure in keeping the ball in the closing minutes. Recovery of the ball by Joe Allen resulted in another Routledge assist for Danny Graham to score his second of the afternoon making the score line a definitive 4-2. We're through to the fourth round which drew us another away tie. This time it will be the winner of Macclesfield vs Bolton who have to play their replay after they drew at the first time of asking. I played the ninety minutes and Orlandi kept his place in the team."

Match Day 21 (15/01/2012): Swansea 3 - Arsenal 2

An interesting fact was being circulated in the papers at the time of this match. Ten years earlier, Arsenal were leading the Premiership while Swansea were rock bottom of League Two, meaning that of the ninety-two teams in professional English football, they were ranked first and last, respectively. A decade on and the Swans would prevail over the Gunners using their own weapon – possession play – against them, in a Premier League match. It was a historic day for Swansea and there was a fantastic atmosphere at the Liberty Stadium. To top it all off, Arsenal legend, Thierry Henry, came on as a sub during his brief return to the club.

- Swansea: Vorm, Rangel, Caulker, Williams, Taylor; Britton, Allen, Agustien (Sigurdsson, 45); Dyer (Routledge, 82), Graham (Lita, 90), Sinclair.
- Arsenal: Szczęsny, Djorou, Mertesacker (Chamberlain, 77), Koscielny, Miquel; Song, Ramsey, Walcott, Benayoun (Rosicky, 63), Arshavin (Henry, 63); Van Persie.
- Goals: 0-1, Van Persie (5); 1-1, Sinclair (penalty, 16); 2-1, Dyer (57); 2-2, Walcott (69); 3-2, Graham (70)

"What a great weekend we've had. My sister, brother-in-law and goddaughter were visiting; I hadn't seen them in such a long time. It was the perfect weekend on a personal and a professional level: it was a historic game.

We won 3-2 against Arsenal and I played the full ninety minutes. It was an intense encounter and the Gunners put themselves ahead 0-1 within the first few minutes. But we quickly equalised with a penalty scored by Sinclair. In the second half, a goal by Dyer put us ahead for the first time. Walcott equalised but within seconds Graham slotted the ball in to finish the match 3-2. It was a great feeling and it was possibly the best atmosphere at the Liberty Stadium I've experienced since I arrived at the club. It was a perfect weekend in every sense."

Match Day 22 (21/01/2012): Sunderland 2 - Swansea 0

After the euphoria of that momentous victory against Arsenal, Swansea were defeated at Sunderland, despite playing well. McEachran, on loan from Chelsea, made his debut, and

Sigurdsson made the starting line-up after having played the second half of the Arsenal match.

- Sunderland: Mignolet, Bardsley, Brown, Richardson, O'Shea, Cattermole, Larsson (Elmohamady, 89), Vaughan (Gardner, 78), McClean, Sessègnon, Bendtner (Wickham, 12).
- Swansea: Vorm, Rangel, Caulker, Williams, Taylor, Britton (Routledge, 78), Allen, Sigurdsson (McEachran, 66), Dyer, Sinclair, Graham.
- Goals: 1-0, Sessègnon (14); 2-0, Gardner (85).

"The journey to Sunderland was short thanks to the private plane laid on by the club as a thank you for the win over Arsenal. Once at the hotel – a Marriott with sea views – we enjoyed the initiation of the new signing from Chelsea, Josh McEachran, who sang an impressive version of Amy Winehouse's 'Valerie'.

We arrived at Sunderland's Stadium of Light on the Saturday, full of confidence after that famous win against Arsenal. It was a cold, windy afternoon, and the pitch was very different to what we're used to at the Liberty Stadium; in fact, it was in a terrible state. Sunderland started strongly with a shot that hit the goalpost.

Although we were enjoying all the possession, we weren't able to finish off the good combinations we were making. Despite the pressure from Sunderland, the team fought bravely for the match and we opened up the pitch as though we were playing at home. That's when our best chance came, as Sinclair hit the ball just over the crossbar after a great pass from Dyer. A minute later, Sunderland scored the opener with an effort that curled into the top-right corner from the left flank; the wind might have helped the ball into the net a little, but we didn't deserve to go behind. Half-time score:1-0.

We knew that we could win the match; we were the better of the two teams on the day. But we needed to take full advantage of our chances, and we came out for the second half with that same mentality. We took control straightaway and looked dangerous when pushing forward. But once again, our domination of the ball came to nothing and we failed to make the Sunderland keeper work very hard. Open play was good, but we all know that football is about goals – and that was the only thing we couldn't find on Saturday. Sadly, with the whole team focused on attacking to earn a draw, Sunderland took advantage of a counterattack to score with a volley from outside the area. It just goes to show how unfair football can be sometimes. The 2-0 loss hurt us because nobody likes to lose. But we returned to Swansea with our heads held high because we knew we'd played a great game.

My notes

1. Passes: Sunderland 226. Swansea 631
2. Possession: Sunderland 31% / Swansea 69%
3. Josh McEachran made a notable debut in the second half, and it was good to see Gylfi Sigurdsson back in the starting XI.
4. I played the full 90 minutes.
5. P.S. I must mention Nicklas Bendtner who broke his nose in an unfortunate incident in the first half. I've been trying to get his phone number so that I can apologise and wish him a speedy recovery."

FA Cup Fourth Round (28/01/2012): Bolton 2 - Swansea 1

Swansea went into the next round of the FA Cup full of hope against a rival that they were harbouring hopes of beating, despite the disadvantage of playing away from home in this one-legged tie. Bessone was the only Spaniard in the starting XI that day. In the opposing team, former Swan, Pratley, a regular in Roberto Martínez's starting XI during the season Swansea were promoted to the Championship, scored against his former club.

- Bolton: Bogdan, Wheater, Boyata, Riley, Ricketts, Eagles (Tuncay, 90), Pratley (Muamba, 80), Petrov, Reo-Cocker, N'Gog (K. Davies, 74), M. Davies.
- Swansea: Tremmel, A. Richards, Williams, Monk, Bessone, McEachran, Agustien, Gower (Allen, 79), Routledge (Dyer, 65), Lita (Graham, 65), Moore.

- Goals: 0-1, Moore (43); 1-1, Pratley (45); 2-1, Eagles (56).

"The fourth round of the FA Cup was at Bolton Wanderers' stomping ground, the Reebok Stadium. This is always an important competition. Despite it not being our main objective, the incentive of playing the final at Wembley is always tempting; everyone dreams of playing in that stadium. Thankfully, I'd already had the fortune to play at Wembley the previous year. I wouldn't have minded playing there again, but sadly we lost the match 2-1. We went ahead in the fortieth minute thanks to a great individual effort from Luke Moore, but Bolton drew level in the last minute of the first half. In the second half, we were more composed and had more chances on goal, but the home side were the ones to advance to the next round with a goal on the counterattack. The dream of returning to Wembley was in ruins, but we all know that our only objective this year is to stay in the Premier League. I had to watch the match from the sidelines as I was being rested before we faced Chelsea at home in the week."

Match Day 23 (31 January 2012): Swansea 1 - Chelsea 1

The Liberty Stadium welcomed another of the big matches of the season against Chelsea, a team put together thanks to Russian owner, Roman Abramovich's chequebook. On this, the last day of January, Rangel was the only Spaniard to start for Swansea, while three were in Chelsea's starting XI: Romeu, Mata and Torres. Luck would intervene for the Londoners in the dying moments of the match.

- Swansea: Vorm, Rangel, Caulker, Williams, Taylor, Britton, Allen, Dyer, Sigurdsson (Agustien, 67), Sinclair (Moore, 78), Graham.
- Chelsea: Čech, Bosingwa, Ivanović, Luiz, Cole, Meireles, Romeu (Essien, 65), Sturridge, Mata, Malouda (Lukaku, 80), Torres.
- Goals: 1-0, Sinclair (39); 1-1, Taylor (own goal, 92).

"Having recorded two consecutive defeats in the league (Sunderland) and the FA Cup (Bolton), we returned to the fortress that is the Liberty Stadium where only one team has so far taken three points from us, and that was Manchester United. Tottenham took a point, while Arsenal left with nothing, despite being the only team able to score two goals against us. In addition, we'd also kept a clean sheet on several occasions. Now it was the turn of Chelsea, who arrived without Terry or Lampard due to injury while Drogba was on African Cup duty. But even without those players, it's still Chelsea, right? Let's not forget Mata, Torres, Sturridge etc. In the first half, we played almost perfect football; we had the possession, the aggression, the pressure...and justice was done when, from a free-kick, Scott Sinclair (ex-Chelsea) volleyed the ball into the net. Half-time score: 1-0.

In the second half, and in freezing conditions, Chelsea came out stronger, pushing to equalise. And in all honesty, they dominated but still couldn't find a clear shot. It was hard for us to get the ball out from behind. We were under pressure from Chelsea, but at the same time we felt comfortable in defence. It looked like we were destined to clinch victory but, in the ninety-second minute, a shot was deflected off one of our players and ended up in the net, leaving us with a draw. The disappointment and sadness in the dressing room made me realise how far we'd come in just a few short years: we were unhappy with a draw against Chelsea! And with the stands pulsating again despite the freezing conditions! The fans gave us a standing ovation as we left the pitch. It was clear that they, as well as the players, were enjoying the great season we were having. I played the full ninety minutes and I was able to swap shirts with a Spanish friend of mine, Oriol Romeu, the Chelsea midfielder.

I got home after the match at around 11.30pm. But by 4am I was at Singleton Hospital with my partner, Nikki; she was having contractions and was about to give birth to our third child: our first daughter. The truth is, I could barely keep my eyes open from the tiredness I felt after playing in such a high-level match. But for anyone who has been present during the birth of a baby, the pain that the mother goes through is indescribable and doesn't compare with any other type of pain. I was there to support Nikki all the way through and, on the first of February 2012 at 12.29pm, our baby girl was born, weighing in at 7lbs 9oz (3.6kg). We hadn't yet decided on a name, although we had picked out a couple we liked. All I can say is that I'm just so proud of Nikki and of our growing family, and being part of that family gives me strength every day. Winning for them is the biggest motivation for me every time I step out onto the pitch."

Match Day 24 (04/02/2012): West Bromwich 1 - Swansea 2

A courageous win for Swansea, even more so considering it was away from home and that so far the team's away results had not been quite so positive. Until this match, Swansea's only away victory had been at Aston Villa, so Swansea's next away victory was won in nearby West Bromwich. With ninety-two completed passes, Rangel was the most influential player, while Sigurdsson was beginning to enjoy playing a decisive role in Swansea games and results.

- WBA: Foster, Reid, McAuley, Olsson, Shorey, Thomas (Tchoyi, 72), Morrison, Mulumbu (Scharner, 64), Dorrans (Cox, 72), Odemwingie, Fortune.
- Swansea: Vorm, Rangel, Caulker, Williams, Taylor, Allen, Britton, Dyer (Routledge, 88), Sigurdsson, Sinclair, Graham.
- Goals: 1-0, Fortune (54), 1-1, Sigurdsson (55), 1-2, Graham (59).

"It might have been cold in Swansea when we played Chelsea, but that Saturday at West Bromwich was even worse. It was so cold it made breathing difficult and there was even some snow. It wasn't easy going out onto the pitch in shorts or getting into our passing rhythm. The weather conditions were difficult for both teams – and for the fans. But, as always, the Swansea Jacks made themselves heard in the stands at The Hawthorns, West Bromwich's home turf.

As seems to happen so often, we had a great first half, dominating possession, but we didn´t have any clear chances. In contrast, the home side created a few chances from free-kicks and corners, which put us in danger on more than one occasion. The scoreline remained 0-0 at half-time and the snow continued to fall, but the Swansea supporters didn't seem to notice the cold. And I know that because my parents were in the stands watching the match live. We continued to dominate, but West Brom took the lead from a corner. A minute later, Gylfi Sigurdsson levelled after a fantastic bit of play which the Iceland international finished with a quality goal. The way the team reacted to that was brilliant because just two minutes later our top goal-scorer, Danny Graham, made it 1-2. The win topped off a great week: a draw against Chelsea, the birth of my daughter and this victory, which put us in the middle of the league table with 30 points, 10 points clear of the relegation zone. I don't think anyone could ask for more than that."

Match Day 25 (11/02/2012): Swansea 2 - Norwich 3

For Swansea, this match was a great opportunity to consolidate their position in the standings. But their opponents, Norwich, another recently promoted team, inflicted a shock defeat on the home side at the Liberty Stadium.

- Swansea: Vorm, Rangel, Caulker, Williams, Taylor, McEachran (Gower, 64), Britton, Sigurdsson, Dyer (Lita, 74), Graham, Sinclair (Routledge, 73).
- Norwich: Ruddy, Naughton, Martin, Ward, Drury (Barnet, 57), Bennett (Hoolahan, 77), Fox, Surman, Pilkington, Holt, Jackson (Morison, 83).
- Goals: 1-0, Graham (23); 1-1, Holt (47); 1-2, Pilkington (51); 1-3, Holt (63); 2-3, Graham (87).

"We returned to the Liberty Stadium on another cold afternoon for an important match between two recently promoted sides, both teams have made an impact in the Premiership – which surprised many people. Norwich, were lying in tenth place in the standings, just one place and two points ahead of Swansea. We knew that winning this match would give us a realistic prospect of staying in the Premiership.

The visitors started the match well; they didn't let us enjoy our usual possession game and soon they were in control. They had several good chances to open the scoreline, but that's football: with our first real chance, Danny Graham scored a quality goal from a great team lead-up. We were heading to the dressing rooms with a goal in-hand, but we knew that it was going to be a complex match, and one in which we were unable to maintain the long periods of possession that we were used to. But the most important thing was to win, come what may.

Unfortunately, almost as soon as the second half kicked off, Norwich equalised. And within minutes they scored again. Unbelievable; it was as though we were still in the dressing room: we just didn't react. And to cap it all, they scored a third on the counterattack, with plenty of time still left on the clock. All the signs were that it was going to be a disastrous afternoon. The coach quickly made some changes and, despite our lethargy and lacking the spark we'd shown all season, we didn't throw in the towel.

With just ten minutes of play left, we reduced the gap to 2-3. And the final five minutes were all about Swansea's efforts to force a draw. Our final chance came with a penalty for Graham, but it grazed the post, just wide. It's bad luck, but these things happen in football. There will always be days like this one, where the team isn't quite a hundred percent. But you can't blame anyone for anything; we gave it everything we had and we were unlucky not to have come away with a point. Once again, our fans were amazing. They supported the team to the very end and, despite losing, they applauded us off the pitch. They recognised that it was just a bad day at the office and respected the team's efforts.

We lost a place in the standings, but we continue to be nine points away from the relegation zone with 30 points. I played for the full ninety minutes."

Trip to Tenerife

Following the defeat, we had a week without a match due to the fact we were no longer in the FA Cup. As a result, the club organised a five-day trip to Tenerife for the entire playing and backroom staff. It was a four-hour flight from Bristol to

Tenerife Sur, and we landed at around 7.30pm on Sunday 12th February. Even at that hour you can still enjoy a bit of sun, which surprised some of the Brits because in Swansea it gets dark around 5pm and all the businesses close for the day.

The trip was from Sunday to Thursday, and the idea was to train together in the mornings at the fantastic sport facilities; after that we could take the rest of the day to relax in the pool, take a walk or whatever we fancied doing. The main thing was that we return to Swansea with our batteries recharged and our minds focused on the upcoming game against Stoke. Once settled in the hotel we ate dinner and had our usual meeting, where the plan for the week was discussed. We all then went to rest up ahead of the next day's training.

Monday morning, dressed for training, we went down for breakfast in the hotel restaurant – and what a spread awaited us: bread, tomato, jamon serrano (Spanish ham), croissants, good coffee… How you miss these things when you're living in a country that's so different from your own. Just seeing the sun from my hotel room, shining on the sea, made me want to get to training – but it also made me feel as though I was on holiday. Another plus point was being able to train in short sleeves or even in a sleeveless top. The Spanish players took full advantage of all this; we understand that where there's good weather there's a better quality of life, and we miss that living in the UK.

After the training session, we returned to the hotel to have lunch together and then had the afternoon free to do as we pleased. Many of the lads went for a siesta; others went for a walk. The Spanish contingent decided to make the most of the weather in hammocks around the hotel pool. Although it was cloudy at times, you could still feel the heat in Tenerife Sur, and we stayed by the pool until it was time for dinner. That evening we had a quiz. We were in four teams, and the two losing teams had to pay for dinner for the other two teams in a well-known Japanese restaurant in the city. Unfortunately for the Spaniards, only Orlandi got away without paying; although he was in a somewhat controversial group!

On Tuesday it was more of the same: training in the morning, free afternoon by the pool and Japanese food for dinner before heading out for a few drinks. The coach gave us

Wednesday off, and once again different groups of players went off to do different things. Some went to play golf; others went to the water park. The Spaniards once again opted to relax by the hotel pool, and later we went for a walk into town to buy gifts for our families. By chance, we bumped into Isabel Pantoja and her son Francisco, known in Spain as Paquirrin. Isabel Pantoja is a very famous folk singer in Spain, and both she and her son are always in the tabloid press. We were about to have our photos taken with them, but we felt a bit uncomfortable. There were rumours at the time that she was about to be sent to prison for money laundering. We weren't used to asking people for photos; usually people asked us.

All good things must come to an end, and usually very quickly. It was already Thursday; we had training in the morning, lunch at the hotel and then we left for the airport. It was another four-hour flight and then two hours on a coach to Swansea. By 10.30pm we were all in our respective homes with our families, and I was very happy to see my partner, Nikki, my two sons, Bailey and Angel Noah, and my newborn daughter who we finally named Isabella Rose."

Match Day 26 (26/02/2012): Stoke 2 - Swansea 0

Another poor result for the only Welsh team in the Premier League. In the duel between two completely opposite styles, the more physical, direct, vertical football won out and took full advantage of the set pieces, including throw-ins from the other side's area.

- Stoke: Begović, Wilkinson, Shawcross, Upson, Wilson, Shotton (Palacios, 88), Whelan, Whitehead, Etherington (Jerome, 68), Walters, Crouch (Delap, 88).
- Swansea: Tremmel, Rangel, Caulker, Williams, Taylor, Britton, Allen, Sigurdsson, Dyer (Moore, 71), Sinclair (McEachran, 71), Graham.
- Goals: 1-0, Upson (24); 2-0, Crouch (39).

"With Stoke playing Valencia in Mestalla in the European League mid-week, we played this game on Sunday. Legend has it that Stoke's ground is one of the most difficult to play in, and not because of the quality of the football they play; in fact, the total opposite. This team's strengths lie in their aggressive, powerful style of play, the way they play the ball straight to Peter Crouch, the way they try to get the most out of all free-kicks, throw-ins and corners to bombard the opposing team's area and take advantage of the height and power that most of Stoke's players have on their side. We have our own game and we started well. We controlled the first thirty minutes of the first half and we had a clear chance on goal from Sinclair, who sent the ball flying over the goalpost from the penalty area after a great assist from Dyer. But suddenly Stoke, who until now hadn't done much of anything, found themselves with a corner. They soon scored, Upson heading in the ball to give Stoke an undeserved 1-0 lead – but that's the nature of football.

We continued attacking but without success in the last few metres. And once again Stoke scored, this time from a throw-in so long and powerful that it felt like a corner, with Crouch converting for 2-0 before half-time. It's difficult to overcome a 2-0 deficit away from home, but we never gave up. We tried everything we could in the second half, but got no joy. We felt we should have had a penalty for a foul on Sigurdsson, and a shot from Caulker hit the bar. The final result: 2-0 to Stoke and our second successive defeat.

My notes

1. Despite two losses and falling to fourteenth position in the standings, we're still nine points above the relegation zone with 30 points and a positive goal average.
2. The Swansea fans who travelled to Stoke to support the team were great, as usual.
3. The next match is crucial: we face Wigan away, and a victory there will take us a step closer to safety. And I'll let you know how it feels to play against my ex-manager, Roberto Martínez.

Match Day 27 (03/03/2012): Wigan 0 - Swansea 2

Swansea improve their away record and secure a brave victory against a Wigan side which included former Swans Roberto Martínez, Jordi Gómez and Iñaki Bergara.

- Wigan: Al-Habsi, Boyce, Alcaraz, Caldwell, Figueroa (Rodallega, 68), Beausejour, McCarthy, McArthur (Diamé, 45), Jordi Gómez, Di Santo, Sammon (Moses, 45).
- Swansea: Vorm, Rangel, Caulker, Williams, Taylor, Britton, Allen, Sigurdsson (Tate, 63), Dyer, Sinclair, Graham (Moore, 75).
- Goals: 0-1, Sigurdsson (45); 0-2, Sigurdsson (54).

"This was an important match for both teams. For Wigan, it was a big opportunity to close the gap between us in the standings and pull themselves out of the relegation zone; for Swansea, it was a chance to extend our advantage over the bottom-of-the-league sides and take a step towards safety. Plus, it is always special to play against a team managed by a man who left such a mark on the careers of so many Swansea players, myself included.

The home side started the match well and, in the first ten minutes, they put us under pressure and had a couple of chances, although we were never really in too much danger. After that flurry of activity, we began to dominate in midfield, opening up the field of play and closing Wigan down in their own half for large periods, as well as creating clear chances to get on the score sheet. But the Wigan keeper, Al-Habsi, kept us out time and time again. It looked like we were heading to half-time goalless, but in the last minute Sigurdsson curled the ball towards the net, and Al-Habsi was unable to get a hand to it. Half-time score: 0-1. Once again, Wigan dominated the opening few minutes of the second half, but we knew how to keep the Wigan forwards in check. A few minutes later, and with us once again in charge of the match, a superb direct free-kick by Sigurdsson from twenty-five yards out slipped through to the left of Al-Habsi, giving Sigurdsson his second goal of the match and putting us 0-2 up.

They threw everything at us then; the home fans were whistling at their players and the manager. But a tackle between Nathan Dyer and Jordi Gómez resulted in Dyer receiving a red card. The referee deemed that Dyer had gone in for a high tackle and with his studs up, and he considered it to be a dangerous tackle. I don't think it was a straight red card but you have to accept the referee's decision. With twenty minutes left and us down to ten men, we had to play more defensively. Wigan enjoyed much more of the possession but couldn't create any real chances, only shots from outside the area, corners and free-kicks that all came to nothing. Final whistle: 0-2.

We were elated with the victory: it was three crucial points. We had come from two consecutive defeats and we knew that if we'd lost to Wigan we would put one foot in the relegation battle zone. But winning gave us an 11-point advantage with eleven matches to go.

My notes

1. Yet again I have to mention the support we received from the 4,000 Swansea fans who made the journey to Wigan. What more can you ask for? It was a perfect weekend.
2. I had the honour of being able to talk to my former teammates who now play for Wigan, such as Iñaki Bergara and Jordi Gómez, and I had a few minutes with Roberto Martínez to talk a little bit about the day and wish each other the best for the rest of the season.
3. Things are looking up, but we need to continue working at it."

Match Day 28 (11/03/2012): Swansea 1 - Manchester City 0

Yet another huge win for Swansea at the Liberty Stadium. Destiny brought the Swans another glorious afternoon in which they overcame Premiership leaders, Manchester City. The Spanish contingent were represented by Silva for Manchester

City and Rangel for the Swans. The right-back is subsequently recognised by FourFourTwo magazine as one of the most influential players of the match. Sinclair missed a penalty seven minutes into the first half, but the goal from substitute Moore, just minutes after coming off the bench, sealed the victory.

- Swansea: Vorm, Rangel, Caulker, Williams, Taylor, Britton, Allen, Routledge (Monk, 88), Sigurdsson, Sinclair, Graham (Moore, 79).
- Manchester City: Hart, Richards, Kolo Touré, Savić, Clichy, De Jong (Johnson, 84), Barry (Agüero, 38), Nasri, Yaya Touré, Silva (Džeko, 87), Balotelli
- Goals: 1-0, Moore (83).

"Well, what can I say? We took on a big team and won, as a result their nearest rival, Manchester United, took the top spot in the Premiership. It was one of those games that just about everyone thinks you're going to lose. And it's to be expected; they were the Premiership leaders, after all, with the biggest budget in the Premier League, in Europe and maybe even in the world! It's such a big team, you could make two teams out of it – and both of those could win the Premier title.

There was a great atmosphere at the Liberty Stadium as the match started. And within five minutes, Swansea had a penalty. But for once, our great penalty-taker, Sinclair, couldn't get the ball past Joe Hart; he'd scored fourteen penalties for Swansea in his time and this was the first time he'd missed since he came to the club. The match continued and we seemed to be dominating in midfield, keeping the lines high up the pitch and well open. City, on the other hand, were suffering at having to chase the ball from one side of the pitch to the other. The half-time score was 0-0.

It was more of the same in the second half, although City did launch two good counterattacks in an attempt to put themselves ahead, but they were unable to convert. However, we exploited a loose ball from City to mount a counterattack on the right touchline and Luke Moore – who'd only come off the bench minutes before – headed the ball home perfectly from a great Wayne Routledge cross to make it 1-0. City kept pushing to the very end and even had a goal disallowed for offside. But we defended brilliantly for those final ten minutes. We recorded our eleventh clean sheet of the season and another David vs. Goliath win at fortress Liberty. It was also another crucial three points in the fight for survival, with ten matches remaining."

Match Day 29 (17/03/2012):
Fulham 0 - Swansea 3

Swansea forged ahead with their third consecutive win, with two away wins and a home victory under their belt. This time they easily overcame Fulham, with Iceland international, Sigurdsson, one of Brendan Rodgers key players in this latter half of the season, scoring a brace. Despite having only arrived in the January transfer window, Sigurdsson had immediately fitted into the team, gelling perfectly in front of the pairing of Britton and Allen and impressing with his scoring ability.

- Fulham: Schwarzer, Kelly, Senderos, Hangeland, Riise, B. Ruiz (Duff, 54), Dembélé, Diarra (Murphy, 72), Dempsey, Johnson (Frei, 67), Pogrebnyak.
- Swansea: Vorm, Rangel, Caulker, Williams, Taylor (Tate, 90), Britton, Allen, Routledge, Sigurdsson (Gower, 90), Sinclair, Graham (Moore, 90).
- Goals: 0-1, Sigurdsson (36); 0-2, Sigurdsson (66); 0-3, Allen (77).

"Almost certain now to remain in the Premiership and with our confidence sky high, we arrived at Craven Cottage to face Fulham. It's another important match as both teams are on the same points (36) and placed tenth and eleventh in the league. A win from either side would move them up to eighth place. The match started very open, with both teams clearly coming out to win the encounter. In fact, Fulham were the more dangerous team in the first few minutes. And that's to be expected: they're a strong team at home. But we survived those dangerous first fifteen minutes when the home team usually applies the most pressure. After that, it was Swansea all the way in all areas of the game: possession, applying pressure, creating goal-scoring opportunities, looking dangerous in the box. Sinclair got past his marker and had a shot on goal: later, after a great cross from

Routledge at the far post, Sinclair dinked the ball to Sigurdsson who headed it in to give us a 0-1 advantage.

We'd done the hardest bit, and we were expecting Fulham to come back hard in the second half. But we came out after the break to play even better than in the first half. Fulham could only watch as we passed the ball from one side of the pitch to the other. You could see the players completely shocked at how difficult it is to keep going after the ball and yet hardly get a touch of it. And after another good bit of play, Sigurdsson scored his second, much deserved, goal. Although there was still plenty of time left on the clock, we focused on doing what we love best and what we practice every day in training: keeping the ball and playing in triangulations. In the end, and following an error by Fulham, Joe Allen took advantage to score and make it 0-3.

We left the pitch to a standing ovation from the Fulham crowd (just like what happened at Liverpool) and with a feeling that was even slightly nerve-wracking: Swansea City, the team everyone thought would likely be relegated at the start of the season, was in eighth position in the Premier League, just three points behind Liverpool and playing great football. I played the full ninety minutes.

My notes

1. Possession: Fulham 32% – Swansea 68%
2. Third consecutive victory and clean sheet.
3. It was our twelfth clean sheet of the season.
4. I have to mention Fabrice Muamba who collapsed on the pitch during the Tottenham–Bolton match and had to be rushed to a London hospital in a critical condition. After two worrying days, he was able to recognise people and talk a little, but it's clear that the guy escaped death after a heart problem. These situations force you to look at life and at football from a completely different perspective; you realise that we're all vulnerable to these types of tragedies and that they seem to happen more and more often. Sending my very best wishes to Fabrice and his family."

Match Day 30 (24/03/2012): Swansea 0 - Everton 2

This match arrived in the middle of a feeling of euphoria at Swansea, with three consecutive victories placing them comfortably in the top-half of the table. The fans were hoping another victory would see them equal Liverpool in the standings, but Everton dug in with both feet at the Liberty to score twice in the second half.

- Swansea: Vorm, Rangel, Caulker, Williams, Taylor, Britton, Allen, Routledge (Lita, 71), Sigurdsson, Sinclair (McEachran, 72), Graham (Moore, 71).
- Everton: Howard, Hibbert, Jagielka, Distin, Baines, Osman, Gibson (Heitinga, 84), P. Neville, Pienaar, Cahill (Fellaini, 58), Jelavić (Stracqualursi, 82).
- Goals: 0-1, Baines (59); 0-2, Jelavić (76).

"On an unseasonably warm afternoon, we faced Everton at home. It was another interesting match; we were eighth in the league – the highest we'd been all season – and a win could have put Swansea on the same points as Liverpool in seventh place. That was an incredible feeling because only the Premier's biggest teams now remained above us in the standings. In addition, there had been much talk all week in the press and among the fans about the possibility of us qualifying to play in Europe next season, but the team knew that our primary objective was to avoid relegation and secondary to that was to finish as high in the standings as we could.

Everton started the game well, immediately applying pressure. We had to work hard to get the ball out from behind but Everton were hardly dangerous. And that's how the first half played out. We had less possession than we're used to because of the tactical system employed by David Moyes to starve us of the ball. Despite that, both Graham and Sigurdsson had several chances, but without success. Half-time score: 0-0.

Everything changed in the second half. Everton continued to apply their stranglehold, and we suffered from our own inaccuracies when it came to building from behind. It had all the makings of a no-score draw until Leighton Baines scored a magnificent goal from a free-kick on the edge of the area to give Everton the deserved lead. We didn´t give up and tried everything we could, but Jelavić scored to make it 0-2. Everton were playing the better football, were better positioned and had clearer ideas. With us on the attack and pushing hard for a draw, Everton could have netted four goals that day but Michel Vorm saved us from catastrophe. We can draw many conclusions from the day, but I will stick with the positives.

This was our third home defeat of the season, but it's a match that will ultimately help us to learn how to improve our football when teams come to Swansea and play in a way that prevents us from building from behind. We shouldn't forget, either, that we were playing a good team with many experienced players. We're still top ten in the standings, closer to playing in Europe than to the relegation zone. Special mention goes to a group of ten people from my hometown, Sant Carles de la Rapita, who came to Swansea that weekend to watch the match live. It was very emotional to see a group of ten shirts emblazoned with 'Rangel 22' in the stands. I would like to thank them for coming and, although they didn't bring me luck in the match, they were great company."

Match Day 31 (01/04/ 2012): Tottenham 3 - Swansea 1

"After the defeat at home to Everton, we entered another festive period in which we had to play three matches in a week and a half, all televised on the UK's most popular cable channel, Sky Sports. The first of these matches was a hard nut to crack: Tottenham, the club rumoured to be Brendan Rodgers' next managerial post for the upcoming season.

- Tottenham: Friedel, Walker, Gallas, Kaboul, Assou-Ekotto (Rose, 88), Van der Vaart (Livermore, 85), Sandro (Lennon, 71), Modrić, Parker, Bale, Adebayor.
- Swansea: Vorm, Rangel, Monk, Williams, Taylor; Britton, Allen (Gower, 90); Routledge (Dyer, 71), Sigurdsson, Sinclair; Graham (Moore, 79).
- Goals: 1-0, Van der Vaart (19); 1-1, Sigurdsson (59); 2-1, Adebayor (73); 3-1, Adebayor (86).

For the first of our three matches we headed to Tottenham's stronghold, White Hart Lane, which played host to Champions League football at the time. The home side won 3-1 despite the fact that we faced them down right up until the last fifteen minutes of the match, when we were drawing 1-1. I have to say what a great match Gareth Bale had; I was tasked with marking him and he amply demonstrated that he was a player destined for a much bigger club. In fact, he's probably the most difficult opponent I'd encountered this season. I should also mention Emmanuel Adebayor who headed-in both of Tottenham's goals in the dying minutes of the match."

Match Day 32 (06/04/ 2012):
Swansea 0 - Newcastle 2

The next match was almost as difficult as visiting White Hart Lane, despite the fact Swansea were playing at home. Newcastle were having a phenomenal run towards the end of the season, largely thanks to January transfer window recruit, Demba Cissé, who proved decisive against Swansea with a brace of goals.

- Swansea: Vorm, Rangel, Caulker, Williams, Taylor; Britton, Allen; Dyer (Sinclair, 66), Sigurdsson, Routledge; Moore (Graham, 66).
- Newcastle: Krul, Simpson, Williamson, Perch, Santon, Tioté (Taylor, 45), Gutierrez, Cabaye (Gosling, 74), Ben Arfa, Cissé, Demba Ba (Ferguson, 59).
- Goals: 0-1, Cissé (5); 0-2, Cissé (69).

"Our next match was at home to Newcastle, another team in the top half of the table that was fighting to get into the top four or to stay in the top six. The result was 0-2 which doesn't reflect the fact that statistically we were the better team, with most of the possession, the better chances and more shots on goal. But the Magpies' big winter signing, Cissé, showed why he is making history, ably taking advantage to convert the only two chances Newcastle had in the match."

Match Day 33 (11/04/2012): QPR 3 - Swansea 0

QPR were fighting for survival in the final stages of the Premier season, something that was not helpful for a Swansea side that couldn't prevent its fourth successive defeat. The result prompted some nervousness for fans and players alike.

- QPR: Kenny, Onuoha, Ferdinand, Hill, Taïwo, Mackie (Bothroyd, 78), Barton, Buzsáky, Diakité, Taarabt (T. Smith, 88), Zamora (Wright-Phillips, 78).
- Swansea: Vorm, Rangel, Caulker, Williams, Taylor (Tate, 45); Britton (Moore, 62), Allen; Routledge (Dyer, 45), Sigurdsson, Sinclair, Graham.
- Goals: 1-0, Barton (45); 2-0, Mackie (55); 3-0, Buzsáky (67).

"The third and final game in front of the cameras took place at Loftus Road, home to QPR who, at that point, were firmly in the relegation zone and fighting for survival in the Premiership. Despite having lost the two preceding matches, the team had played well against far bigger teams who were active in Europe. On this occasion, our opponent was an inferior team compared to those we'd recently faced. Sadly, we lost 3-0 in an embarrassing performance; it was the worst we'd played all season and it gave the teams in the relegation zone some hope. We'd taken zero points from the twelve available, let in ten goals and scored just once. In addition, it was beginning to look as though 39 points were not going to be enough to ensure survival. The fans and the local press started to have some concerns. But as a team we knew it was just a poor run of results and we had to win the next match to end it."

Match Day 34 (14/04/ 2012): Swansea 3 - Blackburn 0

Swansea needed to score some points; although their position above the relegation zone was enough to avoid the onset of panic, it's always dangerous if a negative run of results continues for too long. Their opponents were a Blackburn side that was going through an even worse period of results.

- Swansea: Vorm, Rangel (Monk, 89), Caulker, Williams, Taylor; Britton (Gower, 70), Allen; Dyer, Sigurdsson, Sinclair, Graham (Lita, 85).
- Blackburn: Robinson, Orr, Dann, Hanley (Formica, 45), Lowe, N'Zonzi, Hoilett (Modeste, 56), Pedersen, Dunn, Olsson, Yakubu (Goodwillie, 61).
- Goals: 1-0, Sigurdsson (37); 2-0, Dyer (43); 3-0, Dann (own goal, 63).

"The next match was at home against Blackburn Rovers, a team that was also fighting for survival and, like us, was coming into this match having lost four in a row. This time we didn't let the fans down, winning 3-0 in convincing fashion, with goals coming from Sigurdsson and Nathan Dyer. What's more, the victory gave us almost mathematical certainty to remain in the Premiership with four matches remaining. It will be interesting to see in these final few matches whether we've just had a good campaign or a spectacular season. Coming up we've got Bolton (in twelfth position) away from home, Wolverhampton (in twentieth place) at home, Manchester United (League leaders) away and Liverpool (eighth) at home. The results will speak for themselves.

P.S. To finish today I would just like to mention our great winter signing, Gylfi Sigurdsson, on loan from Bundesliga side, Hoffenheim. He has really come into his own in this second half of the season; his goals and the quality of his touches of the ball, as well as the way he moves within the lines, have made him stand out. He was named best Premier League player for the month of March."

Match Day 35 (21/04/ 2014):
Bolton 1 - Swansea 1

The preceding victory eased the nerves at Swansea, who were now looking to finish the season as high as they could in the table. On this away visit to Bolton the team remained faithful to its playing style with sixty-two percent of the possession, but lacked a bit of luck and shots on target (twenty-six attempts but only four on goal).

- Bolton: Bogdan, Steinsson, Wheater, Ream, Ricketts, Miyaichi (N'Gog, 65), Davies (Klasnić, 79), Reo-Coker, Petrov, Eagles, M. Davies (Vela, 90).
- Swansea: Vorm, Rangel, Caulker, A. Williams, Taylor; Britton, Allen; Dyer (Moore, 29), Sigurdsson, Sinclair; Graham (Lita, 79).
- Goals: 0-1, Sinclair (5); 1-1, Eagles (14).

"It was yet another important match at the Reebok Stadium, home to Bolton Wanderers who were in the relegation zone. They played their hearts out and, all things considered, for us it was good to secure a draw as it was not an easy match by any means.

We couldn't have got off to a better start: five minutes in and Scott Sinclair scored, having cut inside to curl the ball into the top left corner of the Bolton goal. From then on, we continued to dominate but a counterattack from former Manchester United player, Chris Eagles, brought Bolton level. The scoreline remained 1-1 at half-time.

Just like the coach predicted, the second half was a test of time and patience; we could already see that Bolton were lacking in tactical discipline. Essentially, Swansea completely controlled the second half; we created many chances, with lots of movement from Gylfi Sigurdsson – the Icelander receiving the ball between the lines whenever he wanted it – and chances from Danny Graham, including a shot that hit the crossbar. We were clearly in a class of our own when in possession of the ball; Scott Sinclair was all over the left flank, but the winning goal never came.

The 1-1 draw was a bitter pill to swallow considering the great football we'd played. But it was another point and put us on forty-three points – ahead of Norwich and twelfth in the league with three matches to go. The next match would be at home against the already relegated Wolverhampton Wanderers – where former Swan goalkeeper Dorus de Vries now played."

Match Day 36 (28/04/ 2012): Swansea 4 - Wolverhampton 4

Both teams enjoyed a goal-fest, with eight goals scored from thirteen shots on goal. The first came quickly from Orlandi, who also provided an assist in his return to the starting XI. Rangel didn't make an appearance today due to an accident at home.

- Swansea: Vorm; Caulker, Monk, Williams; Allen, Sigurdsson, Britton, Orlandi (Taylor, 45); Dyer, Graham (Moore, 82), Sinclair.
- Wolverhampton: De Vries, Foley, Stearman, Berra, Ward, Kightly, Henry, Edwards, Jarvis (Hunt, 72), Doyle, Fletcher (Ebans-Blake, 76).
- Goals: 1-0, Orlandi (1); 2-0, Allen (4); 3-0, Dyer (15); 3-1, Fletcher (28); 4-1, Graham (31); 4-2, Jarvis (33); 4-3, Edwards (54); 4-4, Jarvis (69).

"We return to the Liberty Stadium with a relatively easy game in that we were facing a Wolves side that had become the first side to be officially relegated. There was also a face we all knew in the Wolves goal: goalkeeper Dorus de Vries played four seasons for Swansea, which included two league promotions, but had decided last summer that it was time for a change.

Unfortunately, I wasn't able to play against Wolves as I'd had a little accident at home: I fell down the stairs with my son in my arms on Thursday night. Thankfully, my son was fine, but I hurt my left leg, although it's nothing serious.

Making the starting XI for only the second time this season was my friend Andrea Orlandi, who scored the Swans' first goal of the match with just twenty-three seconds on the clock. It was his first Premiership goal and the quickest goal to be scored in the league all season. We couldn't have started any better. We continued attacking and after just thirty minutes were already 3-0 up and clearly dominating play. But a defensive lapse saw Wolves score an unexpected goal. We reacted well though, scoring again to make it 4-1. It looked like game over for Wolves, although the visitors did reduce the gap to 4-2 just before half-time.

The second half was a completely different game. We found it difficult to maintain control in midfield and Wolves kept moving forward dangerously. When the scoreline reached 4-3, the doubts were starting to creep in at the Liberty. We tried to fight back, but we couldn't keep hold of the ball – and Wolves were playing like they were in a Champions League final. Maybe they felt they had something to prove, even though they were already relegated. And in the dying minutes they manufactured a fourth goal to secure a 4-4 draw. It was a match that brought much disappointment in the dressing room because of what had happened but, at the same time, much happiness, because mathematically we were now safe. With two matches to go to the end of the season, we can just enjoy them and try our best to finish in the top ten. We face Manchester United next, in a match that could decide the Premier League winners, and we then play Liverpool at home in the last match of the season where the curtain will fall on a great first season for Swansea in the Premier League.

P.S. I'm back training with the team so I will be fit for the coming weekend."

Match Day 37 (06/05/2012): Manchester United 2 - Swansea 0

Àngel Rangel, Fede Bessone and the rest of the Swansea team probably never dreamed that they would one day be staying in a five-star hotel in the centre of Manchester the night before facing Manchester United at Old Trafford. Especially those players who just four years before were playing in League One. The Welsh side, already mathematically safe in the Premier League, could just enjoy the match without worrying about adding to their points tally. And despite the loss, the overall feeling was one of satisfaction because many were expecting a crushing defeat for Swansea.

- Manchester United: De Gea, Jones, Smalling, Ferdinand (Rafael, 88), Evra, Valencia, Carrick, Scholes (Cleverley, 68), Young, Hernandez, Rooney (Berbatov, 79).

- Swansea: Vorm; Rangel, Caulker (Tate, 90), Williams, Taylor, Gower (Britton, 45), Allen, Dyer (Moore, 71), Sigurdsson, Sinclair, Graham.
- Goals: 1-0, Scholes (28); 2-0, Young (41).

"Ahead of the match at Old Trafford, I went for a walk in Manchester city centre, ate and watched video analysis of Manchester United in our pre-match meeting. Fede Bessone came with me for the walk. He was feeling optimistic about the match because he trusted in his teammates – and because he wanted Manchester City to win the Premiership title. United played us knowing the scoreline of its rivals, who were playing Newcastle.

We want to enjoy the experience of playing a match at this hallowed ground, with its amazing pitch, despite the testing opponents we are facing. But it wasn't to be: we lost 2-0, with both goals coming in the first half. In the second half, we didn't let in any goals and, what's more, we had a couple of chances ourselves. At this level, you have to take your chances when they come because just one goal can inspire fear in the opposition. If you can't do that against Manchester United, they will make you pay. But we are happy enough. We did ourselves justice and we left Manchester satisfied that we would live to see another season in the Premier League.

One thing that happened on the trip was that we had to stop at the services because the electricity wasn't working on the team bus!"

Match Day 38 (13/05/2012): Swansea 1 - Liverpool 0

The last match of the season served as a tribute from Swansea to its fans after ensuring survival in the Premiership – in spite of the low expectations many in football had for Swansea at the start of the season. The memorable win rounded off an historic debut season for the first Welsh side in the Premier League, and went some way to erasing the memories of the side's recent poor run of results, having only taken five points from the twenty-four available. Despite that period of poor form,

Swansea achieved a creditable eleventh in the standings, with 43 points, which is no mean feat.

- Swansea: Vorm, Rangel, Caulker, Williams, Taylor, Britton, Allen, Dyer (Routledge, 79), Sigurdsson (Gower, 89), Sinclair, Graham.
- Liverpool: Doni, Johnson, Carragher, Agger, Kelly, Downing (Bellamy, 61), Henderson, Shelvey, Rodriguez (Kuyt, 73), Suarez, Carroll.
- Goals: 1-0, Graham (86).

"A fantastic victory against a big rival – and at home, to boot – meant we finished off this historic debut season in the Premier League in style. Our fans enjoyed the win and we did a lap of honour after the match to celebrate our survival in the Premier League and our impressive season. When all is said and done, the overall result for thirty-eight matches is a positive one, both collectively and personally, in terms of league classification and our playing quality.

When we were promoted from the Championship there were many who didn´t think much of our chances of survival, including someone who said that seeing Elvis Presley alive was more likely. That's why our manager, Brendan Rodgers, asked the fans to come to this last match of the season dressed as the 'King'.

Although Liverpool hadn't been having their best season, they were still an opponent you had to be wary of. Beating them is very special indeed. In the first half we had several good chances, including a shot from Allen and a Sigurdsson free-kick. In the second half, an overhead kick from Andy Carroll was saved magnificently by Vorm. Everything was pointing to a 0-0 impasse, but with four minutes to go Graham scored the winning goal from my low pass into the middle of the area.

Now we can enjoy the summer break, recharge our batteries and get ready for another challenging season in the Premier League. I will take the time to go and visit my family and attend my first camp for children. But I can't go without first saying thank you to everyone who reads this diary; it has been a pleasure for me to write it and share my experience of my first season in the Premier League."

The 2011-2012 Premier League title went to Manchester City for the first time in forty-four years. They won their third league title in a dramatic end to the season. Queens Park Rangers were winning 1-2 at Manchester City, with ninety minutes gone; Manchester City needed to win to snatch victory from Manchester United, who were winning 0-1 at Sunderland. But in stoppage time City produced two minutes of pure magic that the Etihad Stadium will never forget; the stands roared with triumph as Džeko and Agüero scored in the ninety-first and ninety-third minute, respectively. According to the data statistic specialists, OPTA, Swansea stood out for various reasons during the season. Swansea's fifty-six percent possession throughout the season was beaten only by Arsenal's fifty-nine percent, with Arsenal also the highest for completed passes, along with Manchester United and Manchester City (all three recorded eighty-five percent completion rates).

On an individual level, Rangel was the player with the most touches of the ball (3231) in the Premier League, and was also ranked fifth in the league for number of passes (2273), outdone only by his teammate Ashley Williams (ranked first with 2594), Modrić (Tottenham), Yaya Touré (Manchester City) and Arteta (Arsenal). And as if that wasn't enough, Rangel was placed fourth in the league for number of interceptions. Get in!

CHAPTER 10

2012-2013: Swansea 4.0, the first major title

One of the biggest teams in England used Swansea as its model for a playing philosophy that would help it recapture its glory days. In May 2012, Liverpool was in need of a new manager and had whittled the candidates down to just two: Roberto Martínez, the visionary behind "Swanselona" and Brendan Rodgers, who cemented the undertaking begun by the Spaniard in 2007 and engineered Swansea's promotion to the Premier League. It was probably the biggest compliment imaginable for a club that, just a few years earlier, had endured a turbulent period a million miles away from the Premier League.

Rodgers' Exit

Wigan had given Roberto Martínez permission to speak with Liverpool's owners. Dave Whelan didn't want to lose the Spaniard, but he'd always said that if a big club came a-calling he wouldn't stand in his way. Just a few days earlier on the 25th May 2012, a fan had published photographs on Twitter, bringing the issue out into the open. The photos showed Roberto Martínez strolling down a Miami street with Liverpool owner, John Henry.

Hours later, Dave Whelan confirmed that Martínez had interrupted his holiday in the Caribbean to meet with Henry. It looked like an agreement was close, and the Wigan chairman gave him seven days to make a decision. He didn't have to wait that long. On the 29th May 2012, Wigan announced that Roberto would be staying with the Latics.

That same night, the Swansea chairman, Huw Jenkins, received a call from Liverpool's American owners. The day before, Jenkins had denied that Brendan Rodgers was due to meet with them. But in football, especially when it comes to transfers, it's best not to say anything; never say never. On the 18th May 2012, Swansea had issued a statement saying it was pleased to confirm that its manager had declined the opportunity to discuss the role left vacant by Kenny Dalglish. It wasn't the first time that Rodgers had been unequivocal in the face of reports that he was moving to another club. Months earlier, when he had been linked to Tottenham, he dealt with the rumours decisively, saying: "Swansea is where I want to be."

While the rumours continued that Liverpool was signing the Northern Irishman, several people spoke out against the deal. The most vocal was the former France player, Marcel Desailly, who warned Brendan Rodgers not to move from his current role, saying: "It's a shame to leave your baby on the street." But the manager didn't pay him much heed and, on the 30th May 2012, officially accepted the challenge of managing the Reds. Rodgers appreciated that he was being offered a long-term project with the aim of playing attractive football.

Rodgers pleaded for understanding from the Swans fans, explaining that he couldn't turn down an offer from one of the biggest clubs in the Premier League. Swansea was going to lose another manager, but the deal would bring around £4 million into the coffers.

Various media reports suggested that Roberto Martínez had declined an offer from Liverpool because they would not accept his demands for complete managerial control – with everything that that entails in British football. Liverpool's preference was for the new coach to delegate certain functions to other people, which Rodgers was apparently not against. There was talk of partnering him with a director of football, a role that Dutchman Louis Van Gaal was keen to take up.

The search for a replacement

The bets were on in the British press as to the likely candidates, with various names being bandied around, such as Gus Poyet (Brighton), Ian Holloway (Blackpool), Chris Hughton (Birmingham), Michael Laudrup (ex-Mallorca) and Graeme Jones (Roberto Martínez 's assistant at Wigan and at Swansea). Lee Trundle publicly gave his support to the latter candidate, but the transfer never came off. Marcel Desailly, another in the frame, didn't seem to want to make the move either.

The Spanish football journalist Guillem Balagué revealed that Swansea had a dossier on ten managers with links to the Spanish La Liga: "The new manager was going to come from there. And when the current manager leaves, they will once again look for a manager with La Liga experience." According to Balagué, Huw Jenkins spoke with Ernesto Valverde before Michael Laudrup. He also sounded out Luis Enrique. But the possibility that Danish Laudrup was set to become the fourth non-British Swansea manager – after fellow Dane, Jan Mølby; Spaniard, Roberto Martínez; and Portuguese, Paolo Sousa – was gaining traction as time went on.

Although the fans were starting to get restless, Huw Jenkins wasn't overly concerned. In his experience it took, on average, between twelve to fifteen days to sign a new manager. With this same characteristic composure, he took a few days' holiday in Cyprus, leaving the negotiations still ongoing.

Two meetings were enough for Michael Laudrup to sign as manager for two seasons. The agreement was officially announced on the 15th June 2012, the Dane's forty-eighth birthday. During his presentation the following week, he said that he identified with the team's style of play and that his objective was evolution, not revolution. He also admired the calmness and community feel that characterised Swansea and reminisced about how as a child at home in Denmark he used to watch English league matches on television every Saturday.

During the negotiations, he watched numerous team matches and sought advice from some of his compatriots, such as Peter Schmeichel, a former international goalkeeper with a varied career and significant experience in English football. At the same time, he admitted publicly that he did not know much about the team and resorted to humour when he referred to his new home city: "It is a lovely place, although it rains a little more than in Mallorca."

Laudrup's playing career was enough to inspire Swansea supporters and backroom staff alike, but his achievements in the dugout were nothing to be sniffed at either. From 2000-2002, Laudrup was assistant manager to the Denmark manager Morten Olsen. He then went on to manage Danish side Brondby for four seasons, winning four Danish trophies – the Danish Super League, two Danish Cups and a Danish Supercup. He took the reins at Getafe for the 2007-2008 season, leading them to the final of the Copa del Rey and the UEFA Cup quarter finals, where they were beaten in extra time by Bayern Munich. He was sacked from his next club, Spartak Moscow, after just seven months in charge, and went on to save RCD Mallorca from relegation in the last match of the 2012-2011 La Liga season. At the start of the following season, Laudrup resigned citing irreconcilable differences with the director of the Balearic club.

During his first days in charge, and in the face of rumours that he was just using Swansea as a stepping stone to a bigger club, Laudrup professed that he had no ambitions other than to enjoy the season. He also unwittingly showed his zero talent for prediction: "I know managing teams like Getafe, Mallorca or Swansea that I will not win the league or maybe not even the cup. It's other things that have to give you that satisfaction."

Once again, Jenkins had not forgotten John Toshack's ringing endorsement of Laudrup, having worked with him at Sky Sports. "When Huw lost Brendan Rodgers, I told him that Michael liked that style of play and that I thought he could carry it on."

First new signings

No sooner had he arrived than Laudrup had to set himself to the complicated task of preparing the team. Dutchman Ferrie Bodde had left the club at the start of the summer, his injuries having long prevented him from replicating the outstanding form he had displayed under Roberto Martínez. For that reason, his absence was not keenly felt.

In contrast, Laudrup could no longer call on the services of two members of the regular starting line-up from the previous season. Both Steven Caulker and Gylfi Sigurdsson had come to the end of their loan periods and the battle to keep them was fraught with difficulty. The former had fortified a solid defence, forming a superb central partnership with Williams; the latter had brought numerous goals, a physical presence and the injection of pace as the furthest man forward from the midfield line.

But before compiling a shopping list, Laudrup's priority was to get to know the team and the club inside out. The backroom staff were fundamental to that task, including Alan Curtis who subsequently took on a leading first team role in becoming assistant to the Great Dane.

Chairman Huw Jenkins warned that there would have to be a change in the club's policy on signings compared with previous years. The club would now be looking for experienced players who could make an immediate impact, whereas before they had actively recruited youngsters as part of a medium-term plan. Swansea was beginning to need the security of experience to maintain continuity and stay in the elite echelons of football.

Like most managers at a new club, Laudrup turned to players he knew well. And, once everything was signed on the 10th July, he didn't hesitate in confirming his first two signings, who would bring quality and motivation from day one. They were defender Chico Flores – bought from Italian side Genoa for an initial fee of £2 million – and Jonathan de Guzmán – on a season-long loan from Villarreal with the option to make the transfer permanent.

Defender Flores was excited by the prospect of experiencing the Premier League after having played in the Spanish La Liga and the Italian Serie A. Swansea had first piqued midfielder de Guzmán's interest when they beat Manchester City the season before. And he didn't think twice about making the leap when the call came from his former coach.

But, in truth, neither of these two players were Laudrup's first signing. That honour went to Óscar García, a fitness coach he'd worked with at Getafe and Spartak Moscow. "I try and connect the football with the physical preparation; doing everything with the ball," he said. Óscar had never seen his new team play but he had heard of them and knew where to find Wales on a map.

In Swansea's organisation chart, Óscar could call on support from the second team's fitness coach as well as interns from the university for help with data and tests. Straightaway he noticed the demands of British football: "There are fewer pauses, mainly because there are generally fewer fouls than in the continental game, so it's more intense."

Fortunately, language was no barrier in his day-to-day work: "I improved my English in Moscow and my work is not as difficult as Michael's; he needs to be able to provide technical explanations. Most of the time, with a few gestures, footballers understand what they need to do." But the Spaniard recalled how he'd had to sing in front of his new teammates: "I knew it was a custom because I'd had to do it in France. At Swansea I picked "La Bamba" and I think I did it justice. They tried to get Laudrup to do it too, but he hasn't done it yet." Óscar's daily routine included working on the pitch with the players as well as hours in front of the computer preparing for the next sessions.

Pre-season

On the 7th July 2012, the weekend before the start of pre-season training, Àngel Rangel married Nikki, his Welsh fiancée. The first warm-up match was scheduled for the twenty-first of July, just two weeks later. Laudrup's first outing would be at neighbouring team Port Talbot Town. Swansea won convincingly 0-5 with Stephen Dobbie, fresh from his loan spell at Blackpool, scoring a hat-trick.

The team travelled to the United States immediately afterwards to carry out the kind of tour usually reserved for much larger clubs. It was another sign of Swansea's success. Joining them on the trip was the club's third signing of the season, midfielder Miguel Pérez Cuesta. Almost unknown by British fans, the man they call Michu had attracted lots of attention the season before in the Spanish La Liga. The sixteen goals, he scored, for Rayo Vallecano on his debut La Liga season had put him high on the agenda of several big Spanish clubs, but none of them were prepared to match Swansea's £2 million offer.

In the last week of July, on the other side of the Atlantic, Swansea lost 2-1 to the Colorado Rapids, won 0-1 against Ventura County Fusion and drew 2-2 against the San Jose Earthquakes. Jonathan de Guzman, who scored his first goal from a direct free kick against the Rapids, said that the team was still getting to know each other during those first few matches. Chico also got on the score sheet in the United States by scoring the equaliser against San Jose.

After using the games to try out different combinations and resolve any doubts, Laudrup declared publicly that the team would need players who could perform in various positions. And he made it clear that he was aiming for a squad of no more than 22 or 23 players.

In the middle of their American tour, the club issued a statement confirming Liverpool's interest in Joe Allen. The young Swansea academy player, who had been given his debut by Roberto Martínez years before, was now wanted by Brendan Rodgers at Liverpool but, according to the terms of Rodgers's transfer, he couldn't take any Swansea players during his first season. However, there was an exception: he could make an offer for a player if another team had also made a bid. And that's what happened with Allen; he'd caught the eye of other managers. Swansea announced that it would broach the subject with Allen after the Olympic Games where the midfielder, along with Neil Taylor and Scott Sinclair, was competing in London.

The final two friendlies before the start of the Premier League were against Blackpool and Stuttgart. In the first, which was also the official unveiling of Laudrup and his new signings at the Liberty Stadium, Michu rounded off Danny Graham's hat-trick to seal a 4-2 victory. All three new recruits had already experienced scoring in a Swans' shirt ahead of the 3-3 draw against Stuttgart. Israeli striker, Itay Shechter, on a season-long loan from Kaiserslautern, made his debut in this final game before the start of the Premier League.

Days before that match, Joe Allen completed his transfer to Liverpool. While Allen felt he couldn't miss the opportunity to go to such a big club, he was sad about leaving the club where he'd spent his formative years, having joined the academy aged nine. But as a Swansea Jack, Allen was happy that Swansea would receive a record fee – in the region of £15 million – which would undoubtedly help the club grow. Huw Jenkins wished him all the best, but it was a "bitter disappointment" to lose a talented youngster who'd grown up at the club. It was all the more disappointing because Swansea had no pressing financial need to sell. But the chairman went on to say that the club was already getting on with the task of refocusing and reinforcing the squad, the same as when any manager or player left.

Allen's replacement arrived, barely two weeks after his departure, on 24th August 2012. He was Ki Sung-Yueng, and his nickname – the Korean Gerrard – hinted at the type of player he was. "I see a club that is growing and growing, and the style here is very attractive to me," said the twenty-three year-old midfielder, who cost almost a third of the amount received for Allen. Even so, the £6 million price tag for Ki Sung-Yeung was a club record. Just days before the South Korean had signed, two other young players arrived: striker, Jamie Proctor, from Preston; and Arsenal defender Kyle Bartley, who cost Swansea £1 million.

A strong start for Swansea 4.0

On Saturday 18th August 2012, the starting gun sounded for Swansea's 2012-2013 season and the club's centenary – which it would officially celebrate on the 7th September. Expectations for the debut match at Queens Park Rangers were low, not because of the change in management or the loss of players like Allen, but because the players were said to be lacking confidence in Laudrup.

Several media outlets reported that the players had held secret meetings with the chairman to air their grievances about the Dane's training methods and the new style of playing he wanted to impose. According to the players, the progressive intensity of the sessions, which reached their peak every Friday, was the reason for their heaviness and slowness during matches. Laudrup played down the reports. If the meetings took place,

Huw Jenkins would undoubtedly have called Laudrup immediately to get his side of the story.

While the Great Dane didn't believe in the supposed mutiny, he conceded that there were always dissatisfied players in any squad. Later, he admitted holding talks based on psychology with the players. He told them that when things were working well, people were usually more resistant to change. Laudrup felt that if he had arrived at a badly performing club, it would have been easier to introduce the new routines.

Laudrup had already declared that bringing his personal stamp to the club would require an evolution. But Swansea 4.0 wasn't about reducing the possessive style of play; everyone knew the team would suffer if it lost the ball to physically stronger teams. But Laudrup wanted to get away from the pointless passing back-and-forth. He wanted to get to the opposing keeper with more deft and vertical positioning. "Possession has to have an end point. There's no point in playing for playing's sake just so we can say that we had the ball fifty-eight percent of the time but we lost 0-3. Sometimes you need to keep possession, other times you need to attack and sometimes you need to do a bit of both," he said in one of the interviews he gave to El País during the season. Basically, take the game to the opposition and win by attacking upfront. For Laudrup, talk of possession play meant Johan Cruyff, Barcelona and the Spanish national team.

Another significant change in the style of play was the role of the wingers. Laudrup was convinced that a player who knew how to attack and exploit the spaces in the Premier League could be decisive: "I want them to come in and try to find space between lines. They have proved they are so irritating for the other team." The idea was for the wingers to cut in and link up more with the striker rather than stay out wide at the touchline.

In the middle of all these changes, and with so many disagreements in the changing room, nobody could have imagined a better start on the pitch. Not wanting to repeat previously poor starts to the season, Swansea thrashed Queens Park Rangers away 0-5 to top the table after the opening matches on the 18th August 2012. It only took the Swans six shots on goal to secure that scoreline. It was as though the words of Iñaki Bergara had suddenly come true: "In League

One you need five chances to dominate; in the Championship, it's three; in the Premier League if you make one mistake you're screwed."

It took Michu just eight minutes to get on the scoresheet with a low shot in front of goal. It was also the first goal of the 2012-2013 Premier season. In his goal celebration he pretended to pour sidra – the cider from his beloved Asturias which is traditionally poured from high above the pourer's head. The other four goals came in the second half: Michu's second, a perfect curve ball into the net, followed by two goals from Dyer and one from Sinclair. After the match, Laudrup said that the result was a confidence boost for the club and recalled that in the preceding season Swansea hadn't recorded its first league away win until January.

A week later, in the first home game of the season at the Liberty Stadium, the winning streak continued, as did the Spanish influence. Rangel put Swansea ahead and Michu became the Premiership's leading goal scorer with his third goal in two games. Graham rounded off the victory to make it 3-0 against West Ham. Just as in the season opener, Chico, Rangel and Michu made the starting XI, but neither Orlandi nor Bessone figured in either of the two opening games.

Swansea ended the extraordinary August run with another victory at home, this time winning 3-1 against Barnsley in the first round of the Football League Cup, which that year had become the Capital One Cup through a new sponsorship deal. A few days later, in early September, Sunderland took advantage of their only two on target to end Swansea's perfect start to the season with a 2-2 draw at the Liberty Stadium. Once again, Bergara's words had come true. Michu, who was rested for the Capital One Cup game, rescued the point with his fourth goal in three games.

Departures

Worse than the score draw was the red card for Chico; he would now miss the next three matches on suspension. But even worse than that was the serious ankle injury suffered by left-back Neil Taylor which prompted Swansea to search for a replacement outside the transfer window. Laudrup would settle on Dutch player Dwight Tiendalli, who was to be a free agent as of mid-September.

The summer transfer deadline had closed at midnight the night before the Sunderland match. There had been lots of movement, with more players going out than signings coming into the Welsh outfit.

On the 31st August 2012, Swansea signed its most expensive player yet, just surpassing the £6 million paid for South Korean player, Ki, a few weeks earlier. The identity of this last signing wasn't a surprise; it was an open secret that Pablo Hernández was on Laudrup's wishlist. The Spanish international transferred from Valencia and had previously played under Laudrup at Getafe.

A winger who could play on the left or the right, Pablo Hernández was a replacement for Scott Sinclair, who had transferred to Manchester City. The sale of Sinclair, the hero who scored a hat-trick at Wembley to secure Swansea's promotion, earned the club £8 million, including add-ons, meaning that Swansea were still in profit after buying his replacement. Sinclair, who had a goal-scoring average of 28 goals in 82 league matches for Swansea, had refused to sign a new deal offered by the club. As he was in the last year of his contract, Swansea chose to sell him rather than risk losing him on a free transfer the following summer.

Sinclair was by no means the only player to leave before the transfer deadline. On the 31st August, Stephen Dobbie, Andrea Orlandi and Fede Bessone also left. The first two signed for Brighton in the Championship, while the Argentinian signed for Swindon Town in League One.

Orlandi, who had clocked up seventy-nine league appearances in five seasons, was leaving Wales almost exactly five years since he'd become a Swan thanks to that fax he had sent from an opticians in Barcelona. Only this time he signed his new contract well before the midnight deadline.

During his first hours as an ex-Swans player, he talked openly about his feelings for the club: "It's exactly five years since I first joined Swansea in League One. I was a twenty-three -year-old with long hair then. Now I'm leaving with short hair, a baby and the club in the Premier League. I have loved this club from the first day I arrived, and I will always love it. I may not be a Swansea player, but I will always be a Swansea supporter – 'always a Jack' as they say here." He also said that he was confident that he had given his all for the club, despite having had some bad luck with injuries: "I'll always be able to come back to Swansea with my head held high and a smile," he said.

At the end of his first season at Brighton, Orlandi was disappointed that he'd not had any opportunities while Laudrup was in charge: "I also feel a bit angry because I was let go by a manager who had just arrived. The history of the club and of each and every player didn't mean anything to him. I didn't even have the chance to show him anything." In this respect, Orlandi felt that moving to another team was liberating because the situation at Swansea had turned every session into an exam. He felt his future was always in doubt and that every match he'd had to prove that he deserved to play the next. "It's difficult to play well like that," he said.

At Brighton, Orlandi seemed to be rejuvenated: "I don't know if it's a coincidence or not, but at Swansea I was always getting injured. This year, every match was like a party for me, an opportunity to enjoy myself. I never had that feeling at Swansea." In his first season for his new club, he played thirty-eight matches, basked in the support and affection of the fans, avoided picking up any injuries – and enjoyed it all like never before.

Transfer deadline day was also bittersweet for Fede Bessone, who said goodbye again to the team exactly a year since his happy and unexpected return. The left-back with almost forty appearances for Swansea, made the decision to leave because of a lack of playing opportunities in the team's historic first Premiership campaign. At twenty-eight years of age, he felt that he needed to play; but he remained grateful even while he packed his bags: "I've enjoyed every minute of being here and the people in Swansea have been so nice to me." He would forever remember the football chants the fans dedicated to him in the only two matches he'd played in the preceding season – at Bolton in the FA Cup and against West Bromwich Albion in the Premier League.

Mentally, he was already keen to help Swindon win promotion. Swindon's manager, Paolo Di Canio, had persuaded him to sign with a club whose set-up was not a million miles away from Swansea's. But it was only short-term; he was only signed until the 31st December 2012.

Swansea's centenary

Due to international matches, there were no Premier League games the week of Swansea's centenary. The league took a two-week break from the 1st to the 15th September, during which time Leroy Lita joined Birmingham City on a three-month loan. In January, the forward would also be loaned to Sheffield Wednesday until the end of the season.

The club celebrated its centenary on Friday 7th September 2012. Nowadays, only a couple of the original match-day programmes remain of that first match played a century earlier between the Towns, as the then Swansea Town were known, and the Citizens, as Cardiff were known. As time passed, the clubs' nicknames became the nicknames of today: the Swans and the Bluebirds, respectively.

That derby, which ended 1-1, marked the start of the club's hundred-year-long history. The centenary celebrations were commemorated with a special gold-trimmed home kit for the season; a dinner for the Swansea City Supporters' Trust at the Liberty Stadium in July, where the fans were seated among current and former players and legends of the club; the creation of a web page about the club, a joint project between Swansea University and the Swans Supporters Trust; and a book of memories drafted by the club's fans called Swansea 'til I Die – A Century of Supporting the Swans.

But a hundred years of history were not playing out so well for the team on the pitch. The draw against Sunderland was followed by another 2-2 draw, this time at home against Reading, with Michu one of the goal scorers; and three big defeats, losing 2-0 away at Aston Villa and Stoke City, and 0-3 at home to Everton. With eight points in seven matches, Swansea were hovering around the middle of the table and the bad run of results intensified reports of a rebellion in the dressing room against Laudrup.

The only victory in September came in the Capital One Cup: a hard-won 2-3 victory over Crawley Town who had recently been promoted to League One. Swansea went ahead thanks to Michu, but then had to fight back after conceding two goals. The winning goal came courtesy of Garry Monk in the ninety-second minute. The team awaiting them in the next round would be Liverpool, with the added thrill of facing Brendan Rodgers and Joe Allen. Liverpool had not started the season well with two draws and three defeats in their first five Premier League matches.

The knock-out tie would be played on the 31st October at Anfield, undoubtedly making Liverpool the favourites to win. But Swansea opened the scoreline in the thirty-third minute from a corner, with Chico nudging it in with a powerful header. The shock was further compounded in the seventy-second minute when Michu and Pablo Hernández set Dyer up to score. Four minutes later, Luis Suarez reduced the deficit with a header from a Gerrard free-kick. Rodgers had brought his two star players off the bench after half-time. But it wasn't enough and Swansea rounded off their victory to make it 1-3 in extra time. De Guzman, assisted by Michu, guided the ball into the net in an almost exact replica of the second goal. With that, Swansea reached the quarter finals of the competition for the first time in the club's history. Laudrup was beginning to win the plaudits, especially for his key signings; four of his recruits had played a decisive role in the important victory.

A controversial celebration

A few days before the victory at Anfield, Pablo Hernández scored his first Premier League goal in the 2-1 win at home to Roberto Martínez's Wigan side. The other Swansea goal in that match came from Michu: his sixth goal in eight league matches only adding to the celebrations.

The four Spaniards had by now all scored in the Premiership. They posed with three shirts, each adorned with a drawing of the Spanish flag and which, when read together, spelled out "ES-PA-ÑA". "Chico was the one who made them. It was just a simple idea to celebrate a goal; there was no double meaning behind it. One of the ball boys was holding them for us on the touchline," said Michu. But Catalonian player, Rangel, was heavily criticised on social media for the gesture and he felt obliged to provide an explanation and declare himself both one hundred percent Catalan and Spanish at the same time. He emphasised that the celebration had nothing to do with politics.

Although Roberto Martínez initiated the Spanish Swansea phase in 2003, the link between the club and Spain dates back to 1927. In May of that year, the team toured Spain, with stops in Madrid, Bilbao and Barcelona. There, they played several matches against Motherwell – on two separate occasions –the Spanish army, Athletic Bilbao and Athletic Catalunya, with the aim of introducing British football to the Spanish public.

After the victory against Wigan, Swansea lost 1-0 at the Etihad Stadium against Manchester City and then drew two games in quick succession, both one-all draws, away at Southampton and home to Chelsea. In the latter match, Pablo Hernández pulled a point back with a superb individual goal in the eighty-seventh minute. The Spaniard was improving with every match; the new role that Laudrup had created for the wingers suited him.

Pablo Hernández respected the confidence and freedom that Laudrup gave his players on the pitch. Laudrup had been one of Hernandez's idols as a child, so he was happy to have him as manager and also to have a kick around with him: "He hasn't lost an ounce of his quality," he said.

He had also been curious to find out what it was like to play in another league; he characterised Spanish football as more tactical, and the Premier League as more intense. "The Premier League is different to Spain, a bit more physical but I am enjoying it here." He also thought it was important for his family, especially his son, to experience a different culture, country and language. "There is plenty of time to go back home once this experience is over," he said.

Swansea had taken a gamble on Hernandez, paying the biggest transfer fee in their history at the time for him, but the ex-Valencia player didn't feel any added pressure as a consequence. Instead, he felt proud and he wanted to return the faith the club had in him on the pitch. He also felt the immediate warmth of the fans, who were thrilled at the prospect of having a Spanish international in their team. Although he had not been lucky enough to play for Spain in the UEFA European Cup or at the World Cup, he had been given the call up at the last minute in the FIFA Confederations Cup after Andres Iniesta picked up an injury.

At Swansea's modest facilities, Pablo Hernández quickly became accustomed to sharing the locker room with people from the local community. "It would be considered a bit strange in Spain, but here it's just normal to be with the fans and the media. The fans greet you, they wish you luck and are always very respectful." He also loved it when two or three thousand Jack supporters followed them to away matches and drowned out the opposition home fans.

Hernández felt more and more comfortable at Swansea, far more so than at Valencia where twenty-odd journalists always crowded around the exit at every training session. In Wales, though, he rarely even saw a photographer except at the weekly press conference.

Hernández got on well with his new teammates. In fact, he already knew Chico and had previously played against Michu. Having them and Rangel close had helped him a lot. So too Lakie, who had been his first contact in the city and had helped him sort out the necessary basics, such as finding a house and furniture and opening a bank account.

"It was glorious sunshine for the first three days. Then it began to rain and I realised it had just been an illusion," he said sadly. He keeps to his Spanish schedule and eating times, except when he goes to the shops and restaurants in Swansea. The city pleasantly surprised him, especially its small and friendly city centre. But the Swansea players didn't catch him out with the infamous karaoke initiation, which he faced in Birmingham ahead of his first away match at Aston Villa. Juan Mata had warned him about the tradition in England: "I went for an easy song, 'La Macarena', which is what Mata sang when he signed for Chelsea."

Nice to Michu

The day Swansea faced Arsenal, Michu was keen to swap shirts with his fellow Asturian, Santi Cazorla. But the former Villarreal and Malaga player was not in the mood for making friends. Arsenal had lost the match 0-2, with Michu scoring both goals for Swansea. Despite that, in the days that followed both players messaged each other and Michu finally got to swap shirts.

"Before, we were the Arsenal of League One, then the Championship, and now we're the Arsenal of the Premier League," claimed the Jacks fans on the social networks. Along with the victory at the Emirates, two other events seemingly supported the excited comments: Swansea had scored twenty-two of their twenty-three first league goals in open play and in only three games had they had less than fifty percent of the possession.

That day, Rangel and Michu were listed along with Messi in the Yahoo Eurosport European leagues fantasy XI. Rangel described his teammate as "caviar for the price of peanuts." And he wasn't the only one full of praise for Michu. Swansea legend, John Toshack, considered him one of the stars of the season, not only for his goals but also for his style of play: "He's a number 9 that falls back to midfield to receive the ball and enable his teammates to get into the game."

His statistics were impressive and they were up there with the best. Michu scored another brace of goals in the subsequent 3-4 loss to Norwich, making him top Premiership goal scorer in December with twelve goals in eighteen matches. Only Thierry Henry, Van Nistelrooy, Anelka, Drogba and Van Persie had equalled or bettered that goal rate in their first eighteen 18 games in the Premier League.

Although Michu is known internationally for his attacking flair, Real Oviedo captain, Diego Cervero, said that he'd never stood out as a goal scorer at Oviedo. Michu's playing position had been the subject of much debate. He himself thinks he plays best behind the striker, but Laudrup gave him the number 9 position because he thought he could become Swansea's top goal scorer. Cervero still remembers Michu's first match as striker – and how he scored five goals. It was only a practice match, but Cervero still called him up to congratulate him.

Oddly enough, José Ramón Sandoval, the Rayo Vallecano manager who had played him at number 9 that day, didn't think Michu was suited to that position because he didn't have the right movement to spin with the ball. "He can do more damage coming in from behind the striker because when he's running he's unstoppable, and he knows how to take advantage of the spaces created by a striker. He plays well in the space between the holding midfielder and the two centres," said his ex-trainer. "He is highly skilled when it comes to ball control and finishing."

Diego Cervero and Michu became firm friends at the Oviedo youth academy. Cervero played alongside Hernan, Michu's older brother, for three years. Later, he would drive the younger brother who, at eighteen had no other way of getting there himself, to the Requexon, Oviedo's training facilities. During their car journeys they would talk about continuing their studies – they couldn't pin their hopes for the future on football alone. Cervero decided to follow in his father's and grandfather's footsteps by studying medicine, while Michu began a business administration and management course.

For Michu, Oviedo still holds a special place in his heart. He even contributed to the capital increase needed to save the club in 2012, a situation not dissimilar to the one Swansea went through a decade earlier. Along with Santi Cazorla and Juan Mata, Michu persuaded many Brits to buy shares to save the club from collapse. Diego Cervero can bear witness to the footballer's worries about the club at that time; Michu was calling him almost every day to get the latest on the situation. But the Swansea striker had already made an even bigger indication of his devotion to Oviedo: he'd rejected the chance to play in the Spanish La Liga for Sporting Gijon – Oviedo's hated rivals.

Many thought he'd passed up the opportunity of a lifetime by rejecting the offer, especially as he wasn't getting regular playing time at Celta Vigo in the Spanish Segunda B. But then Rayo Vallecano – managed by Sandoval – entered the frame. It took two weeks of almost daily calls for Sandoval to locate Michu, who had cut himself off from the world after missing a penalty for Celta Vigo in the playoff against Granada for promotion to the Spanish La Liga.

"I want you to come and play for Rayo," Sandoval told Michu. "You'll be in my starting XI. I'm gambling on you to do well. I can't offer you any money right now, but it'll come your way in the future." And with that, he convinced Michu to sign.

Michu wasn't just bringing his attacking style of play and an eye for a goal but defensive skills too, especially when pushing forward. "He's more comfortable pressurising the opposing team when they are initiating play rather playing defensively. His size makes it easy for him to steal the ball," said Sandoval. He could still recall the first half of a match at the Nou Camp which saw Pep Guardiola change Barcelona's system three times. He did that partly because of Michu, who had been marking Gerard Piqué.

The talent scout, Antonio Gómez, who was at Rayo Vallecano at the same time as Michu, also knew where the player's talents lie: "His best feature is knowing when to get into the box and how to shake off his marker in quick play." Although he doesn't consider Michu particularly fast or powerful, he reckons that he has great movement considering his height and he's difficult to stop when on the break.

Neither Sandoval nor Gómez were surprised at their protégé's progress. In fact, in an interview with FourFourTwo magazine in February 2012 when Michu was still playing for Rayo Vallecano, Sandoval had not only predicted that Michu was ripe for the national team but also that he was a good fit for the British game.

Michu's a team player; he doesn't complain and will happily play in any position; he's professional, looks after his nutrition and gets enough rest. And he continuously demonstrates his professional commitment. Like the week Sandoval found out from the Rayo Vallecano doctor that Michu was sneaking in for extra training. He hadn't wanted the manager to know because he'd wanted to play at the weekend. For Michu, players who trained hard played better during the match. His philosophy was always: train well, play well.

The same desire to learn that he showed by enrolling in a business administration course came through in abundance every match. "He was always trying to get information from the opposing players he'd played against, wanting them to tell him areas he needed to improve on or errors he'd made," Gómez said.

At the close of June 2012, Michu had not had any offers from other clubs, and he was worried. If nobody was interested in him after the 15 goals he'd scored in a fantastic debut season in La Liga, it would be difficult for him to get another opportunity for progression. He even attended two weeks' of pre-season training with Rayo Vallecano after Sandoval's departure. But then came the call from Swansea – and he accepted their offer.

What tipped the balance in favour of Swansea was the Welsh team's style of play, his childhood dream of playing in the British Premier League and the fact that he was joining other Spanish players and Michael Laudrup was at the helm. "Laudrup demands a certain amount of responsibility, but he also gives you freedom both on and off the pitch. When he gets involved in training or whenever he touches the ball, he shows his class," Michu said. In addition, Rangel had told Michu all about the city and his new club. Michu's former Rayo Vallecano teammate, Piti, had put him in touch with the most experienced Spanish Swan, Rangel, who Piti had played with at Reus.

But Michu's Swansea career didn't get off to a good start. When he landed at Bristol airport, an error in communication at the club meant there was no one there to meet him; not even the ubiquitous Lakie. "I started my adventure by taking a taxi at one in the morning," he recalls, but as none of the hotels accepted bookings at that late hour, he had to sleep at the home of one of the club's kit men.

Months later, Michu was not only being taken seriously in the UK, where he was associated with the play on words "Nice to Michu", but also in his home country. In Spain there were even whispers of him being a target for the national team.

Despite all the goals he'd scored in the Premier League, Michu was still with his childhood sweetheart and hadn't lost an ounce of his humility. When he left Rayo Vallecano, he just became another one for dinner at UD Logroñes, Cervero's new club, so that he could spend some time with his good friend. During the brief period he'd spent in Oviedo over Christmas 2012 he was catching up and having dinner with various friends.

Michu's personality enabled him to easily adapt to the limitations of Swansea's modest facilities. "Sharing the dressing rooms with the locals or training on a pitch that wasn't in great condition is unusual in the Premier League. And it wouldn't even happen in the Spanish Segunda B. But I can't do anything to change it so I have to adapt; it's not a problem. You might even make a few new friends out of it." His humility also showed when he attributed his run of goals to sheer good luck.

But his personality meant that he didn't exactly enjoy his initiation at Swansea. Like all newcomers, he had to sing a song to his teammates on his first away trip with the team. He sang "Stand by me" by Ben E. King.

Given that Swansea is a fairly small and quiet city with limited leisure activities his daily routine was simple: "For someone who wants to channel everything into their football, it's good," he said. Away from the pitch, Michu spent his free time taking classes in English (going twice a week during the first few months), sleeping, reading, watching television shows or browsing the internet. He was particularly grateful to his parents who brought him home comforts every time they visited, such as Asturian fabada, a rich stew of pork and beans. His father, who used to travel all over Spain to watch him play, even drove his Spanish car to Swansea for him. Initially, while he was getting used to driving on the left, Michu made sure he was not the first in the queue at traffic lights or at the entrance to a roundabout to avoid making a mistake at the wheel. Much later, the club would give him a right-hand-drive car.

His trademark goal celebration became an instant classic; he opens his mouth and cups his hand to his ear. The action originates from a famous Rayo Vallecano win against Granada. The Granada fans were daring him to take a penalty, taunting him about his failure to convert from the spot for Celta Vigo in the promotion playoffs, also against Granada; the reason he had wanted to cut himself off from the world. But Michu silenced them with a goal and the gesture; a challenge to the rival fans to go on and taunt him again.

Diego Cervero mimicked his celebration after scoring on his return to Oviedo. It was his homage to the Oviedo academy player who had come so far. Sandoval has a more poetic interpretation of the gesture, telling Michu: "It's like you're saying that you want to take on the world." He was proud to say that seeing Michu grow and excel has been one of his biggest sporting achievements. "One day we will work together again," he says – although it would be impossible right now as Sandoval is manager of Sporting Gijon.

The allure of silverware

Swansea's league results immediately before the 0-2 win at Arsenal were a no-score-draw against Liverpool at the Liberty Stadium and two wins: 1-2 away at Newcastle and 3-1 home against West Bromwich Albion. For Leon Britton, the latter was the team's best match in the Premiership so far. The subsequent defeat against Norwich left Swansea eighth in the table, with 23 points from sixteen matches.

In the League Cup, Swansea advanced to the next round after a 0-1 victory away against Middlesbrough on the 12th December 2012. A Middlesbrough own goal in the eighty-first minute brought the prospect of a mouth-watering but challenging two-legged semi-final against Chelsea. The away leg at Stamford Bridge was set for the 9th January 2013, just seventy-two hours after Swansea hosted Arsenal in the third round of the FA Cup. The Welsh side was going all out for silverware.

But before that, they needed to focus on the Premier League. After the home defeat to Norwich, Swansea suffered another loss against Tottenham at White Hart Lane as well as two draws: the first, a laudable 1-1 draw at home against Manchester United, with Michu scoring for Swansea; the second, a no-score-draw at Reading on Boxing Day. The 2012 sporting calendar drew to a close three days later with a brave 2-1 win away at Fulham. Playing in London wasn't a cause for concern for Swansea, even though they had recently lost away to Spurs. Laudrup's team saw out the year ninth in the table with 28 points from twenty matches. The Swansea fans were particularly happy that the team were three points clear of Brendan Rodgers' Liverpool.

Ahead of the two cup matches looming large, Swansea earned a point at home on New Years' Day against Aston Villa, although it felt like a win because Swansea's equaliser came in the ninety-fourth minute, deep in extra time. The goal scorer was Graham, who had given away a penalty just ten minutes earlier.

And so the 6th January came round – the Day of the Three Wise Men in Spain – and the elimination match against Arsenal in the FA Cup. Although the Day of the Three Wise Men is not celebrated in the UK, Michu made himself the fans' wise man almost as soon as he came off the bench. In the fifty-seventh minute and with the scoreline at 0-0, the fans welcomed Michu onto the pitch, singing "He scores when he wants." It took Michu just one hundred and ten seconds to prove the fans right; in his first effort, with just three touches of the ball, he scored to make it 1-0. Arsenal equalised and then took the lead, with two goals in quick succession in the eighty-first and eighty-third minutes. But Swansea fought back to force a replay with another goal from Graham right at the final whistle.

Just three days later and with little time to recover, Swansea was thrust into another of the big games of the season: the League Cup match at Stamford Bridge. Before that match, Laudrup would gladly have taken a 1-0 defeat in the hope that his team could score one or more goals in the home leg of the tie. But the players far exceeded Laudrup's expectations.

While Chelsea failed to hit the target, Swansea scored two goals courtesy of Michu and Graham, both of whom had scored in the match against Arsenal. Michu put Swansea ahead with a shot in front of goal, which hit the post before going in, after De Guzmán had stolen the ball. Graham sealed the victory with a cheeky goal in injury time, taking advantage of a mistake by Ivanovic to dodge Petr Cech and score. The headline in The Mirror after Chelsea lost 2-0 was 'Ivan the Terrible!'

No one could have expected the reaction that the result would generate. It was like David beating Goliath. Some newspapers made much of the difference in the spending power of both teams since the Premier's first season in 1992-93. Chelsea had spent £744 million; Swansea had spent just £14 million, most of which had gone on the 2012-2013 squad. In addition, Swansea players had the lowest wages in the Premiership. The Jack Army joked about the financial disparities, singing: "I don't care too much for money, money can't beat the Swans!"

And the praise just kept coming. The former England striker and football presenter, Gary Lineker, tweeted that Laudrup deserved manager of the season just for signing Michu, who he considered the bargain of the century.

Not long after, one paper published a list of the five best buys in the Premiership's history. Michu was at the top of the list, followed by Eric Cantona no less, who transferred from Leeds to Manchester United for around £1.2 million. Next came Robin Van Persie, bought by Arsenal from Feyenoord for some £3 million; Joe Hart, bought from Shrewsbury Town by Manchester City for £500,000, the same amount Arsenal paid Paris Saint-Germain for Nicolas Anelka.

Another article picked Swansea's top ten best buys in its history. Swansea player-turned-manager Roberto Martínez came top; Michu was second and Leon Britton was third. The top three were followed, in order, by Lee Trundle, Àngel Rangel, Ashley Williams, Garry Monk, Alan Tate, Michel Vorm and Scott Sinclair.

In the midst of all the excitement, Swansea had to host Chelsea in the home leg of the League Cup semi-final on Wednesday 23rd January 2013. The result from the away leg had been good, but Laudrup didn't want to make any predictions about the match. The players knew that if they strayed too far from their philosophy they risked losing the match. They were not accustomed to defending head-to-head; their weapon was the ball.

Chelsea had more of the control of play with fifty-two percent of possession, but didn't have a shot on target until halfway through the second half. Even with the seven minutes of extra time added by the referee, Swansea held on for a no-score-draw. With that, Swansea had reached its first cup final, and in its centenary year to boot. The club's only other semi-finals were in 1926 and 1964 in the FA Cup, which Swansea had lost to Bolton and Preston North End, respectively.

The lengthy seven minutes of extra time were added because of an incident that saw Eden Hazard red-carded in the eightieth minute. The Belgian player had kicked a ball boy who had held on to the ball for too long. It subsequently came to light that the teenage ball boy was the son of Swansea director, Martin Morgan, owner of Morgans hotel in Swansea and the holder of an estimated £42 million fortune.

The incident brought teenage Charlie Morgan instant fame; he gained thousands of new followers (from 600 to 100,000 in a matter of seconds!) on Twitter where, hours earlier, he had announced that the 'king of all ball boys' was about to make his final appearance. Laudrup denied that the club had given the ball boys any instructions but said that Hazard's victim should have released the ball. But he also suggested that the Belgian international should never have reacted like that.

For the most part, the media directed its fury at Hazard, although the Belgian also had his defenders. The journalist John Carlin, for example, wrote in El País that "few times in the history of the sport had a kick been more justified," and described Charlie Morgan as a "spoiled brat". Harry Redknapp, QPR manager, described the ball boy's behaviour as "disgusting". In any case, both the footballer and the youngster apologised in the Chelsea dressing room, and Charlie decided not to press charges against Hazard.

Before the victory against Chelsea, Swansea had been knocked out of the FA Cup having lost 1-0 to Arsenal at the Emirates in the replay of the third round tie. They had also played two Premiership matches ahead of the home tie against Chelsea, recording a no-score draw at Everton and a 3-1 win over Stoke City, with De Guzman scoring twice. One of his goals, scored from a direct free kick, would, in May 2013, be selected as Swansea's best goal of the season.

The last day of the January transfer window brought the surprise transfer of Danny Graham to Sunderland. The forward would lose his chance to be in the historic final at Wembley, but his transfer put £5 million into Swansea's coffers. Meanwhile, Swansea had brought in reinforcements in the form of Belgian left-winger, Roland Lamah, on loan from Osasuna for eighteen months.

Before facing League Two minnows Bradford in the final of the League Cup on the 24th February 2013, Swansea had four more Premiership matches to overcome. The one home game resulted in a convincing 4-1 win against the same team they beat 0-5 in the opening game of the season – Queens Park Rangers. The goal-fest was led by the Spanish contingent: the in-form Michu scored two, and Rangel and Pablo Hernández scored one each.

Perhaps the players were too focused on the upcoming cup final, or distracted by the praise heaped on them, because the three away matches brought largely negative results. There was a no-score draw against Sunderland, a 1-0 defeat at West Ham and an embarrassing 5-0 thrashing by Brendan Rodgers's Liverpool at Anfield.

That day, 17th February 2013, exactly a week before the biggest game in Swansea's history, the team suffered its worst defeat in over a decade. Although he'd made seven changes to the starting eleven that had overwhelmed QPR, Laudrup didn't use that as an excuse for the poor performance. Instead, he apologised to the fans who had travelled to watch the game in Liverpool, saying that it had been a nightmare match and that they could easily have conceded ten goals.

Development and facilities

The first three matches Swansea played in 2003 were against Bury, York City and Lincoln City. Back then, the average number of spectators at Swansea's ground was 4,000. A decade later, Swansea's first opponents of the year were Arsenal, Chelsea and Everton, the average match attendance was more than 20,000 fans and the stadium was full match after match. The club's meteoric rise on the pitch was undeniable and its progress could be seen off the pitch too.

Until halfway through the 2012-2013 season, Swansea's training ground was at the Glamorgan Health and Racquet Club in Llandarcy. The club used to hire two grass pitches, an artificial pitch and a leisure centre with a pool, sauna, Turkish bath and gym. But the players shared all the facilities, including the showers, with the other members of the centre.

The Swansea manager's office was tiny, but Laudrup just had to put up with it: "It's smaller than the bathroom and we don't have a meeting room either. Thankfully, the club wants to grow and develop and these things will be fixed," he said in an interview with El País. The Dane insisted that Rodgers had taken the same complaints to Huw Jenkins. A proper training facility would improve training for upcoming local players and strengthen the first team.

Laudrup's prayers were answered in the second half of the season when training sessions moved to Landore, the sports complex built as Swansea's training academy. The facilities cost almost £6 million and included two grass pitches and an artificial pitch, as well as several areas used for group work or goalkeeping drills.

The building next to the training pitches was still being built, and for several months the players had to get changed at the Liberty Stadium nearby. Once the renovations were complete, the players had access to multiple dressing rooms on the ground floor as well as other services on the first floor, such as meeting rooms, offices, a restaurant, kitchen, physiotherapy room and a gym.

But the first team's use of the facilities at Landore was just a temporary measure while a bigger sports complex at Fairwood was being built. In July 2012, the club announced that it had signed an agreement with Swansea University to use its pitches in the west of the city. The deal included access to eight full size pitches and another exclusively for first team training, as well as a pavilion that housed changing rooms, offices, seminar rooms and areas for use by the team's medical staff. At last, Swansea's facilities were on a par with those of its Premiership rivals.

In February 2013, Laudrup arranged for the players to go to Dubai for five days of sunshine and relaxation. Brendan Rodgers had done something similar part-way through the 2011-12 season when he took the team to Tenerife for a few days. It was further evidence of the leap forward that the team had made.

Next on the list were plans to increase capacity at the Liberty Stadium. In the summer of 2012, a mere seven years since it was opened, the club announced it would add a further 11,500 seats to the existing 20,500. During the 2012-13 Premier season, only QPR's ground at Loftus Road was smaller than Swansea's. The proposals for expansion were being supported by Swansea Council and was forecast to cost in the region of £15 million. Three parties were to be involved in the project: Swansea City FC, the Ospreys – the rugby club that shares the ground – and the local authority.

The project would ultimately result in the renovation of the north, south and east terraces during the 2014-15 season. Thanks to Huw Jenkins' good management skills, the club had emerged from bankruptcy to solvency with an annual turnover of £65 million in the 2011-12 season. John Toshack extolled the virtues of the chairman's perseverance with the club's prudent financial approach: "If you earn ten, you can't spend twelve. It's a financially healthy club and it lives very comfortably within that philosophy."

Jenkins knew that the club needed to stay in the Premier League for several seasons at least if its many plans were to be feasible. The Swansea chairman bemoaned the fact that most people link ambition with clubs spending instead of placing the emphasis on hard work and common sense.

The club's impressive rise through the ranks was also beneficial for the city of Swansea itself as well as for its neighbouring localities. The results of a study by the Welsh Economic Research Unit, part of Cardiff University, suggested that the club's first season in the Premier League generated £58 million for the region. Having the club in the footballing elite had, for example, helped create around 400 jobs, mainly in the restaurant and pub sector in Swansea.

The study also surveyed hundreds of visiting fans and found that some forty-four percent had spent a night in the city, either the night before or the night after watching their team play at the Liberty Stadium. The club was therefore also supporting a large proportion of indirect jobs – such as transport, hotels and restaurants. In addition, the increase in global television audiences would help advertise Wales to a wider number of potential tourists, and Swansea University confirmed that it had received more applications from foreign students attracted to Swansea because they'd seen the team playing in the Premier League.

It's Chico Time

The four-and-a-half weeks between the semi-final against Chelsea and the final of the League Cup may have passed slowly for the Jack fans. But they flew by for one member of the team: Chico had torn two exterior ligaments in his knee in the match against QPR on the 9th February 2013.

Although he was told that it was likely he'd need three or four weeks to recover, he trained morning, noon and night and did everything he could to try and be ready for the final at Wembley on the 24th February. There was no way he was going to miss his first professional football final. He documented the whole process by publishing photos on his social networks, be it going to Swansea Bay beach at 6 a.m. or travelling to the sport complex at Barcelona for cold compression therapy. He also trained in the pool and even applied herbal remedies to his knee.

But he got through it with a smile, especially when the media began to link him with a future move to Pep Guardiola's Bayern Munich. Chico had worked with Guardiola in the Barcelona B team: "He's a great manager and a really nice person, and he knows how to control the dressing room."

He wasn't short of praise for his current manager, Laudrup, who himself played alongside Pep Guardiola. "It's understandable that Laudrup would dream of managing a big team," he said. He was referring to a widely reported rumour that Real Madrid was interested in signing the Dane as their new manager.

Before entering British football, Chico had played in Spain and Italy: "It's more about possession and technique in Spanish football, whereas in Italy it's a more physical, tactical and defensive game. English football is also very physical, but it's also very fast." Chico also liked the organisation of English football, the shared football rights, the footballing calendar and the atmosphere of the Premier League.

For Chico, the good atmosphere and humility within the team were key to the progress the club was making. Nobody complained about not having their own private locker in the sports complex or about having to share the changing rooms with the Swansea locals. Like many Andalusian's, Chico thought himself quite outgoing.

His teammates had a bit of a fright during the pre-season tour in the USA when Chico suddenly grabbed a knife towards the end of their first meal together. "Those sitting next to me backed off in shock, but I told them that I was only going to use it as a microphone. I sang "We are the Champions" because I don't know many songs in English." If he'd known the song, he might have picked 'It's Chico Time,' the 2006 debut single of The X-Factor contestant, Chico. When the footballer from Cadiz signed for Swansea, the headlines made the most of the song title to announce the signing: 'It's Chico Time!'

The League Cup

But unfortunately, and despite his best efforts, Chico Time was not in time for the League Cup final. Inaugurated in 1960, the League Cup doesn't have the footballing tradition of the FA Cup. Since 1967, the final has been played at Wembley, and in 1968 it was decided that the winner would also play in a European league.

Michael Laudrup described the 2013 cup final as a showdown between a small fairy tale ending and a big fairy tale ending. Swansea was eighth in the Premier League; Bradford was eleventh in League Two, or rather, seventy-ninth out of the four professional English leagues. Strangely enough, it was the reverse in the 1999-2000 season, with Swansea playing in the fourth division and Bradford in the Premier. The last time the two teams had faced each other was six years earlier in League One. At Wembley, Bradford's Nathan Doyle and the Swans' Leon Britton were the only players who had started in both games.

In the press conference before the match, Michael Laudrup refused to answer any questions about the rumoured interest from Real Madrid. Everyone had been talking about it; Mourinho's tumultuous season in charge ended up being his last as Real Madrid manager. But for Laudrup, talking about it was disrespectful, particularly when the most important match in Swansea's history was three short days away.

The shocking defeat at the hands of Liverpool in the league had been a warning for Swansea not to get too confident. And while the Swans had left both Liverpool and Chelsea by the wayside on the road to the final, Bradford had also defeated three Premiership teams: Wigan, Arsenal and Aston Villa. Bradford manager, Phil Parkinson, said ahead of the match that his players were like kids in a sweet shop.

The sheer excitement of the Bradford players was their biggest weapon on the pitch. The team had cost less than £8,000 – the amount paid for striker James Hanson. The rest of the players had been free transfers. That figure was in stark contrast to the almost £1 million that the club would earn from the gate and TV rights just for making the final, with around £250,000 of that destined for players' bonuses.

Bradford took inspiration from various personal, human stories, approaching the clash with a great deal of emotion. The team's mascot, nine year old Jake Turton, led the players out onto the Wembley pitch. The youngster had suffered from a brain tumour and had spent several weeks in a coma. The image of Gary Jones, team captain and former Swansea player, kissing the boy on the head after Bradford had toppled Aston Villa in the semi-final made the front pages of all the UK papers. The goalkeeper's story was another source of inspiration for the team: Matt Duke had been diagnosed with testicular cancer in 2008, and eighteen months before the cup final he was unemployed.

There was another dimension to the poignancy of the event for the Bradford players. The tracksuit jackets they wore during the ceremony before kick-off were emblazoned with the number 56. It was a tribute to the number of people who had died at the Valley Parade stadium in May 1985. The tragedy happened during the last match of the season; a season that saw Bradford promoted to the Second Division. An unextinguished cigarette started a fire in the stands, the cigarette ignited the rubbish that had accumulated under the seats setting fire to the wooden stands.

Tasked with snuffing out Bradford's fairy tale ending, Swansea's team orders were to move the ball around quickly, hence the inclusion of midfielder Ki, in a central defender role as a replacement for the injured Chico.

With just a few minutes left before kick-off, pyrotechnics and the roar of 35,000 fans accompanied the teams as they made their way on to Wembley's revered pitch. The privilege of making the Swans' starting XI that day fell to Tremmel, Rangel, Ki, Williams, Davies, Britton, De Guzman, Dyer, Routledge, Pablo Hernández and Michu.

Amongst the many supporters that day were the proud family members and friends of the players. Almost everyone was there. The cup final being played on a Sunday was great for most workers – except for other footballers. Diego Cervero had been one of Michu's invited guests, but Oviedo also had a match on the 24th February in the Spanish Segunda B.

Ten days before, Cervero had picked up an injury – always unpleasant for a footballer but on this occasion it potentially had a silver lining; it increased the possibility that Cervero might be able to travel to Wembley after all. However as team captain, he was obliged to attend all home matches, even if he was just on the sidelines. But the forward wasn't ready to give up: "I even tried to see if the Oviedo match could be moved to the Saturday," he said. But his efforts were in vain. While he'd been able to see his friend's debut in San Mamés in the Spanish La Liga at the end of August 2011, he was sadly unable to watch Michu play at Wembley in person.

Other footballers, however, were lucky enough to go to Wembley as spectators. Just twenty-four hours after playing in the Brighton v Burnley match, Andrea Orlandi was travelling to London, along with his teammate Iñigo Calderon, to celebrate the historic meeting as a Swansea fan. Meanwhile, goalkeeping coach, Iñaki Bergara, was settling down in front of the television in Manchester: "with some snacks and a Coca-Cola. A great plan." Among the other Spanish ex-Swansea contingent, Guillermo Bauzá was also watching the match at home; Jordi López was following the proceedings from Ukraine via his mobile phone; others, like Albert Serrán, weren't able to follow the match live.

Swansea came out firing from the get-go. The team was not about to give Bradford an inch to create any chances. The League Two side were chasing shadows, while the Swansea players were performing their famous triangulations. They were perfectly executing Laudrup's orders to move the ball around quickly. Just thirteen minutes in, Swansea threatened to score with a Ben Davies header that was deflected.

At the quarter of an hour mark, Swansea picked up the pace. Michu got clear of his marker, making a dash diagonally towards the left of the area where the ball found him. Instinctively, as is so often the case with Michu, he fired a low cross with his left foot. Matt Duke deflected the shot, but the ball was still in the area. The explosive Nathan Dyer was ready and pushed it into the net, making it 0-1 for the Swans. The match was looking good for Swansea; Bradford needed to open up more and the Swansea side were taking advantage of the spaces to play around with possession.

The minutes passed by until Pablo Hernández, nutmegged the ball, and found Michu in the same area he'd fired that low cross from before. Once again, the Swansea number 9 got clear and fired another shot that went through a Bradford player's legs before crossing the line for Swansea's second goal. Fate had conspired to pay tribute to the late Besian Idrizaj at Wembley. With echoes of what happened in 2011 against Reading, the fortieth minute had seen another Swansea goal.

Although both Ki Sung-Yueng and Wayne Routledge had their chances, the scoreline remain 0-2 at half-time. Having learned the lessons from their past promotion playoffs, Swansea came out of the dressing room for the second half with as much intensity and ambition as for the first. So much so that it took barely two-and-a-half minutes to create the best goal of the match. Dyer pushed forward on the right towards the area and played the ball to Michu. Michu let the ball pass between his legs for Wayne Routledge to collect. Routledge did a one-two, allowing Dyer to cut back inside and make it 0-3 with a shot that went in off the post.

But the final wasn't over yet. Swansea's prowess overwhelmed a Bradford side that was feeling the pressure of such a momentous occasion. To cap it all off, less than ten minutes later, Bradford goalkeeper Matt Duke was sent off for bringing Jonathan de Guzman down in front of the goal.

That's when Swansea committed the only blemish of an otherwise flawless game. Dyer wanted to take the penalty to complete his hat-trick, but de Guzmán wouldn't let go of the ball. De Guzmán was the usual penalty-taker, and he was the one who'd won the penalty in the first place. The row between the two teammates deepened to the extent that Michu had to pull Dyer away from the spot. Leon Britton and even the referee also approached Dyer to speak to him while he continued gesticulating from outside the penalty area. In one way, his reaction was understandable; he was unlikely to get another chance to score a hat-trick in a Wembley final. Despite the controversy around him, de Guzmán calmly slotted the ball in to make it 0-4. On the touchline, Michael Laudrup and Alan Curtis were still discussing the situation as they embraced each other.

There was still thirty minutes to go when Michu slotted in the fifth with a shot that glanced the goalpost. The scoreline seemed fair if a bit cruel against a modest Bradford side.

Laudrup brought captain Garry Monk on for the last half hour of the match. That Sunday was the highpoint of Monk's and Britton's careers; both had represented Swansea in all four English professional leagues. Lamah and Tiendalli also took to the pitch in the last third of the match which ended with a definitive 0-5 victory for Swansea in extra time. A last goal from de Guzmán, assisted by Rangel, finished off the match. Swansea had won its first big title in its history. And they'd done it exactly six years to the day that Roberto Martínez first took over as manager; six years since that League One match against Yeovil that marked the starting point for the current project.

What's more, it was only the second time that a non-English club had won an English football final; the first time had been in 1927 when Cardiff won the FA Cup. And Michu became the first Spaniard ever to score and win an English cup final.

Not wanting to take the captain's armband away from Ashley Williams when he came on the pitch, Garry Monk would share the traditional captain's honour of lifting the cup in the director's box. Afterwards, the team posed for their official photographs on the pitch, accompanied by so much fanfare that the memories Monk had of the Autoglass Trophy in 1994 in the same stadium paled in comparison. The celebrations continued in the stands and on the pitch, where all the members of the Welsh club were taking photos of themselves with the cup.

Chico mimicked a matador with a cape, the flag of Cadiz and the flag of Spain around his waist. The Andalusian defender was wearing a t-shirt in tribute to four Spanish footballers who'd recently died: Puerta, Jarque, Miki Roqué and Preciado. Fitness coach, Óscar Garcia, kept his promise and had his hair cut by Chico, Agustien and Michu in the dressing room.

Back at home in Manchester, Iñaki Bergara was smiling; he felt that he'd just witnessed something big. Swansea had not only won the first big title in its history, it would also now compete in next season's Europa League.

From the stands, Orlandi was ecstatic, not only for his best friend Rangel, but also all his former Swans teammates, the fans and for a club that he still thought of with great affection. Perhaps he even felt like he'd contributed to the victory? "Some people say that," he says, "but I don't see it that way. I don't feel that I contributed in any way, although I am fortunate to have been part of the development of a club that was a generous and humble team of people when I arrived."

"Can we play here more often?" Laudrup asked in the subsequent press conference. This was his third win at Wembley. The first had been in 1983 in a match between Denmark and England; the second was in 1992 when he won the European Cup with Barcelona and now, in 2013, he'd won the League Cup as manager of Swansea City. The Dane considered this last win to be particularly special; it was one thing to win a trophy with Barcelona or Real Madrid, it was quite another to do it with a club like Swansea. He was proud of having achieved that, and also proud of his players; they'd shown themselves capable of playing their best football when it mattered the most.

Britton made some tongue-in-cheek ambitions for the next season: "But why can't we have a crack at Europe? There is nothing else on a Thursday night apart from EastEnders."

Swansea's victory parade took place two days later. Thousands of people were on the streets to follow the open-top bus on its two-kilometre route through the city. Spaniards Chico and Pablo Hernández finished the night at Itay Shechter's place along with Spanish singer Huecco, who tweeted the following to his followers: "Flamenco party here in #Swansea with the best @phernandez19 and @ChicoFlores12 at #ItayShechter's place. 1.15am!"

During the afternoon's celebrations, the chairman, Huw Jenkins, issued the following statement: "We want Laudrup to stay for a few years. We don't want to have to go through the same reorganisation process every summer. We need continuity and to plan where we're going." Since 2007, none of Swansea's managers had stayed at the club for more than the two-and-a-half seasons Roberto Martínez spent in charge. The club was convinced it should invest in all its key players, starting with the manager.

Contract renewals, the team and the angel of Swansea

A month before the final, Michu re-signed with the club until 2016. On the club website Michu said that all the speculation about his future didn't interest him: "It was an easy decision for me; I'm living a dream here." In March, Rangel extended his own contract to 2016 as well. He was building a home in Wales and he liked the efforts the club was making to keep its important players. "I am settled here, I am enjoying my football, I have married a Welsh girl and I'm building a house in Swansea – I feel like a Welshman now. I am very happy on a personal and professional level," he later commented.

A day later, it was announced that Laudrup would be staying until at least 2015. "I've always said that I am happy here and I never had any doubts I would stay," he said. He wanted to continue with the plans that had so far been successful. It put an end to the rumours of him going to Real Madrid, despite the fact that, according to the Spanish press, he was the fans' favourite for the job, ahead of Carlo Ancelotti and Rafa Benitez. "He's not in a rush to manage at the upper echelons of football just yet. He's young and as a player he's won everything. When things go wrong at a big club, they can quickly bring in a new manager. Laudrup wants stability, to make Swansea bigger and to do well in the Europa League," Rangel said after Laudrup decided to stay.

The rumours linking Chico with a move to Bayern Munich also faded away when, in April, he became the third Spanish player to extend his contract to 2016. But the Spanish players weren't the only ones confirming their commitment to Swansea. Leon Britton also re-signed until 2016 in the hope of seeing out his playing days at Swansea. He felt that he was enjoying his best years at Swansea. Season after season he'd overcome the physicality of the three divisions below the Premier, and now he was enjoying the increased space and better pitches in the top division. Wayne Routledge, Ben Davies and Michel Vorm extended their contracts to 2016, while Ashley Williams and Garry Monk re-signed until 2015.

Also staying in Swansea until 2015 was Swansea's only Spanish international: Pablo Hernández. The club's other three Spanish players, particularly Michu, had come close to making the Spanish national team. Spain's manager, Vicente del Bosque, attended the match against Everton in early 2013 to see Michu in action. The shortage of right-backs in the then-World and

European Champions side meant that Rangel didn't go unnoticed either.

The newspapers speculated that Michu, who had a shot hit the crossbar during that no-score draw at Everton, and, to a lesser extent, Rangel were odds-on favourites to be called up for Spain's friendly against Uruguay on the 6th February 2013 in Doha. In the end, neither player was selected. Many in Spain were at a loss as to explain Michu's absence, while in Wales there was surprise that Rangel, being chased by Arsenal at the time, didn't get the call up.

Rangel would carry on working hard in the hope of attracting the interest Vicente del Bosque had already shown in him. His performance and playing profile were a perfect fit for the national side. His match statistics, which showed his consistency in number of passes made and touches of the ball, proved it, as did the number of teammates who spoke out in his defence, such as Lee Trundle.

With a Welsh wife and children, Rangel might have been forgiven for paying more than a passing attention to the rumour that he might get a call from the Wales manager. "I feel like a Welshman now," he said in front of the BBC microphones after winning the League Cup. But when they met during an international match at Cardiff's Millennium Stadium, the president of the Football Association of Wales himself told Rangel that it wouldn't be possible: "He told me that the rule on country residence had changed so having lived here for more than five years and being married to a native didn't qualify." Although he held a British passport, Rangel couldn't play for the national side. The only way to represent Wales was to have been born in Wales, have native Welsh parents, have native Welsh grandparents or have attended five years of compulsory education in Wales.

The Catalan defender was also admired for his behaviour off the pitch, like the occasion he helped the homeless community in Swansea. It was a particularly cold day when the owner of a café told Rangel and his wife, Nikki, that he would have to throw sandwiches away because they were due to go past their best before date. The couple asked if they could take the sandwiches and they went round the streets looking for homeless people. When they couldn't find anyone due to the snow that had fallen in the preceding hours, the footballer asked his Twitter followers for help: "Anyone knows the location of homeless people in Swansea? I got food going spare! #randomtweet." At the time, he had no idea of the impact his gesture would have. The New York Times was just one of the media outlets that picked up the story of how the couple ended up giving out sandwiches at a homeless shelter.

Àngel the angel of Swansea also organised charitable events such as a fundraiser in aid of three cancer charities which took place in April 2013 at the Liberty Stadium. Cancer had affected several of Nikki's close relatives. The event, which was attended by several of his Swansea teammates, featured an auction with prizes including the chance to attend the Swansea v Manchester City match in the defender's own box in May, and a week's holiday on the Costa Brava. The event raised over €20,000.

Final stages of the season and the future

After the League Cup final, Swansea had eleven Premiership ties left that season. With 36 points, and lying eighth in the league table, only a catastrophe would prevent Swansea from staying in the Premier League for another season. Thankfully the first game after that memorable cup win was a 1-0 home win, courtesy of Luke Moore's solitary goal, against Newcastle. But after that match, Swansea endured a bad run of results that would continue to the 19th May 2013, the last day of the season.

The final stretch of the season began with three consecutive defeats, losing 2-1 away at West Bromwich Albion, 0-2 home against Arsenal and 1-2 against Tottenham. Luke Moore scored Swansea's only goal at West Brom, while Michu scored against Tottenham. Both players also scored in the subsequent draw at Norwich. Swansea failed to score a single goal in any of the next three matches – the longest Swansea had gone without a goal all season – with two no-score draws at home against Southampton and Manchester City and a 2-0 defeat against Chelsea at Stamford Bridge.

By the 4th May, Swansea were on 43 points, having taken just three points from a possible 21 with four defeats and three draws. Despite that, they were still ninth in the league. Plus, they had faced four of the top five teams: Arsenal, Tottenham, Chelsea and Manchester City. But they still had to face the league leaders Manchester United, who were already champions mathematically, in the penultimate game of the season.

But before that they had to play away at a struggling Wigan side. Roberto Martínez's team needed a miracle to avoid relegation. Wigan were pinning their hopes on taking full points from each of their final three matches. Swansea were almost safe, having an eight point advantage over the teams at the bottom of the league, which included Wigan. As if that wasn't enough pressure for Wigan, they were playing in the FA Cup final at Wembley just five days later.

Both teams had a similar style of possession play. But while the Latics recorded twice the number of shots on target (eleven to Swansea's six), the visitors' efforts had been the more effective – something that had characterised the team since Laudrup's arrival. As a result, Swansea came from behind twice to earn a 2-3 victory and deal a blow to their former visionary manager's current Wigan side. To make matters worse, Rangel, one of Martínez's favourites at Swansea, was one of the goal scorers. The Spaniard would say after the match that Wigan had hurt themselves.

Not long after, the Latics would experience sheer joy and heartbreak in four short days. On Saturday the 11th May they were crowned FA Cup champions after a last-gasp goal against Manchester City. But they could only half-celebrate the club's first major title. A final of a different kind awaited them on the 14th May, this time against Arsenal at the Emirates. Arsenal were lying in the crucial fourth place in the league, qualifying them for the Champions League. While Wigan still had hopes of victory up until the sixty-eighth minute, the final 4-1 scoreline sealed their fate and their return to the Championship, eight seasons since their promotion.

It was a cruel twist of fate that Swansea's only win in their last ten Premiership matches contributed to relegation for three former Spanish Swans. Iñaki Bergara recovered from the blow with his characteristic optimism. "Lessons in life: a good breakfast and we'll start the journey over afresh," was one of the messages he took inspiration from as he began to show signs of life. But at least Bergara, Roberto Martínez, Jordi Gómez and the rest of the Wigan squad could always be proud of having been crowned champions at Wembley. They did it in the same season and in the same place where the Swans had been crowned winners of the League Cup a few months earlier. In addition, winning the League Cup and the FA Cup qualified Swansea and Wigan to play in the Europa League.

For the penultimate match of the season, Swansea were part of an historical event in British football: it was the last home game for Sir Alex Ferguson after twenty-six years in charge of Manchester United. Laudrup confessed that even his own son wanted Manchester United to win so that Ferguson could bow out on a high. For his part, the Scot had recently praised Swansea as the Premiership team of the year. He also admired Michu. Numerous football professionals and newspapers, such as the Daily Mail, picked the Swansea number 9 as their player of the year. And Michu came close to taking the shine off Ferguson's farewell home match with his eighteenth goal of the season. But Ferdinand stole victory for Manchester United with a goal in the eighty-seventh minute to make it 2-1.

A week later on the 19th May Swansea played the final match of the season to a home crowd. Swansea were the better team and had more chances than Fulham, but suffered a crushing 0-3 defeat. It was a disappointing end to a good season for the Swansea Jacks, who had come out in force to turn the Liberty Stadium black and white. A year earlier the fans had watched the last home match of the season wearing Elvis Presley costumes – a scheme of Brendan Rodgers.

Swansea closed the season with a negative record of two wins, three draws and six defeats since the League Cup final against Bradford. Before that final, Swansea had recorded only eight defeats in twenty-six matches. The Welsh side finished ninth in the league with 46 points – two points higher than in the debut Premier season – despite having finished with a point less than the season before. Perhaps having won a title and knowing that they were almost certainly safe in the Premiership, all by the end of February, lessened the players' competitive spirit in the final stages of the season. Elsewhere, Brendan Rodgers' Liverpool finished seventh – outside the European qualification places – and Roberto Martínez's Wigan ended up eighteenth.

The 2013-2014 season would bring the first Welsh derby in the history of the Premier League, between Cardiff and the Swans. But it would also produce another derby of interest for some other of the protagonists of this book: the long-established clash between the two big Liverpool teams: Liverpool and Everton. Brendan Rodgers was in his second season for the Reds, but now with the objective that the team push on after a season of transition. Meanwhile, Roberto Martínez was now the occupant of the manager's role left vacant by David Moyes, who'd left Everton to take over from Sir Alex Ferguson at Manchester United.

Taking Iñaki Bergara and the rest of his backroom staff with him, Roberto congratulated Moyes on the magnificent achievement of having created a team with its own identity. After deciding that it was time to leave Wigan, Roberto signed with the Toffees for four seasons with the aim of finishing in the top four. "It's not going to happen next season, but it is the aim for the future," he said at his presentation.

Bill Kenwright, chairman of the club that has spent the most seasons in the highest level of English football at one hundred and ten, revealed that during the negotiations Roberto passed the audition by beating Manchester City in the FA Cup final. Yet again, Roberto's footballing strategies, as well as his ambitious and optimistic disposition, had opened the door to another management role.

Swansea's good performance in the league made many of the players a target for other teams during the final stages of the championship. But the chairman, Huw Jenkins, wasn't intimidated by the buying power of the other Premier League teams: "We don't need to sell," he said. And it was all thanks to the club's financial efficiency and the proceeds it received from television rights, which are distributed more fairly than in the Spanish La Liga. Swansea received almost £50 million from television rights; eighteen of the twenty teams in the Spanish La Liga received less than that, with Barcelona and Real Madrid being the biggest recipients.

With Swansea competing in four competitions in the coming season – the Premiership, the League Cup, the FA Cup and the Europa League – Laudrup was conscious of the fact that he needed to strengthen his team. He said he was aware of the areas for development and that he was aiming to strengthen the starting XI, although he was keen to avoid having too many players. The club had already started to put things in motion in January. Laudrup had earmarked five or six potential signings and his priority was a forward to share scoring responsibilities with Michu.

Before the end of the season, Swansea signed another Spanish footballer who they'd tried to sign during the January transfer window: Jose Alberto Cañas, Swansea's sixteenth Spanish signing. Cañas began to study English at the start of the year and had been watching Swansea's matches since he'd heard the club was interested in him: "I've seen many of the games on television and I know their style of play, which suits me very well. They've had a great season and we hope to improve on that and enjoy playing in the Europa League."

After various discussions with Laudrup, the midfielder admitted that working for the Dane was one of the reasons he'd decided to sign: "In footballing terms, he was a fantastic player." The chance to play in the Premiership was also a deciding factor, after having spent several seasons in the Spanish La Liga. And if any niggling doubts remained, his conversations with Chico and Alvaro Torres tipped the balance. They both knew the Welsh club well and spoke favourably about the club, the fans and the city. But that didn't mean it was an easy decision for him to make; it was never easy to leave home – he had originally found it difficult to leave his former club Real Betis where he'd come up through the academy. To stop him feeling homesick, Cañas and Chico had already joked about starting a carnival in Wales to rival his hometown of Cadiz's famous February carnival.

After his holiday in Sant Carles de la Rapita, Àngel Rangel had been available, as ever, to help as many Spanish footballers as he could to adapt to a new team and culture. More than half a dozen of his compatriots had been linked with Swansea during the previous few months, something Rangel attributed to the economic situation in Spanish football: "There are many talented players in the Spanish Liga who want to make the jump to the Premiership because of the crisis. In football terms, La Liga is strong but the Premier is still a big attraction."

Rangel considers the 2012-2013 season as one of the best in the club's history. And it would be difficult to beat a season in which Swansea won the League Cup and finished in the top ten teams in the Premier League, but he's still confident at bettering it. After all, every one of Swansea's previous six seasons had been better than the one before it.

At the team's final dinner of the season, Michu picked up four awards: players' player of the year, fans' player of the year, top goal-scorer and best player at home. "He has been a key player and the goals speak for themselves. I hope that the club scouts have been working hard and that we're lucky enough in the future to sign more aces like him for peanuts," said Rangel. De Guzman's free-kick goal against Stoke City won goal of the season and Chico was awarded best new arrival. According to Opta, the sports data agency renowned for its advanced performance analysis technology, Chico had also made the European leagues' fantasy team alongside Xavi Hernandez, Santi Cazorla, Cristiano Ronaldo, Lionel Messi and Franck Ribery.

Àngel Rangel, Chico Flores, Pablo Hernández, Michu, Óscar García, Andrea Orlandi, Guillermo Bauzá, Albert Serrán, Gorka Pintado, Jordi López, Roberto Martínez, Iñaki Bergara, Jordi Gómez, Óscar Brau and Fede Bessone are the fifteen Spanish Swans who've contributed over the last decade to the story of a modest Welsh club that rose from League Two – the bottom of the professional English football leagues – to the elite Premier League, going on to win the League Cup title at Wembley. As the Swansea fans' saying goes: "Once a Jack, always a Jack".

ACKNOWLEDGEMENTS

To Libros del K.O. for taking a chance on this project and to Àlvaro Llorca, a magnificent editor. To Artur Galocha for his beautiful front cover.

To Roberto Martínez for opening the way for the Swans and for his collaboration with this project, taking time out even during the most challenging parts of the season.

To the Rangel family, especially Àngel and Xavi Cruz, and to Andrea Orlandi.

To Iñaki Bergara, Guillermo Bauzá, Albert Serrán (and Marta F. Andrés), Óscar García, Jordi López, Fede Bessone, Gorka Pintado, Jordi Gómez, Óscar Brau, Chico, Pablo Hernández and Michu.

To Swansea City and, in particular, to Jonathan Wilsher and Huw Jenkins.

To John Toshack (and Mai Angulo), Brendan Rodgers, Leon Britton and Huw Lake.

To the Swans Trust, especially Alan Lewis. To John van Zweden, Huw Cooze, Eirian Wyn, Tim Lewis, Guillem Balagué, Andrew Gossy and Gwyn Rees.

To Jordi Cruyff, Gustavo Poyet, Álvaro Torres (You First Sports) and José Alberto Cañas, Diego Cervero, José Ramón Sandoval and Antonio Gomez.

To everyone who made this book possible. Thank you!

Bibliography

The bibliography used to write this book is available on the following webpage:

librosdelko.com/2013/los-cisnes/

This book was originally printed in Spanish on 24 June 2013, two-and-a-half years after Javier Cambronero met with two undocumented journalists – in his office at UDL, Alcalá de Henares – who presented him with the publishing project that would go on to be called Libros del K.O. Javier Cambronero listened patiently to these two novices, and gave them not only his blessing but also some old school advice that they've never forgotten. He was nothing like the cartoon-esque financial ogre they'd expected him to be; instead, he became an indispensable father figure who provided stability, advice and commercial coverage to a generation of independent Spanish publishers. In the words of Eduardo Riestro, editor of Ediciones del viento: "Javier Cambronero did more for reading in this country (Spain) than any of the ministers of the Spanish democracy". Rest in peace, friend.